Perspectives on Education

Edited by Allen D. Calvin
University of San Francisco

Addison-Wesley Publishing Company
Reading, Massachusetts
Menlo Park, California · London
Amsterdam · Don Mills, Ontario · Sydney

To the Calvin family:

David, Dorothy, Jamie, Kris, Scott, and Zelda

ISBN 0-201-00878-5
ABCDEFGHIJ-MA-7987

Preface

It has been said that every professor has one outstanding lecture he or she gives during a course. This book is an attempt to bring together a collection of such lectures. The chapters in this book consist of original articles written to introduce students to an area of contemporary education in such a fashion that they can see some of the problems and challenges in that area, and hopefully be encouraged to continue their studies in those areas that are of particular interest.

Because this is a collection of original articles (rather than a reprint of manuscripts that were already published in professional journals), the authors were able to write them specifically for students rather than for their professional colleagues. The authors have worked extremely hard to present complex ideas in such a fashion that they can be understood and appreciated by students who do not have a familiarity with highly technical language.

The educators who wrote these chapters not only are outstanding researchers and academicians but they are also committed to seeing that the educational system here in the United States succeeds in its attempt to become truly responsive to the needs of each individual. They have taken the time from their careers to share their own knowledge and experiences. Their primary reason for doing so is to persuade additional talented students to enter the educational profession and assist in finding new and better ways of improving the educational process.

San Francisco, California   A.D.C.
January 1977

Contents

Robert E. Roemer

The social conditions for schooling

1

In this first chapter, Dr. Roemer helps us understand the assumptions that lead a society to establish schools and, particularly, to demand universal schooling for its young. As Dr. Roemer points out, because these assumptions can be questioned, they create inevitable controversies in the area of race and bilingual/crosscultural programs. Dr. Roemer's chapter also helps to prepare us for the issues raised by Davy and Llanes (Chapter 10) and Green, Brydon, and Herndon (Chapter 12).

Robert E. Roemer

Dr. Roemer received his Ph.D. from Syracuse University in 1973. After teaching philosophy of education for two years at the University of San Francisco, he took a position with the University of Texas at San Antonio, where he now serves as Coordinator of Cultural Foundations of Education. His research interests have centered on the contemporary problems of higher education, an area in which he has both published and delivered papers.

Are Schools Necessary?

For those of us living in contemporary American society, a world without schools is hard to imagine. First of all, going to school is a common experience we all share. From the age of about seven until we finally assume adult roles in society, most of us are going to school. During this time, if asked what we do, our immediate response is, "I go to school." Many of the basic skills we depend on in our daily lives were acquired in school. For most of us the ability to read the words printed on this page was developed in school. School has so touched our lives that part of our personal identification depends on what schools we have attended and, more important, what degrees we have earned, or failed to earn. If we had never been to school our lives would be far different. We would have had different experiences in our adolescence, we would think differently about ourselves, and we would have different beliefs about the nature and means of human growth.

It is difficult to imagine our society without schools. Entry into occupational roles depends on the amount of schooling a person has received, and the general belief is that anyone without a high-school diploma is severely handicapped when seeking a job. Schooling is even more necessary for entry into the professions. Few people would attempt to become doctors or lawyers without going to school. Thus the common expectation of those in school is that their schooling is a decisive factor in determining the type of job they will hold after finishing school. Because a strong relationship between schooling and occupational status is generally assumed to exist, the normal way that the poor or underprivileged seek to improve their status in our society is through the acquisition of more or better schooling.

Try to imagine our society without schools. How would occupations be allotted? How would training for highly technical occupations be acquired? What changes would be introduced into our social relationships if it were never possible to ask others how much schooling they have had? Certainly both those offering employment opportunities and those seeking employment would have to restructure their approaches to one another. Furthermore, in the universities in our country, highly sophisticated research is done that is of considerable importance to the well-being of our society. Research in many fields such as medicine, advanced economics, nuclear physics, and learning psychology is largely concentrated in the graduate departments and research institutes connected with universities. If there were no schools, either this research would have to be undertaken by other agencies or the progress and development of our society could no longer depend on advances in these fields.

Schools also provide employment for large numbers of people. These people include not only teachers and school administrators but also government employees working in state departments of education and the United States Office of Education, and people who work for textbook publishers and other companies that sell goods and services to the schools. Schools are a major industry in our society. If they were to vanish, a huge displacement would occur in the employment force.

Though it is difficult to imagine our society without schools, it is not impossible to do so. In fact, such societies are not only possible but have existed in the past and continue to exist today. Sometimes they are described as being primitive or underdeveloped. They are, certainly, considerably different from the society with which we are familiar. Nevertheless, large numbers of people may socially interact with one another in a stable manner even though none of them ever received any schooling.

Perhaps this point can be made clearer if we try to imagine an ongoing society without education. Now this is impossible, just as it is impossible to imagine a square circle. A society cannot endure for more than one generation without education. By *education* we mean that process by which a society transmits to new members the values, beliefs, knowledge, and symbolic expressions that make communication within the society possible. And communication is necessary if a society is to continue and endure. Without communication, there is no social interaction, and thus no society. However communication is developed, it is an educational task—but it need *not* be performed within the context of schools.

What, then, are schools? Basically, schools are specialized institutions in which the general educational tasks of a society are formally undertaken. It may be helpful to societies to sponsor schools and to devote special attention to the accomplishment of educational tasks. But though our own lives and our society would be considerably different without schools, in neither case are schools necessary in the same way that education is necessary.

The Conditions for Establishing Schools

If schools are not necessary in society, why are they ever established? Before attempting an answer, let us consider the nature of the question itself. Even though the central activity of schools is teaching and learning, schools are commonly given all sorts of purposes beyond that of imparting knowledge, skills, beliefs, and attitudes. In fact, all of the following functions have at one time or another been assigned to the schools: to train personnel to fill occupational roles in society; to promote social mobility in society; to raise the morality of society by developing in youth virtues deemed important; and to maintain national superiority by training vast numbers of engineers and technicians. This list is by no means exhaustive and can easily be extended. It simply represents some of the reasons why schools are established. Those who talk about the goals of schools, school policy, or what schools should be answer the question of why schools exist by stating the purpose of schools.

But let us try to answer this question in a far more general and fundamental way. Let us interpret the question in the following manner: under what social conditions are schools established, no matter what purposes they are given? Seen in this light, the question of why schools are established becomes focused on the basic conditions that must prevail in a society before schools can be developed. Given that schools, unlike education, are not necessary for the continued existence of a society, what are the conditions under which a society is likely to make the transition from the absence of schools to the institution of schools?

The answer to this question lies in the necessity for education—the obligation every society has (if it wishes to continue in existence) to educate its members in such a way that they will be able to participate in and continue the society. The content of education varies from society to society. Each society has its own sets of beliefs and values that have to be imparted in order for the continuity of the society to be maintained. In our society, for example, belief in democracy as a way of life and the right to hold private property are basic, but this is not so in some other societies. Similarly, for full participation in the life of a society, certain basic skills and knowledge are necessary. Full participation in modern society demands, among other things, literacy and the ability to deal with technology. But whatever the necessary skills and knowledge are, they are essential components of that society's educational program. Thus the content of the educational task in every society is determined by two considerations: the beliefs and values necessary to ensure continuity of the society, and the skills and knowledge necessary for full participation in the society.

A society may deem certain items to be essential in its educational program; however, this alone is not sufficient to generate schools. The learning necessary for the continuity of and participation in some societies can be acquired without the formal instruction offered in schools. Even in our society, each of us learns to speak our native language before we ever attend school. We learn to speak as we engage in the life of our family and our neighborhood. What will generate schools, however, is when a society determines as essential in the educational process certain items that *cannot* be learned in the casual life of the society. There are two possible reasons why these items cannot be picked up in the ordinary course of events: first, the material could be so difficult that its mastery depends on sustained attention over long periods of time by the learner and specialized preparation for the teacher; or second, the material, though not especially difficult, is not efficiently acquired if left to chance. As an example of the first case, consider the knowledge necessary to be a medical doctor. While each of us has picked up certain health tips and knows cures for the common cold or a hangover, none of us expects to act as a physician on the basis of this knowledge, which we have *happened* to acquire. The knowledge needed by a doctor is too sophisticated to be picked up in everyday life, and even if it were available in that context we could not acquire it without dedicating ourselves seriously to its study. Thus the acquisition of this knowledge demands formal instruction. In contrast, almost everyone knows how to cash a check, and that knowledge is easily acquired in everyday life.

As an example of material that is not especially difficult but would not be efficiently acquired if left to chance, consider arithmetic and spelling. Most of our parents know the rudiments of mathematics and can spell ordinary words correctly. If we just hung around them long enough, or around other adults who know these things, we would pick up the same knowledge, but we can do it much more quickly if we can concentrate our attention on these studies. Our parents could take the time to teach us this material, but if they did so they would have less time for other interests, especially as we got past the beginning stages. If all parents were responsible for seeing that their children had mastered the three Rs, a great many working hours in our society would be spent on this task. It is much more efficient for all concerned to designate certain people to teach these subjects and to stipulate as well certain times of the day and periods of the year when this is to be done—in short, to set up schools.

These, then, seem to be the fundamental social conditions necessary for the establishment of schools. In other words, if among those items that a society considers to be essential components of its educational program are some that are too difficult to be picked up in everyday life or that are more efficiently acquired under a formalized arrangement, then the moment has come for the society to undertake the establishment of schools.

Universal and Extended Schooling

Notice that the social conditions that lead to the establishment of schools do not at the same time generate a particular type of school. A society can respond in any number of ways to these social conditions and establish various types of schools. A society could intend its schools for only one segment of the population, say those who belong to the aristocracy. In fact, in the history of western civilization it has often been the case that only the sons of the wealthy and socially elite received formal instruction. On the other hand, a society could establish schools that almost everyone attends but only for limited periods of time. In many underdeveloped countries, school attendance is universal for only the first few years of school; most of the population does not finish elementary school, and very few people graduate from college.

Let us examine a society in which schooling is universal, a society in which almost everyone attends school. Let us also suppose that schooling in this society is also extended—that most people are in school for a long period of time, say around twelve years. This is, of course, the type of school system the United States has come close to creating. The normal expectation in the United States is that a young person will complete at least twelve years of schooling. Ironically this is one reason why there is a dropout problem in the United States. If everyone terminated schooling at an early age there could be no dropout problem. If almost no one received very much schooling there could be no serious social disadvantage in not having much schooling. But in a society where just about everyone finishes high school and where the acquisition of most social benefits such as income, prestige, and status is believed to depend on having at least a high-school diploma, the dropout definitely becomes a problem. Thus the very existence of a dropout problem indicates not only that most people attend school but also that most are in school for extended periods of time.

Given the existence of universal and extended schooling, let us examine what sort of society is likely to establish schools with these characteristics. (Notice that we are now dealing not with the mere existence of schools as such, but with the existence of a particular type of arrangement for schooling.) First, any society that sponsors universal schooling must be committed to the belief that schooling is good for everyone. Without the widely held conviction that schooling is good for everyone, a society would most probably establish schools that would be elitist in character and serve only a privileged segment of the population. Second, a society that keeps most of its youth in school for a long period of time must also be committed to the belief that the more schooling one receives the better. Without widespread commitment to this belief, schooling, although universal in scope, would be typically abbreviated in duration, perhaps lasting only a few years. Thus in attempting to determine the type of society that would sponsor universal and extended schooling, we are really asking what type of society would be strongly committed to the beliefs that schooling is good for everyone and the more schooling the better.

Before answering this question, let us map out a strategy to guide our analysis. Rarely is it possible to hold a completely isolated belief. Most of our beliefs are embedded in other beliefs or are supported by various claims. If we believe that every man has the right to life, liberty, and the pursuit of happiness, then we also believe that life, liberty, and the pursuit of happiness have a special place in the hierarchy of goods. Holding this to be true we are also likely to believe that society should facilitate the preservation of life, liberty, and the pursuit of happiness. In short, this single belief is embedded in other beliefs. Noting this, our strategy at this point will be to investigate the belief systems that support the two fundamental beliefs that schooling is good for everyone and the more schooling the better. Another way of stating our strategy is this: If a society is committed to each of these two beliefs, it must be committed to other beliefs as well. If we can determine what these supporting beliefs are, we will be well on our way to determining the type of society that would dare sponsor universal and extended schooling.

Let us start with the conviction that schooling is good for everyone. In order to get at the other beliefs needed to support this conviction, let us consider the ways in which it is possible to *deny* that schooling is good for everyone. The first way is to assert that the schools teach matter that certain persons are incapable of learning. For example, someone might say that there is no point in sending to school the children of families in the lowest socioeconomic class because such children do not have the backgrounds necessary to profit from the instruction offered in school. A second way to deny that schooling is good for everyone is to show that the social benefits derived from schooling are not available to members of certain classes. Thus, in a society that maintains a caste system it could be argued that schooling is not good for those who are members of the lowest caste because they have no access to the benefits that normally come to those who have been schooled. A third way of denying the value of schooling is to point out certain occupations in which the knowledge and skills acquired in school are of no use. Thus it might be felt that those who wish to be ditch diggers would profit very little in that occupation from the experience of schooling.

A fourth, and more direct, way of denying that schooling is good for everyone is simply to claim that schooling in itself is harmful to the individuals who receive it. This claim can be advanced for many reasons. A religious group might feel that what the schools teach is contrary to their central beliefs. Or parents might be afraid of what will happen if their children become very learned and sophisticated. Or it could be felt that children, once they are away from parental guidance, will acquire bad habits in school. But whatever the reason, the basic claim here is that schools are bad because they in some way harm the students.

Although there may be other ways to claim that schooling is bad for everyone, it is possible to determine from these four some of what is involved in commitment to the belief that schooling is *good* for everyone. That conviction must be supported by the following beliefs: (1) that schools teach something everyone can learn, (2) that schooling is profitable for all classes, (3) that schools teach knowledge and skills useful for all occupations and life interests, and (4) that schooling in itself is not harmful. If these are in fact true statements, then the belief that schooling is good for everyone is warranted. But notice that these statements describe a particular type of school and to a certain extent a particular type of society as well. Let us next consider the type of school and society described by these statements in order to determine what conditions have to be realized before the belief that schooling is good for everyone is warranted.

First, in order to teach something everyone can learn, schools must offer a curriculum sufficiently diversified that everyone's learning potential can be exploited in some way through this schooling. This means that the offerings of the schools have to cover the spectrum of human learning potential. Therefore, the schools cannot limit their instructional content to material that could be mastered only by students coming from a particular cultural background, nor can the medium of instruction be a language that the students do not understand.

Second, in order for schooling to be profitable for all classes, the society must grant to all classes access to the benefits associated with having gone to school. The society in which this condition is realized must be of the sort that does not deny to anyone, regardless of race, religion, or sex, the social goods that derive from having gone to school. Only in a society that meets this condition can it be said that if schooling is profitable for anyone it is profitable for everyone.

Third, in order to teach knowledge and skills useful in all occupations and life interests, schools must offer an array of instruction broad enough to respond to everyone's interest. This instruction can be broad in either of two ways: first, in the nature of the subject matter, such as reading that everyone finds useful; or second, in the variety of the offerings. Note that there is a basic assumption present here: namely, that learning of some sort bears on whatever a person may do. Stated most simply, this assumption would assert that whatever people can do they can *learn* to do, and in fact learn to do better. Hence the ditch digger can, through learning, improve himself or herself precisely as a ditch digger. Thus this third condition not only describes a type of school (one that offers a broad array of useful instruction), but also assumes that whatever activity a person is engaged in, learning can facilitate the performance of that activity.

Finally, if schooling is not to be regarded as harmful, then whatever transpires in school must be seen as compatible with the way human beings should live. What is learned in school must be harmonious with what is widely accepted as the good life, and the personal transformation that results from having gone to school must be enhancing rather than detrimental. If a society feels that its schools are not harmful it is, then, basically satisfied with the schools and finds that the schools embody in a substantial way the ideals of the society.

Up to this point our attention has been focused on the belief that schooling is good for everyone. But this is only one of two basic beliefs that are needed to support universal and extended schooling. Let us turn now to the second belief, the belief that the more schooling one receives the better.

It should be noted at the outset that this belief cannot be held as absolutely as the belief that schooling is good for everyone. The reason is simply that a moment arrives in the educational career of everyone when it is no longer true that the more schooling one receives the better. For each of us there is an appropriate time to be done with schooling. Education may be a lifelong process, but schooling certainly is not. Thus, though it may be true in a general way that the more schooling one receives the better, this cannot be absolutely true. Addressing a group of fifth graders, we might unhesitatingly announce that the more schooling the better, but we would be much more cautious in making such a statement in front of seniors graduating from college.

A second feature to note about the belief that the more schooling one receives the better is that it is very similar to the belief that schooling is good for everyone. In fact it is really a stronger version of the belief in universal schooling, in that it asserts not only that schooling is good for everyone, but also that it is good for everyone for substantial periods of time. Thus the statements that warrant the belief in extended schooling are merely stronger versions of the statements needed to support the belief in universal schooling.

To make this apparent, let us use the same strategy employed before and consider the ways in which it is possible to deny that the more schooling one receives the better. First, this belief could not be held if the schools featured a single curriculum that favored only a certain type of learning interest and potential. For example, if the higher levels of schooling increasingly concentrated on mastery of the Greek and Latin classics, for those who had no inclination nor ability to master such material it would not be true that the more schooling they received the better. Second, this belief could not be held if for certain classes of people advanced schooling brings no greater share in social benefits. For example, there would be no point for a woman to stay in school long enough to complete a doctorate in mathematics if the world is not yet ready for a woman mathematician. Third, this belief would not be valid if staying in school for a long time would be of little profit for a person whose occupation or life interest is not given extended preparation by schooling. Quite obviously, some occupational performances are not improved by extended schooling. Does acquiring an advanced degree in engineering help a person to be a better window washer? Finally, those who reject extended schooling might contend that it is eventually detrimental—that those who stay in school eventually acquire a very constricted emotional life, or they lose touch with reality, or they begin to rely on what they can read in books rather than what they can see with their own eyes, or they come to consider themselves superior to those who are not educated.

Therefore, if a society is to be committed to the belief that the more schooling one receives the better, it must be willing to accept as true the following four statements as well: (1) schools are fully responsive to all types of learning potential, (2) extended participation in the schools increases access to social benefits for everyone, (3) extended schooling provides preparation for all occupational and life interests, and (4) staying in school for a long time does not adversely affect a person. Clearly, all of these are stronger statements of the propositions needed to support the belief in schooling as good for everyone. What was originally stipulated for the initial levels of schooling is now extended to other levels. In place of the assertion that all people can learn something in school, the belief in extended schooling assumes that everyone's learning interest and potential can be fully developed in school. Instead of merely indicating that social benefits are open to all because of their schooling, it is now stated that this is true no matter how much schooling one receives. Instead of suggesting that learning is helpful in every occupational and life interest, this second belief states that this holds true even for great amounts of learning. Finally, not only is schooling not harmful according to this belief, but staying in school for a long period of time is not incompatible with what is considered to be proper human growth. What all this suggests is that the conditions that have to be realized in order for the belief in schooling as good for everyone to be credible are the same conditions that made credible the belief that the more schooling one receives the better. Thus a society that can warrant its belief that everyone should go to school can also warrant the belief that everyone should go to school for substantial amounts of time.

The Location of Educational Controversy

One of the benefits to be derived from analyzing the conditions for schooling is that such an analysis indicates the likely areas for serious educational controversy. The operation of the schools produces an oversupply of controversy. But some conflicts are more serious than others. What time the school day should end is not nearly as serious a matter as whether children should be bused in order to attain racial balance in the schools. Is there a way of distinguishing a serious educational controversy from one that is trivial besides that of gauging the emotional involvement of the combatants? The suggestion here is that the most serious conflicts in schooling are those that bear directly on the social conditions for schooling.

The preceding analysis was an attempt to demonstrate that a society that wishes to sponsor universal and extended schooling is committed to the maintenance of certain social conditions. It must, first of all, maintain a relationship between the schools and the individual learner such that the learning potential of everyone can be developed through the experience of schooling. Second, the society must so distribute its benefits that if anyone can lay a claim to those benefits on the basis of the schooling received, everyone who has the same schooling can make the same claim. Third, the society must establish schools whose programs of instruction are relevant to a great variety of occupations and life interests. If the schools are universal and extended they must, then, be in some sense relevant. Finally, the society must make sure that the life within its schools is harmonious with the style of life favored in the society at large. Only in this way will the schools be perceived as not being harmful. In short, any society that wishes to sponsor universal and extended schooling must maintain a certain relationship between the school and the learner, between the school and the distribution of social benefits, between the school and occupational and life interests, and between the school and the accepted forms of behavior in the society. These relationships form the basis for serious educational controversy. An educational controversy that centers on these relationships is serious rather than trivial because it is intimately connected with the social conditions that warrant the beliefs that support universal and extended schooling.

Several contemporary educational controversies would appear to be serious by this criterion because they involve a denial that the social conditions needed to sustain universal and extended schooling are in fact realized. Let us consider some of these controversies.

With regard to the relationship between the school and the learner, two controversies are especially prominent today. The first of these centers around the suggestion that certain races cannot learn as well as others, and the second derives from the claim that the present structure of the schools works to the disadvantage of certain ethnic groups. In recent years some specialists in genetics have claimed that the difference in the average IQ scores of groups distinguished according to their racial membership can in part be explained by the different genetic endowments of the groups. The implication is not only that intelligence is inherited to some degree, but also that certain races are on the average less intelligent than others. The central educational issue here is whether, for genetic rather than environmental reasons, schooling is as good for some groups as it is for others.

The second most prominent controversy arises from the complaint by some groups that the schools favor students who come from a particular culture, usually described as the white, middle-class culture. The claim here is that the instructional methods and content of the schools are biased against students who do not have this cultural background. Because of this, these students are not able to learn in the schools as they are currently operated; given other instructional methods and content, however, they could learn. This complaint leads to demands for courses in ethnic studies and bilingual, cross-cultural programs of instruction. Essentially, of course, these are demands that the schools teach something everyone can learn.

This recognition of the relationship between schooling and the distribution of social benefits has given rise to several recent movements. The first movement assumes that there is a strong relationship between schooling and the acquisition of social benefits. Given such a relationship, this movement attempts to ensure that equal opportunity for education is accorded to all. Some of the aspects of this movement have been the efforts at desegregation of the schools, including the use of busing to achieve a racial balance, and the institution of various compensatory programs such as Head Start and Upward Bound. All of these programs of action take seriously the relationship between schooling and the distribution of social benefits and attempt to guarantee that the opportunity for schooling is given equally to all.

The second major movement arising from the relationship between schooling and the distribution of social benefits seeks to ensure that this relationship will not be weakened because of race or sex. Recent legislation, namely Title VII of the Civil Rights Act of 1964 and the Equal Employment Opportunity Act of 1972, aims at ensuring that the employment opportunities that come from the schooling one has received will not be denied because of one's sex or race. This legislation, along with demands by women's liberation groups and ethnic minorities, has served to strengthen the relationship between schooling and the acquisition of social benefits.

Ironically, another aspect of the effort to keep employment opportunities open works to weaken the relationship between schooling and the acquisition of social benefits. Quite obviously the requirement of some educational credential, such as a high-school diploma, for employment or advancement in employment can be used to discriminate against groups that do not possess such a credential. This would be especially true if there were no relationship between the performance expected in an occupation and the skills and knowledge connected with, say a high-school diploma. In fact, the Supreme Court has recently ruled (*Willie S. Griggs, et al.* v. *Duke Power Company*) that in those instances in which some group can demonstrate it is adversely affected by the educational requirements imposed by an employer, then the burden of proof rests with the employer to show the job-relatedness of the educational requirements. Failure to do so would mean that those requirements could no longer stand. The final effect would be to decrease the relationship between the acquisition of social benefits and the amount of schooling one has received.

Another contemporary movement in education, if successful, would have just the opposite effect. This is the movement to expand programs of career education and to increase the number and variety of professional schools. Both of these developments aim at articulating more closely the work done in school with performances outside of school. Certain types of schooling have always been highly relevant to occupational performance, of course, notably the professional schools, such as medicine, law, nursing, business, and education. It is noteworthy that in higher education the recent decline of enrollments in liberal arts colleges is matched, in general, by rising enrollments in the professional schools. With the continued growth in professional schools and the development of programs of career education, the relationship between schooling and occupational performance is kept strong, and this then provides a basis for requiring at least certain forms of schooling as a prerequisite for job employment.

The relationship between schooling and the nonworking life of the larger society does not ordinarily occasion much controversy, simply because society would not long support schools that were not to its liking. But now and then what school officials feel is best for the students differs from what the community feels is best, and then controversy does arise over whether the schools are harmful to children. Recently some communities have complained about the courses of instruction offered in school, especially sex education classes, and they have also complained about the science textbooks used in school when passages in those textbooks contradict some religious belief widely held in a community. In these instances there is agitation to ensure that the schools are not harmful and that what transpires in the schools accords with the lifestyles and beliefs approved of in the society.

All of these are serious educational issues because they have direct bearing on the beliefs that schooling is good for everyone and the more schooling the better, both of which beliefs are necessary to sustain universal and extended schooling. There is no judgment here as to whether these beliefs should or should not be maintained, only the suggestion that if they are maintained they need to be supported by certain social conditions. Serious educational controversies will be those that focus on these social conditions, because these are the social conditions for schooling as we know it.

Suggested Readings

Bereiter, Carl. *Must We Educate?* Englewood Cliffs, N.J.: Prentice-Hall, 1973.

Goodman, Paul. *New Reformation: Notes of a Neolithic Conservative.* New York: Vintage Books, 1971.

Illich, Ivan. *De-Schooling Society.* New York: Harper & Row, 1971.

Perkinson, Henry J. *The Imperfect Panacea: American Faith in Education, 1865–1965.* New York: Random House, 1968.

Spring, Joel H. *Education and the Rise of the Corporate State.* Boston: Beacon Press, 1972.

Young, Michael. *The Rise of the Meritocracy.* Baltimore: Penguin Books, 1961.

Edward Bispo
Frank Wallace

A career in education: will there be any jobs?

2

This chapter by Dr. Bispo and Mr. Wallace has some very important career
information for prospective teachers. It states, for example, that by 1983
there will be a shortage of teachers. As you read through many of the other
chapters in this book, you will find that the information presented in this
chapter will be particularly useful to you if you are considering education
as a possible career. Even now, as the authors point out, there are openings
in early childhood education (see Chapter 3) and bilingual education (see
Chapter 10).

Edward Bispo, Frank Wallace

Dr. Bispo and Mr. Wallace work closely together in developing education programs and reform strategies for the California State Department of Education. Dr. Bispo has had experience at all levels of teaching, curriculum development, and education administration in school, district, state, and national educational settings. Mr. Wallace has had a wide variety of experience in educational program development, systems design, and organizational management at state and national levels, along with experience in international education in South Asia.

You are twenty. Are you considering becoming a teacher, and wondering what kind of college program you should choose? Most people would say that considering a job in education is ridiculous. Everyone knows that there are no jobs, that there is an incredible surplus of qualified teachers. You have read about teacher layoffs throughout the country during the past few years. The media has highlighted the closing of schools due to declining enrollments. The odds are you will not get a job. Right?

Wrong. This chapter presents a number of different perspectives that may encourage educational job seekers, not only regarding prospects over the next five years but also regarding prospects in the immediate future. We argue that preparing for a career in education may be more rational than most people think. The chapter is divided into three parts. The first provides a schematic model for assessing your chances and applies this model to both the present situation and that of the 1980s; the second part surveys specific job opportunities now; and the third discusses the impact of unpredictable worldwide events on education.

Each part is intended to give you—the potential job seeker—additional analytical skills that will help you make a better decision about a most critical subject—your career.

A Schematic Model for Assessing Your Chances

The education labor market is not much different from other job clusters. There are a variety of predictive data that influence the number of teaching jobs available and the number of people qualified to fill them. A few are quite obvious and well publicized; others are much more subtle.

Essentially our schematic model provides three major categories of data that can help you to determine your opportunity of finding a job: the number of students; the number of qualified teachers; and the amount of money available. In general, when the number of students goes up, more jobs are available; when the number of qualified teachers goes down, competition is minimal and the job seeker is more likely to be successful; when more money is pumped into the system, obviously more jobs result. In each case, when the reverse condition prevails, the number of available jobs declines and competition for jobs becomes more intense.

How does this basic analysis help you? The schematic model presented in Fig. 2.1 is organized into three major categories, each of which can be divided into specific data indicators that you should obtain locally (as we have nationally) so that you can predict your community's particular situation and your potential success in finding friendly personnel offices in an often outwardly inhospitable career situation. Most of the indicators we analyze can be obtained from school districts, from other local governmental agencies, or, in some cases, from state agencies. Thus, your survey should not require extensive re-

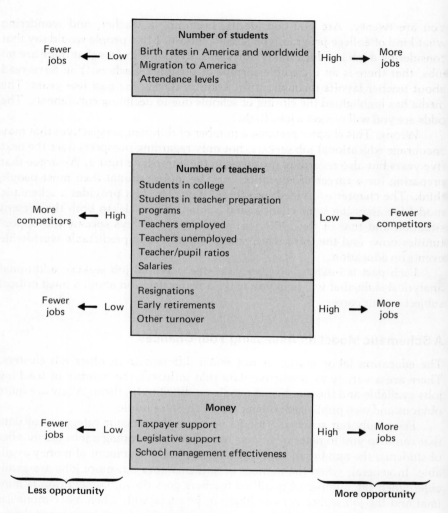

Fig. 2.1   A schematic model for assessing the education labor market

search. And, if you do become an active job seeker, your knowledge of the state and local situation will be a useful asset as you describe your interests and skills to potential employees.

Applying the Model to the Present Situation

As you can see in Fig. 2.1, there are several data indicators in each category. Most of these are not particularly impressive as individual bits of information, but, pieced together in a schematic model, they provide a comprehensive analytical tool for predicting what has happened or will happen to the educational labor market. Let's take a closer look at the data indicators in each of the three categories.

1. Number of students

The first contributing factor to the number of students is the birth rate. The well-publicized baby boom that began in the late 1940s resulted in a rapid increase in school-age children during the ensuing fifteen-year period. The baby boom then slowed and finally resulted in a baby "bust"—at least in the eyes of new teachers seeking jobs. The bust was a result of several factors: the development of practical birth-control methods and their widespread acceptance; the extensive publicity about the dangers of a population explosion throughout the world; and the growing desire among many young couples to have greater personal freedom. These young people, in growing numbers, have chosen not to have children.

A second contributing factor is migration. America ceased to accept significant numbers of immigrants after the late 1940s. In the past, such immigrations had included a substantial number of families having numerous school-age children.

Finally, with regard to attendance levels, the general assumption that all children go to school is not valid. For a variety of reasons, an ever-increasing number of children are not attending school even though every state except one has compulsory school attendance laws. Quite shockingly, the 1970 census reports that nearly 2,000,000 school-age children, or 4.2 percent, were not enrolled in school for at least three consecutive months prior to enumeration. More than one million of these children were between the ages of seven and fifteen. And in the eleventh and twelfth grades alone, the number of dropouts or nonenrollments is now estimated to be well over 900,000. In far too many schools, percentages of nonenrollments are reaching epidemic levels.

In summary, the critical data indicate a clear trend: school enrollments have declined drastically during the past six years. This decline, although at a lowering rate, will also continue for another four to five years. Without further details, it is easy to conclude that the decreasing number of students has resulted in a rapid decline in the number of new jobs available. Indeed, many teachers who previously held jobs have been laid off as a result of the decrease.

2. Number of teachers

The student data are also helpful in assessing the number of qualified teachers seeking work during the past few years. First, because of the earlier baby boom, college and university enrollments experienced their greatest growth in the mid-1960s and many of these students chose education as a career, generally because of the number of jobs available and because increasing salary levels made education an attractive career choice. The number of new teachers eligible to enter the job market is still high today. Second, because these young teachers have been recently employed and because the economic situation now requires many young mothers and potential early retirees to continue working, the amount of turnover has dropped. And finally, because those laid off have not easily found other jobs, the number of unemployed teachers still seeking jobs remains high. Thus the competition for existing openings continues to be intense, especially for a new college graduate with no teaching experience.

3. Money

Throughout most of the 1960s, the American economy experienced a sustained rate of economic growth. As a result, available new money was pumped into education to provide for increasing numbers of students and to provide additional services to students with special needs: those from disadvantaged homes, those desiring vocational training, those from Spanish-speaking homes, those with physical and mental handicaps, and so forth. These new programs were possible because both taxpayers and legislators, as well as educators, gave strong support to the need for improving our educational programs.

Since then, rapid inflation combined with an economic recession has resulted in severe personal economic constraints. Increases in real incomes have not kept pace and standards of living have dropped accordingly. For these reasons alone, local property taxpayers are unwilling to tax themselves at increasingly rising rates. In addition, however, for a number of reasons that are interwoven throughout our social environment, the public has lost confidence in the overall educational system. School unrest, vandalism, and racial conflicts have increased. The specially funded programs have not resulted in significant educational achievement. Traditional school management methods also have been questioned. Similarly, increased teacher militancy has resulted in several well-publicized strikes or walkouts that have not always been received favorably.

Because of these problems, individuals from several vantage points have begun to criticize existing programs and organizational characteristics in our public schools, even suggesting that our schools cannot and should not expect to meet the needs of all children. Some have postulated that schools simply do not make a difference in educational achievement for most children—bright or slow. The result is that public and political confidence in education and educators has declined to a serious degree. And the "bottom line" is that new resources for education have not been forthcoming. The consequences for the educational labor market should be obvious.

All these data contribute to the present, very grim, job-market situation. The U.S. Bureau of Labor Statistics predicts that 4.2 million teachers will be seeking jobs during the 1970s. Only 2.1 million jobs (200,000 annually) will be available. Overall, a huge teacher surplus exists and most people predict that it will increase. The general message for you who may be thinking about a career in education is: Forget it. Seek another way to earn a living. But wait a minute. . . .

Applying the Model to 1983

By 1983, there will be a shortage of teachers. "Impossible!" you say. Not so! Let's take another look. Using the same categories of data in our schematic model, we can illustrate that the present gloomy publicity is really quite short-sighted. Some interesting possibilities emerge.

1. Number of students

Census data show that our total population is still continuing to grow. Presently, overall school enrollments continue to decline. However, the decline has already reached bottom in classes below the fifth grade, and total enrollments will start to increase by 1980. And, for approximately ten years—due to the momentum of total population growth—the growth rate of total enrollments will equal the twenty-five-year rate experienced between 1940 and 1965! Surprised? We were too.

We also expect to see a drop in the number of school-age youth who are not in school. Increasing attention is being given to the rights of children (and their parents) who have been excluded from school. It seems safe to predict that administrators will be forced to develop better means of meeting the educational needs of "problem" children who are now being excluded. These changes will also result in an increase in the number of students in school.

2. Number of teachers

The production of new teachers is our second key variable. Contrary to what most of the general literature suggests, there was a 12-percent decline in the production of new eligible graduates between 1968 and 1972. Currently, the annual decline is approximately 7 percent. We predict this rate of decline will increase during the next five years. Interestingly, the number of college freshmen indicating teaching as a likely career dropped by half between 1968 and 1972.

Second, while the total number of available jobs will grow, during the immediate future the number of currently unemployed teachers seeking jobs in education will drop significantly. They will have been forced to seek other careers, many in personally satisfying social service occupations.

Finally, although the trend has yet to emerge, the education programs in the 1980s will demand far greater numbers of specialists—learning diagnosticians, gaming and simulation technicians, electronic media curriculum developers, research specialists, coordinators of classroom volunteers and teacher aides, and bilingual and multicultural specialists. The use of more sophisticated individualized instruction techniques and learning machines will also create a need for new teachers with special classroom management skills.

3. *Money*

Quite obviously, the increase in the number of students will also result in additional resources. Beyond this, however, there are growing legal pressures for giving students and their communities access to an acceptable level of educational opportunity. In program terms, this means that all communities should be given the same opportunity to obtain the basic resources needed to adequately educate each student. In budget terms, this means new resources must be made available. While it seems likely that more precise accountability procedures will be required in order to ensure effective use of such resources, it also seems clear that substantial increases in state educational aid will be forthcoming in the reasonably near future, at least in the states where legal decisions have been announced.

The contrasts between the present situation and that predicted for 1983, for each major set of data influencing the education labor market, are great indeed. Analyzing the job situation using these data, we can be almost certain that there will be a shortage of teachers at least by 1983, perhaps before. It would appear that the continuing negative headlines, and most of the general literature, that bemoan the total shortage of jobs tell an incomplete story. In terms of overall opportunity, you might well decide to prepare for a job as a teacher in the near future.

You Might Have a Good Chance Now

What if you need a job now? Can you compete with four million other job seekers? Perhaps you have a better chance than you think. Or perhaps with a little additional planning and preparation, your chances could be improved. Let us take a closer look.

First, does the schematic model help us to predict individual situations? Obviously not. The model and the data used are based on national statistical reports. On a nationwide basis, they can be extremely helpful as planning tools. However, they are often poor predictors of specialized labor market needs, whether at the national level or for a specific region or school district. The national statistics are almost useless for you since your particular skills and attitudes may be directly suited to the demand for such skills in a specific district.

The information presented in Table 2.1 was obtained through a comprehensive review of numerous specialized reports, surveys, and other job-market literature. We could discern no particular pattern in this labor market informa-

Table 2.1
The job market today—questions and answers

Where are jobs most likely to be found?
    The South
    Rural areas
What levels offer greater opportunity?
    Preschool
    Early childhood } especially for males
    Adult
What personal characteristics are sought?
    Black
    Chicano or Spanish-speaking
    Persons with crosscultural sensitivity and experience
    Persons able to handle "alternative" programs, such as an open classroom format
    Persons with strong positive attitudes toward children
What subject matter expertise is most needed?
    Environmental education
    Natural and physical sciences
    Chemistry
    Mathematics
    Spanish
    Speech and reading
    Career education
    Vocational education (especially distributive education and agriculture)
    Industrial arts
What specialized teaching skills are in particular demand?
    Ability to work with handicapped and exceptional children (special education programs)
    Remedial reading and math specialization
    Bilingual education specialization
    Diagnostic specialization
Are there some areas of subject matter expertise in very low demand?
    Art
    Business education
    English (general language arts)
    Foreign language
    Home economics
    Physical education
    Social studies

tion, so we have not tried to provide a detailed analysis of the causes for the favorable conditions we discovered.

For example, we found that there are regions in which competition for jobs is low. In particular, there generally is a balance between graduates and new jobs throughout the South. As late as 1973, 1,000 new teachers were hired from outside areas. Similarly, there are fewer competitors for jobs in rural areas than for those in most large cities. And there are certain kinds of specialties and subject matter areas in which competition for available opportunities is significantly lower. Finally, there are a number of personal characteristics to which administrators continually give particularly close attention.

Naturally, some of the characteristics are related to the needs of special areas, such as those regions emphasizing bilingual education for Spanish-speaking students. And, as mentioned above, general statistics are only useful as broad predictors. We would encourage you, if you are considering education as a career, to do your own analysis. Look at your own needs and interests—and your own commitment. Then conduct a survey in those areas where you might consider teaching. It is essential that you do this kind of preplanning to determine what to emphasize in your own educational preparation. Finally, the effective career planner and job seeker should know what skills are likely to be powerful—or worthless—calling cards when interviewing for a job.

Unpredictable Events: Their Impact on Education

Our schematic model for analyzing the education labor market is a useful tool if you want to be systematic in planning your career in education. This section provides an additional perspective on the vast American—and international—educational establishment. It presents some of the many challenges that face any educator—certainly any educator trying to develop long-range plans.

All of us have been exposed to "future shock" publicity. It is indeed clear that during the past three decades change has become the dominant characteristic in our lives. Inevitably, before we die we will experience events even more incredible than men walking on the moon, the transplanting of a human heart, or the horrifying events of war broadcast on the living-room television.

"So what?" you ask. There is a special message for all of us in education: these dramatic events inevitably affect the education system, often in very direct ways. When a Sputnik is lifted into space, our schools are given an immediate challenge to produce scientists. When business, industry, and government recognize the value of computers, a vast new array of skills are included in our educational programs. When sixteen-year-olds are given the right to drive, the educational system must respond. When eighteen-year-olds

125274

are given the right to vote, there are consequences for our schools. When thousands of Vietnamese refugees flee to America, our schools are directly involved.

Invariably, these kinds of social, political, and economic events result in the need for new teachers to fill new jobs. Also invariably, there tends to be an ebb and flow of such educational programs. The race to space has slowed, and thus the space engineers, scientists, and moon walkers have been forced to find other jobs. The development of scientists is no longer the first priority in our schools. The "new" math has been revised or put in the back of the closet. Now bilingual teachers and reading specialists are needed to teach Vietnamese children how to cope with an American social environment and prepare term papers in English.

We are in a superindustrial society that has many new capabilities. One result is that we are only partially able to anticipate change and its consequences. Therefore, our ability to plan a long-range educational program and predict what kinds of new teaching jobs will be needed is also limited. No matter how good our analytical model is, unforeseen events will have a now unanticipated but direct impact on the educational labor market.

As a specific example, one such set of events seems to be unfolding now. Briefly, the oil-rich "developing" nations are rapidly amassing huge fortunes. They are now able to buy the many, often highly complex, manufactured goods that are necessities (or status symbols) of the so-called "developed" nations. They also have begun to buy the *teaching services* needed to educate their people to use these goods. Thus, while specific policies and programs have not yet emerged, the potential opportunities for American job seekers willing to consider international careers are already obvious. The implications for our educational system may also be extensive.

A Word of Advice: Be Aware!

The various perspectives on the education labor market presented in this chapter have a clear message: be aware! Be aware of how social events can have a frequently unpredictable impact on our schools. Be aware of the numerous factors that influence the availability of jobs in education. And be aware that if you do plan ahead, you will likely be successful in preparing yourself to meet the most pressing needs of the educational system, wherever you happen to enter it.

A final word: This chapter has not dealt with the broad issue of the quality of education in America. Nevertheless, be aware that the education job market is concerned with quality, especially while a surplus of qualified teachers continues to exist. There seems to be one primary characteristic that affects the quality of teaching and of learning everywhere. A teacher must have a deep concern about children. Children's confidence to succeed, their desire to learn, their sense of self-motivation, are all directly and powerfully influenced by their teachers' desire to have them learn to succeed. We would urge you to look for some other career if you cannot convey these feelings to our children.

James J. Gallagher

Early childhood education

3

r. Gallagher's chapter focuses its attention on an area of instruction that
ould grow rapidly in the near future. It is becoming more and more ap-
rent that the beginning school age will continue to drop, and it appears
ely that in the not-too-distant future the schools will be involved with
ree- and four-year-olds to a much greater extent than at present. The im-
ications for children with special needs (as discussed in Chapters 10 and
) are becoming more and more apparent. In addition, as we noted in the
evious chapter, there are increasingly positive implications in this area for
e career-oriented student.

James J. Gallagher

Dr. Gallagher has been active in the field of early childhood education f
a quarter of a century, and has conducted numerous research projects
on the thinking processes of gifted children.

He is past president of The Association for the Gifted and the
Council for Exceptional Children, and has served on a number of governmental policy and advisory boards.

He is currently Director of the Frank Porter Graham Child Development Center.

One of the strongest trends in American society over the last two decades has been the steady movement toward early childhood education.[1] Like most major social trends, it is the result of diverse forces. This chapter will try to identify some of these forces and will discuss some of the current goals and objectives of early childhood education.

Figure 3.1 shows the continuing growth of organized child services in the decade from 1964 to 1973. During that period, the number of five-year-olds in organized nursery school and kindergarten programs increased from less than 60 percent in 1964 to over 75 percent in 1973. The estimate for 1975 is 85 percent, thus continuing this steady growth.[2] The presence of four-year-olds in organized programs, while at a smaller percentage than that of the five-year-olds, showed a clear trend upward as well, more than doubling in number over the ten-year period. There is little doubt that America has accepted the desirability of such program efforts, not just as strategies by which the handicapped or disadvantaged children get head starts in coping with life, but for all children.

The forces generally credited with the continuation of that increase are (1) our growing experience with preschool programs; (2) our drive for social reform, with these programs as instruments for reform; (3) new information with regard to the importance of early childhood; and (4) changing family roles in modern society.

Historical Threads

The earliest recognized attempt to provide special experiences for young children in organized fashion is generally recognized as the kindergarten. Friedrich Froebel, a German educator, has been credited with the origination of the kindergarten in 1837.[3] The basic idea of the Froebelian kindergarten was not to prepare the child for future schooling, but rather to represent an extension of a healthy family life. The emphasis was on the use of group activities and special materials by which the youngsters learn about their environment, but the emphasis was on *play*. By learning how to play, children learned how to adjust to their peers and to the larger society, and learned the rules of the game of life in a painless and generally enjoyable environment. Froebel's kindergarten offered the first full expression of the need for peer group socialization.

Social Reform

In the latter part of the nineteenth century and the beginning of the twentieth century, the urban slums in large American cities stimulated many social reformers to begin a different kind of kindergarten as a means of trying to save the slum children from the unhealthy, crime-ridden, constricted environment

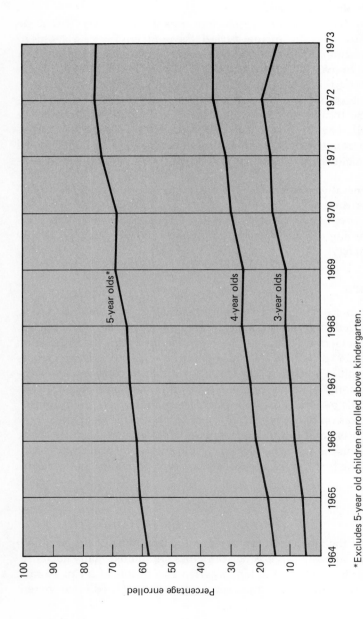

*Excludes 5-year old children enrolled above kindergarten.

Fig. 3.1   Preprimary school-age children enrolled in nursery school and kindergarten, October 1964 to October 1973 [From K. Snapper et al., *The Status of Children* (Washington, D.C.: George Washington University, 1975)]

of the streets. In effect, these kindergartens, often placed in settlement houses and churches, provided an island of affection and attention for the young child in a threatening world. On that island these children received affection, food, and the opportunity, through play, to learn social habits of cooperation and personal care habits such as cleanliness.

The basic objectives of these programs were *not* to stimulate and accelerate the intellectual abilities of children, but to provide them with social habits by which they could become effective members of a society, habits that they would not learn from the neighborhood environment in which they lived.[4] An important dimension of social reform was the attempt to provide constructive programs for handicapped children and thus give them a fighting chance in life.

Many strong movements in this country originated elsewhere. A good example was the movement originated by Dr. Maria Montessori, a physician who first became interested in preschool children through her work with mentally defective children. Much of Montessori's later work was influenced by that early experience.[5] She extended her work from the retarded to children who lived in abject poverty in Italy. In contrast to the kindergarten emphasis on general love and affection, Montessori stressed the need for specific objectives and the design of the materials for learning. Her emphasis on sensory education—the ability to learn through touching, seeing, and hearing—was a natural outgrowth of her work with children who were developmentally delayed. Through the use of a wide variety of materials, the children could proceed at their own pace in such a program. The emphasis was on individual development as opposed to the group-learning, social-play concept of the traditional kindergarten.

Head Start: A Noble Experiment

The use of early childhood programs as devices for social reform carries on in the present. We are still being influenced by one of the most extensive efforts ever undertaken—Project Head Start.

Head Start was one of the key campaigns in the War on Poverty announced by President Lyndon Johnson in 1964. Begun as a summer program for culturally deprived preschool children, it was proclaimed an instant success by an eager president only two months after it had begun.

> *This program which began as an experiment has been battle tested—and it has proved worthy. . . . The success of this year's program and our plans for the years to come are symbols of this Nation's Commitment to the goal that no American child shall be condemned to failure by accident of his birth.*[6]

The design of the program was based on earlier work on the debilitating effect of social class.[7] The typical haste with which America grasped and financed this program caused rapid expansion all over the country of programs based on a simple and somewhat incorrect idea—namely, that poor children had been deprived of experiences available to middle-class children, and that Head Start would compensate for the early lack with a program to fill those experience gaps. Although there was great diversity among Head Start programs, most emphasized good health care, language development, and social skills.

More deliberate evaluations by a variety of scientists and educators have made clear that such intervention does provide meaningful but limited increases in functioning intelligence.[8] Such gains can be eroded, however, unless the programs are continued.

A later report, which tested over 1,400 Head Start children before the program began and then again a year after, revealed modest gains in Stanford-Binet IQ (an average of +5 points), along with gains in skills related to schooling (vocabulary and numerical skills) and more positive attitudes toward education on the part of the parents of the children.[9] Opinions on the total impact of Head Start are still divided.

Increased Knowledge of Early Childhood

One of the reasons for increased interest in early childhood education is that the more research conducted on the capabilities of infants and young children, the more impressive become the conclusions.[10] Many important events appear to take place quite early in a child's life. An early truism, often repeated, was that the infant's world was "a buzzing, blooming confusion." Investigators now know that that statement grossly underestimates the young child's capabilities. A typical example of a summary statement of research findings is as follows:

> One could conclude from the research that the infant and young child is not a helpless blob waiting for the powerful internal engine of maturation to turn him or her into a human being. From the very beginning, the young child is a learner, a selective responder to stimuli, who is developing patterns of responses that cast long important shadows into later childhood and adulthood.[11]

In many cases, the statements of the investigators as they describe the infant and young child are tinged with awe as they marvel at what the young child is able to do. An example of this is provided by the description of the incredible obstacles a child has to overcome in learning the language:

> The plight of the infant or young child is not an easy one. He emerges in the midst of a group of native speakers of a language who do not speak his

language nor do they have the slightest intention of doing so. He has no aids in terms of dictionaries, interpreters, programmed language training textbooks, or even a rudimentary alphabet. He is exposed to intermittent bursts of verbal output in a veritable stream of sound. His task is to segment this stream of speech into the primary sounds (phonetic elements) and sound categories. He must identify the boundary markers of the meaningful units called words as well as the inflectional changes that can apply to the various words and classes of words. He must also learn how these sounds and words are distributed within lengthy monologues.

The job is not made easy for the infant by the native speakers (even his own mother), who do not themselves speak in carefully sequenced words which are well articulated. They speak quickly and efficiently and in the process run words together in almost monotonic streams with hardly a pause between separate sentences. Somehow the child overcomes these difficulties, and most children learn this complex system with relative ease over a period of three or four years.[12]

Bloom claimed in a much-quoted analysis that 50 percent of intellectual development takes place between conception and age four.[13] So the more that research showed the potent role played by early years, the more the realization grew of how our later years might be influenced by what happened in that period.

Family Role Change

Another clear influence in early childhood education has been the increased tendency for women to want to combine marriage and motherhood with a career. Figure 3.2 shows the steady growth of the percentage of mothers in the labor force with children under six. Whether they were working because they wished to or because they needed to, these working mothers needed to have some organized care for their young children while they were at work. They, therefore, became a strong voice for the increase and improvement of child education and related services.

Hess and Shipman have pointed out:

The current growth of programs in early education, and the large scale involvement of the schools and federal government in them, is not a transitory concern. It represents a fundamental shift in the relative roles and potential influence of the two major socializing institutes of the society—the family and the school.[14]

The cumulative effects of our increased knowledge, our desire for social reform, and changing roles for family members have led to public action.

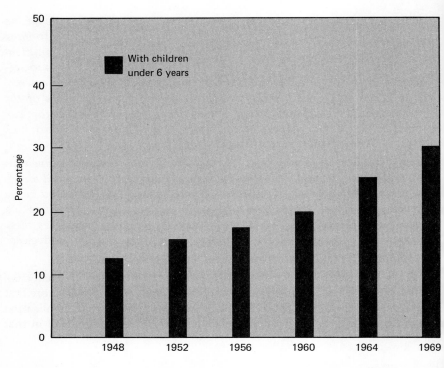

Fig. 3.2 Percentage of mothers with children under six years of age who were in the U.S. labor force, 1948–1949 [From *Profiles of Children* (Washington, D.C. White House Conference on Children, 1970)]

Plowden Report

Another overseas effort that became influential in this country was the study conducted in the field of early childhood by the Central Advisory Council of England under the direction of Lady Plowden, which has since become known as the Plowden report. In the field of nursery education, this report is note worthy for its strong recommendation favoring the expansion of early educa tion opportunities and its call for the responsibilities for such programs to be placed in education rather than the health departments. A few of the pertinent recommendations from that report are listed below:

1. *There should be a large expansion of nursery education, and a start should be made as soon as possible.*

2. *Nursery education should be available to children at any time after the beginning of the school year after which they reach the age of three until they reach the age of compulsory schooling.*

3. *Low priority should be given to full-time nursery education for children whose mothers cannot satisfy the authorities that they have exceptionally good reasons for working.*

4. *The education of children over three in day nurseries should be the responsibility of the education rather than health departments.*

5. *Nursery groups which are under the supervision of a teacher or head teacher of an adjoining primary school should be part of that school. Groups not attached to a school should form a single nursery center with the other groups which are supervised by the same qualified teacher.*

6. *Ideally, all services, including nursery, for the care of young children should be grouped together and placed near the children's homes and the primary schools. The planning of new areas and the rebuilding of old should take account of nursery education. The emphasis on good nursery programs did not imply a lack of interest in home based services which were also recommended.*[15]

Program Design for Early Childhood Education

The forces described above have provided the impetus for early childhood programs, but the professionals must design the content of such programs.

So what is the nature and content of early childhood programs? There is a wide spectrum of program activities and emphases currently in practice. To some extent, there would seem to be a tendency to emphasize the differences between programs rather than their commonalities. Without wishing to minimize differences in philosophy and program content, we present here some important points that are included in practically every American early childhood program.

1. An emphasis on language development, both receptive and expressive, as the basis for social communication and future academic performance.

2. An emphasis on social skills development. The importance of having the child learn the elements of cooperative play, of sharing, of appreciating the feelings of others, is a universal element in whatever program one finds.

3. The development of good physical habits and nutrition. Practically every early childhood program tries to provide nutritious snacks, lunches, and so on, to help the child to a healthy beginning, but also to encourage the development of habits of good eating.

4. The establishment of good relationships between the child and a caring adult or adults. The element of trust and respect between child and adult

is an integral part of the programs so that the child gains personal security from being close to a trustworthy and predictable adult.

5. A desire to involve the parents in the program to whatever degree they wish to participate. This means that the parent may act as a teacher's aid or a community volunteer or whatever. There is a clear expectation that these programs should enhance the parent-child bond and not substitute for it.

However, within these broad general objectives there is plenty of room for different emphases and strategies.

Crosscultural Influences on Early Education

An interesting survey was conducted by Robinson and Robinson that reviewed early childhood programs in eleven countries.[16] These countries were the United States, England, France, Switzerland, Sweden, Cuba, India, Israel, Soviet Union, Hungary, and Poland. In each of these countries the organization and style of management of early childhood programs fit into the general political system, as did the nature of the program content. There are many similarities among the programs of different countries. For instance, in every nation infancy and early childhood were acknowledged to be of critical importance.

Building a sound body and developing a healthy orientation toward oneself and others is a universal objective of early childhood programs, but in countries like England, France, Sweden, and Switzerland the goals for early childhood are for more individual and creative expression, whereas in socialist countries, such as the Soviet Union, the emphasis is more on the joyful sharing of the work of the group. Thus in the socialist preschool the children assume many of the duties of the classroom: "Preparing and serving food, clearing the tables for meals and activities, caring for the animals and plants in the nature corner, doing routine housework, cultivating the garden and so on."[17]

In the Soviet system there are explicit goals, and exercises to reach them, that are taught only by example in American programs. The very specific interest in the Soviet programs in hygiene and courtesy are presented as indications of these goals:

> The children are trained to wash their hands and faces thoroughly in the morning, before going to sleep, before meals, and whenever else they get dirty. They should know the proper order to observe in washing and they should know how to wipe their mouths and eat by themselves, take the food in small quantities and chew it well with their mouths closed. . . .

> The children should greet adults and other children affably and say "good bye" to them, not interfere in a conversation between their elders, and not interrupt a person who is speaking. It is essential for them to ask for things politely and to say "thank you" for any help they have received.[18]

In contrast, although Americans expect their children to grow into hard-working, productive adults, many Americans often feel that childhood is the last opportunity for an individual to be free of the burden of hard work. Therefore, there is an emphasis on joy and play as ways of expressing oneself before having to embark on the onerous world of work. The structure of the early childhood programs in various cultures becomes a kind of mirror of that society, of its values and its perceptions of the young child and his or her role in that society.

These various cultural streams of the past come together to form the river of the present, and much of our current effort in early childhood education is clearly the product of these earlier efforts, always altered somewhat, of course, by current circumstances and current values.

Programs for Handicapped

As much as one might agree on the value of starting early to stimulate development in normal children, the enthusiasm for beginning early is even more intensified for children who are handicapped.[19] A major breakthrough in federal legislation for the handicapped occurred in the late 1960s, and one of the characteristics of this legislation was a strong emphasis on the early childhood programs:

> The long range objective of the Handicapped Children's Early Education Program is to stimulate services to all 1,000,000 preschool age handicapped children by the end of the decade (1970's).[20]

This program established demonstration centers across the country to illustrate exemplary practices for the preschool mentally retarded, sensory handicapped, blind, deaf, emotionally disturbed, and so on. Some of the particular emphases are noted below:

> Few parents are prepared psychologically or financially to shoulder the enormous burden of care or treatment of a handicapped child. They need help in understanding their child's disability and in working with their handicapped child. Activities and services are designed to encourage active and varied parent participation.

> When possible, demonstration centers will be established in settings so that they may be used for the training of teachers, speech pathologists, and audiologists, clinicians, psychologist physicians, and other supportive personnel whose contributions are required in good effective early childhood education of the handicapped.

> This relatively new program ... is designed to develop and demonstrate effective approaches in assisting handicapped children during their early years and is structured so that other communities can replicate or adopt exemplary program components to meet their own needs.[21]

Just as the content and tone of the early childhood programs were influenced both by the special needs of the children involved and the background of
the professional, so are they also influenced by the broad general trends of
society. As Akers has pointed out,

> In the 40's and 50's, concerns for the young child were essentially directed
> toward his psychosocial development—a healthy, well-adjusted personal-
> ity. Heavily influenced by Freud and Erikson, early childhood educators
> and, perhaps to a slight lesser degree, researchers were preoccupied with
> such aspects of development as trust, autonomy and the acquisition of
> affective social skills. [22]

However, the 1960s were again the scene of massive social reform. The
awareness of the prevalence of school failure among children from culturally
different backgrounds deepened the concern of teachers and scientists about
whether these children had an adequate intellectual foundation to meet the
school on appropriate terms. Thus in programs like Project Head Start and the
Compensatory Education programs, the emphasis was placed on learning
those skills necessary to adequately master the school program at the first
grade level.

Controlling the Effects of Poverty

One of the strongest stimuli for the expansion of programs for early childhood
rested on the specific desire to combat early unfavorable experiences that children reared in conditions of both urban and rural poverty were suffering. Two
separate sets of information added impetus to that effort. First was the growing notion that potentially critical emotional, linguistic, and cognitive patterns
were associated with social backgrounds that were already present by age
three. [23] The professional world was also substantially impressed by Bloom's
contention that much of the intellectual growth of the human being takes place
during the first four to six years of life. [24]

The second issue that disturbed professionals was that there were demonstrable differences in the ways in which children were reared in lower-class and
middle-class families. For example, Bernstein [25] and Hess and Shipman [26] found
very different language interchanges among mothers and children from different social classes. The lower-class mothers focused attention on the use of
language to control the behavior of the child and to give directions. The
middle-class mothers tended more to explain the situation to the child and give
reasons for various behaviors.

Bee asked the mothers of preschool children to help their children do a
particular task, and then analyzed the language exchanges between mother
and child as they worked together to complete the task. [27] She found that the
middle-class mothers tended to allow the children to work on their own while

offering suggestions that helped the children find the solution. The lower-class mothers made suggestions quite specific to the solution of the problem, sometimes depriving the children of the opportunity to solve the problem themselves. These patterns observed in other settings caused concern that children would not develop the language facility (or behavior patterns) necessary to play the important role of student in their early school years.

Different Program Emphases

The Montessori Approach

There have been a number of identifiable approaches to the design of early childhood programs that have stressed special elements as important and unique. One of the best known approaches has been that of the Montessori movement.[28] An extraordinary burst of interest and enthusiasm for this approach was initiated in 1960 in the United States with the organization of the American Montessori Society. Over seven hundred schools are now identifying themselves as Montessori schools, with almost two hundred affiliated with the AMS organization.

The basic notion of the system that seems to appeal most strongly to American parents and child-care workers is that of *freedom within structure*. The child has the opportunity to explore his or her environment, but that environment is carefully constructed and materials provided so that the child will naturally learn important ideas and skills without dreary didactic approaches. The key premises of Montessori education are as follows:

1. *Children are to be respected as being different from adults, and as individuals who differ from each other.*
2. *The child possesses unusual sensitivity and mental powers for absorbing and learning from his environment that are unlike those of the adult in both quality and capacity.*
3. *The most important years of growth are the first six years of life when unconscious learning is gradually brought to the conscious level.*
4. *The child has a deep love and need for purposeful work. He works, however, not as an adult for profit and completion of the job, but for the sake of the activity itself. It is this activity which accomplishes for him his most important goal: the development of himself, his mental, physical, and psychological powers.*[29]

Piagetian Approach

Hooper[30] reports on a curriculum that places special stress on the work of Piaget.[31] Piaget is well known for his charting of developmental skills from early childhood. His basic ideas stress that intelligence is rooted in biological adaptation and that there is a complete, unbroken continuity between the baby's reflexes and his or her higher mental processes. Intelligence grows as an integrated whole structure and the child's socioemotional and cognitive life are inseparable.

The early childhood programs that are based on Piaget's work featur organized and planned experiences for the child, each proceeding in a hierarchy of difficulty as the child succeeds at the lower levels in areas of par ticular importance. The exercise noted in Table 3.1 is one of a series of seven

Table 3.1
Seriation training

Session I

Materials: Three bowls; four pitchers

1. Introduce two bowls of obvious size difference.
    a. Comparison between two bowls. "Can you tell me which one is biggest smallest?"
    b. Introduce middle-size bowl. Compare it to the smallest. "Is this bowl smalle or bigger than this one?"
    c. Compare middle bowl with largest bowl. "Is this bowl smaller or bigger tha this one?"
    d. Ask one child, "Remember the story of Goldilocks and the three bears? Thes bowls look like they belong to Papa bear, Mama bear, and Baby bear. Coul you put them on the table for the three bears? First the biggest for Papa bear the next biggest for Mama bear, and then the smallest one for Baby bear."
    e. Let each child have a turn. Repeat with each child, "The biggest, the nex biggest, and the smallest one for Baby bear."
2. Introduce two pitchers of obvious size difference. "What are these?"
    a. Compare two pitchers. "Can you tell me which one is the biggest, smallest?"
    b. Introduce middle-size pitcher. Compare with smallest, largest.
    c. Ask one child, "If you were a Mother and were putting these pitchers away o the shelf, show me how you would put the biggest, next biggest, an smallest."
        For boys—"If you were a man working in the service station, etc."
3. Introduce fourth pitcher of a different size. "Look, I have another pitcher—wher shall we put this one on the shelf? Why?"
4. Teacher lines them up the wrong way and asks if that is the right way. Let th child correct mistake. Repeat.
5. Have each child take a turn in seriating pitchers. Repeat biggest, the next bigges and the smallest one, if necessary.

From J. Hooper, "An Evaluation of Logical Operations Instruction in the Preschool." In R. Parke (Ed.), *The Preschool in Action* (Boston: Allyn & Bacon, 1973). Reprinted by permission.

teen that explore increasing refinements of *seriation training*, or training in the understanding of ordered sequences.

Developmental Programs

Out of the earlier efforts to chart the various developmental stages of children across multiple developmental dimensions such as motor coordination, language, and social development[32] came another philosophy of early childhood education. This point of view used developmental information to design activities especially to stimulate the child's performance in those various developmental channels.

One example of such an approach is provided by Lillie in his Carolina Developmental Profile. Figure 3.3 shows a developmental profile built around various items that can be checked off for each child to show where that child is in the mastery of the various developmental milestones. For example, we can see that one particular expressive language task was still not completed by this child at age three. This would be the basis for an instructional program, as would be the information on fine motor skills. By means of such a profile, the teacher in an early education program would be able to identify the needs of the child and have available the particular tasks that the child would be expected to do next.

Table 3.2 shows the types of instructional activities that follow through on the specific instructional objectives in the area of receptive language. In addition, there are particular activities noted that would help the teacher carry out the instructional objectives. Also given in Table 3.2 are the materials needed for the activity. An added advantage to this approach is that it makes it easy to assess the child's attainments precisely.

Programming for Socioemotional Development

Another example of the increasing specificity in terms of objectives in early childhood education programs is indicated in Table 3.3. The emphasis in this program is less on motor or language skills and more on the ability of the individual to participate constructively in social interaction.

This approach to socioemotional development is also based on a developmental stage model. We should be able to locate at which stage the child is operating, and which stages they have yet to reach. For example, a child may be observed to be using words to express herself or himself in the group but not really be able to express awareness of the relationship between feelings and behavior in self and others. That would place the child between stages 3 and 4 in communication and give the teacher some clues as to the kind of experiences the child may need to help move him or her to the next stage of communication. Similar identification of a child's progress in socialization can be made. This is especially important when the child is behind.

CAROLINA
DEVELOPMENTAL
PROFILE

A Criterion-Referenced Checklist for
Planning Early Childhood Education

Name *Jonathan Jenkins*

Date of birth *5/9/70*

Date *10/25/74*

Developmental age level

	Gross motor	Fine motor	Visual perception	Reasoning	Receptive language	Expressive language
5	(20) (19) (18) (17) 16̷	(15) (14) (13) (12)	(12) (11) (10)	(12) (11) 10̷ (9) 8̷ 7̷	(12) (11) 10̷	(12) (11)
4	(15) 14̷ (13) 12̷ 11̷	(11) (10) 9̷ (8)	(9) 8̷ 7̷	6̷ 5̷ 4̷	(9) 8̷ 7̷	(10) 9̷ (8) 7̷
3	10̷ 9̷ 8̷ 7̷ 6̷	7̷ 6̷ 5̷	6̷ 5̷ 4̷	3̷ 2̷ 1̷	6̷ 5̷ 4̷	6̷ (5) 4̷
2	5 4 3 2 1	4 3 2 1	3 2 1		3 2 1	3 2 1

Priority Long-Range Objectives (by area and task number): *Fine motor tasks 8, 10, 11, 12, 13, 14, 15. Expressive language tasks 5, 8, 10, 11, 12.*

Fig. 3.3 Carolina Developmental Profile [After C. Lillie, *Early Childhood Education* (Chicago: Science Research Associates, 1975)] Reprinted by permission.

Table 3.2

Developmental objective (by task no.)	Instructional activities
10. Touches the pictures with the knives on request Materials for activities 1. Two long pieces of yarn; common objects 2. Flannel board and cutouts 3. Pictures of single objects; pictures of multiple objects	1. Using yarn, mark off on a table two areas approximately 6 × 6 inches square. In one area put two or more forks. Then ask the children to show you the forks. Be sure that you do not always put the single object in the same place. 2. Follow the same procedure as activity 1 above except use the flannel board. 3. Have several pictures that show each object as a single unit in one picture and as a multiple unit in a second picture (one boat, two or more boats). The teacher says, "Point to the boat; point to the boats; point to the knives; point to the knife."
11. Touches the one that is dark but not little on request Materials for activities 3. Sets of objects (objects in set should be the same color but different sizes)	1. Child must be able to discriminate between big and little, between dark and light, and know the meaning of *not* before he can pass this objective. 2. Play altered version of Simon Says. Use familiar objects in the room. "Simon says touch the chair but not the table." 3. Gather sets of several objects. Examples: Two red apples, one very big and one little. Say to the children, "Show me the one that is [color] but not big [or little]."
12. Touches the picture of the one who will be hurt, on request (is able to understand the concept of "will") Materials for activities 1. Calendar 2. Pictures that indicate a future event 3. Pictures of objects in the process of being made; pictures of the completed objects	1. During the opening activities many teachers discuss the days of the week. "Yesterday was ____; today is ____; tomorrow will be ____." 2. Show the children a set of three pictures: a boy swimming, an apple, and a Christmas tree. Ask the child to show you which picture tells us that Santa will come. You can use the same procedure with other holidays. 3. Present the children with pairs of pictures such as cookie dough and finished cookies, cake batter and finished cake. Ask the children which picture will be cookies.

After D. Lillie, *Early Childhood Education* (Chicago: Science Research Associates, 1975). Reprinted by permission.

Table 3.3
Developmental therapy goals for each curriculum area at each stage of therapy

Stage	Behavior	Communication	Socialization	Academic skills
I	To trust own body and skills	To use words to gain needs	To trust an adult sufficiently to respond to him	To respond to the environment with processes of classification, discrimination, basic receptive language concepts, and body coordination
II	To successfully participate in routines and activities	To use words to affect others in constructive ways	To participate in activities with others	To participate in classroom routines with language concepts of similarities and differences, labels, use, color; numerical processes of ordering and classifying; and body coordination
III	To apply individual skills in group processes	To use words to express oneself in the group	To find satisfaction in group activities	To participate in the group with basic expressive language concepts; symbolic representation of experiences and concepts; functional semiconcrete concepts of conservation; and body coordination
IV	To contribute individual effort to group success	To use words to express awareness of relationship between feelings and behavior in self and others	To participate spontaneously and successfully as a group member	To successfully use signs and symbols in formalized school work and in group experiences
V	To respond to critical life experiences with adaptive, constructive behavior	To use words to establish and enrich relationships	To initiate and maintain effective peer group relationships independently	To successfully use signs and symbols for formalized school experiences and personal enrichment

From M. Wood (Ed.), *Developmental Therapy* (Baltimore, Md.: University Park Press, 1975)
Reprinted by permission.

Alternative Early Education Programs

One of the most innovative ideas of the late 1960s came out of an organization known as the Children's Television Workshop. There are few citizens in the United States who are not aware of that organization's most famous product, the television program *Sesame Street*. Designed to be a combination of entertainment and education, *Sesame Street* was created to reach the preschool child (particularly the child without middle-class advantages) with the fundamental learning building blocks to prepare the child for the school experience. The popularity of the program left little doubt as to its entertainment value, but was it a viable alternative as a device for early education?

A major evaluation study was commissioned to answer that question.[33] If the answer was *Yes*, then children could receive adequate preparation for school without the necessity for a major program in a day-care center or early education center, but merely by turning on the television set at home. The potential of educational television for education was suggested by the results of the evaluation study.

1. The children who watched the most, learned the most.
2. The skills that received the most time and attention on the program itself were . . . the skills that were best learned. (It was in the area of letters and numbers that the children's gains were most dramatic.)
3. The program did not require formal adult supervision in order for children to learn in the areas that the program covered. Viewing at home was as great as viewing under supervision.[34]

While the TV program was shown to be successful in what it attempted to teach, there remain interesting questions as to whether TV programs can teach important social skills or more complex cognitive skills that seem to be part of the normal repertoire of early education programs. It must be noted that even the original results are now being questioned by critics of the approach.[34]

Another form of alternative early education programs are the home training or parent training programs. In these programs the emphasis is on the training of parents to perform the teaching role in the home or the introduction of parent surrogates in the home who can carry out some of the major teaching roles to achieve early education goals. Various projects [35] have demonstrated that some of the same gains that have been made in special early education programs can also be made by providing a well-organized home stimulation or training program.

Diversity as a Desired Goal

There seems to be little doubt that there are many different paths to success in the early education of children. Given the wide variety of opinions and values concerning early education it seems clear that the best approach is to provide the widest variety of options to parents. A diversity of options would satisfy the parent's own particular philosophy and value system, and still provide the necessary building blocks to children so that they can progress into the preparatory phase (school) of the modern society ready to respond appropriately to that challenge.

Summary

There has been a strong and continuing trend toward more provisions for early childhood education in the United States over the past fifteen years. This trend seems to be supported by a variety of forces; most notably the increased knowledge of the importance of early childhood for later development, a strong desire to use early education as a vehicle for social reform, and changing family roles.

The various programs, while presenting differences in philosophy, have major areas of agreement. Almost all programs in the United States focus on language development, the practice of social skills, the formation of good health and nutritional habits, and the establishment of good adult-child relationships. Specific program content does vary according to the values and philosophy of the supporting culture.

There are a number of alternative programs for early childhood that do not require the establishment of nursery schools or day-care centers. These include a variety of home training programs where parents are given specific training or home visitors come to work with the children in the home setting. Some additional experiments with the use of TV to reach children are also visible.

Since the current differences in attitudes and values regarding early childhood education are impressive, a diversity of program approaches seem called for so that the children can receive the necessary instruction within the framework of the family's own value system.

References

1. See, for example, I. Gordon (Ed.), *Early Childhood Education* (Chicago: University of Chicago Press, 1972).

2. K. Snapper, H. Barriga, F. Baumgartner, and C. Wagner, *The Status of Children* (Washington, D.C.: Social Research Group, George Washington University, 1975).

3. M. Lazerson, "The Historical Antecedents of Early Childhood Education." In Gordon (Ed.), *Early Childhood Education*.

4. Lazerson, "The Historical Antecedents of Early Childhood Education."

5. M. Montessori, *The Montessori Method* (New York: Shocken, 1964).

6. L. Johnson, "Remarks on Announcing Plans to Extend Head Start," *Published Papers of the President*, No. 467, August 31, 1965 (Washington, D.C.: Government Printing Office, 1966).

7. See particularly A. Davis, *Social Class Influences upon Learning* (Cambridge, Mass.: Harvard University Press, 1961).

8. J. McDavid, *Project Head Start: Two Years of Evaluation Research* (Washington, D.C.: Division of Research and Evaluation, Project Head Start, 1968).

9. *Effects of Different Head Start Program Approaches on Children of Different Characteristics: Report on Analysis of Data from 1968–1969 National Evaluation.* Prepared for Project Head Start (Systems Development Corporation), Office of Child Development, Department of Health, Education, and Welfare, Washington, D.C., 1972.

10. See B. Caldwell, and H. Ricciuti, *Review of Child Development Research*, Vol. 3 (Chicago: University of Chicago Press, 1973).

11. J. Gallagher, *Teaching the Gifted Child* (Boston: Allyn & Bacon, 1975), p. 62.

12. K. Ruder, W. Brecker, and C. Ruder, "Language Acquisition." In J. Gallagher (Ed.), *The Application of Child Development Research to Exceptional Children* (Reston, Va.: Council for Exceptional Children, 1975), p. 2.

13. B. Bloom, *Stability and Change in Human Characteristics* (New York: Wiley, 1956).

14. R. Hess and V. Shipman, "Early Experience and the Socialization of Cognitive Modes in Children," *Child Development* 36 (1965), 869–886.

15. *Children and Their Primary Schools* (Plowden Report) (London: Report of the Central Advisory Council on Education, Her Majesty's Stationery Office, 1967), Vol. 1, pp. 132–133.

16. N. Robinson and H. Robinson, "A Cross-Culture View of Early Education." In Gordon (Ed.), *Early Childhood Education*.

17. H. Chauncey (Ed.), *Soviet Preschool Education*, Vol. 1 (Princeton, N.J.: Educational Testing Service, 1969).

18. Chauncey (Ed.), *Soviet Preschool Education*, p. 78. Reprinted by permission.

19. S. Kirk, *Educating Exceptional Children* (Boston: Houghton Mifflin, 1972).

20. E. Martin, "Thoughts on Mainstreaming," *Exceptional Children* 41 (1974), 150–153.

21. *Handicapped Children's Early Education Program* (Washington, D.C.: Report of the Secretary's Committee on Mental Retardation of the Department of Health, Education, and Welfare, 1971), pp. 1–3.

22. M. Akers, "Prologue: The Why of Early Childhood Education." In Gordon (Ed.), *Early Childhood Education*. Reprinted by permission of the National Society for the Study of Education.

23. J. Bruner, "Poverty and Childhood." In Parker (Ed.), *The Preschool in Action* (Boston: Allyn & Bacon, 1972), p. 8.

48   *Perspectives on Education*

24. Bloom, *Stability and Change in Human Characteristics.*
25. B. Bernstein, "Social Class and Linguistic Development: A Theory of Social Learning." In A. Halsey, J. Floud, and C. Anderson (Eds.), *Education, Economy and Society* (New York: Glencoe Free Press, 1961).
26. Hess and Shipman, "Early Experience and the Socialization of Cognitive Modes in Children."
27. H. Bee, "Social Class Differences in Maternal Teaching Strategies and Speech Patterns," *Developmental Psychology* 1 (1969), 726–734.
28. See T. Banta, "Montessori: Myth or Reality?" In Parker (Ed.), *The Preschool in Action.*
29. Banta, "Montessori: Myth or Reality?", pp. 220–221. Reprinted by permission.
30. F. Hooper, "An Evaluation of Logical Operations Instruction in the Preschool." In Parker (Ed.), *The Preschool in Action.*
31. J. Piaget, *The Origins of Intelligence in Children* (New York: W.W. Norton, 1952) and *The Construction of Reality in the Child* (translated by Margaret Cook) (New York: Basic Books, 1954).
32. See, for example, A. Gesell and F. Ilg, *Infant and Child in the Culture of Today* (New York: Harper, 1943).
33. G. Bogatz and S. Ball, *The Second Year of Sesame Street: A Continuing Evaluation* (Princeton, N.J.: Educational Testing Service, 1971).
34. T. Cook, H. Appleton, R. Corner, A. Shaffer, G. Tamkey, and S. Weber, *Sesame Street Revisited* (New York: Russell Sage Foundation, 1975).
35. S. Gray and R. Klaus, "The Early Training Project: A Seventh Year Report," *Child Development* 41 (1970), 909–924; and E. Schaefer and M. Aaronson, "Infant Education Research Project: Implementation and Implication of a Home Tutoring Program. In Parker (Ed.), *The Preschool in Action*, pp. 410–430.

Suggested Readings

Caldwell, B. and H. Ricciuti (Eds.). *Review of Child Development Research.* Chicago: University of Chicago Press, 1973.

Gordon, I. (Ed.). *Early Childhood Education* (Seventy-First Yearbook for the National Society for the Study of Education, Part 2). Chicago: University of Chicago Press, 1972.

Kirk, S. *Educating Exceptional Children.* Boston: Houghton Mifflin, 1972.

Lillie, D. *Early Childhood Education.* Chicago: Science Research Associates, 1975.

Parker, R. *The Preschool in Action.* Boston: Allyn & Bacon, 1972.

Ryan, S. (Ed.). *A Report on Longitudinal Evaluation of Preschool Programs*, Vol. 1. Washington, D.C.: Office of Child Development, Department of Health, Education and Welfare Publications (OHD) 75–24, 1974.

Jane A. Stallings

What teachers do does make a difference – a study of seven follow through educational models

4

r. Stallings' chapter is the only one that deals primarily with a single emrical study. We asked Dr. Stallings to write this chapter because we think e project that she directed and the data she obtained represent one of the ost important single studies conducted in American education. The con-ntion that schools can markedly affect the growth and development of ildren has been seriously questioned by Coleman, Jencks, and others. his study clearly indicates that classroom activity is a crucial variable in e development of the child.

Jane A. Stallings

Dr. Stallings is presently manager of Classroom Process Studies at Stanford Research Institute. She was trained as a teacher at Ball State University, and taught in the classroom for nine years. Her graduate work in educational research and child development was conducted at Stanford University.

Do classroom practices make a difference in how children grow and develop? In order to answer this kind of question, the government over the past seven years has funded a group of planned educational experiments. A variety of educational theories have been put into practice in a program called Follow Through Planned Variations.

The program began when the government invited educators to submit plans for establishing their various teaching models in public schools in order to test whether their individual approaches could improve the educational achievement of economically disadvantaged children. From the group who came forward, twenty-two were eventually selected to implement their programs in the Follow Through study. These educators are called "sponsors" because they each sponsored a particular model of education. Although the project varied somewhat from year to year, ultimately Follow Through models were implemented in 154 Follow Through projects within 136 urban and rural communities in all regions of the country.

The theory and practices proposed by the various educational sponsors were quite diverse, and from the program's inception in 1969, government agencies and educators asked: "Does planned variation exist, and, if so, how do the various educational programs effect children?"

The purpose of a recent report by Stallings and Kaskowitz[1] was to study the classroom implementation* of seven Follow Through sponsors' models to evaluate whether or not the planned variations were in existence. Three previous studies of Follow Through implementations were limited to one or two locations per sponsor. With such small samples, few generalizations could be made regarding the sponsors' performances at other locations. Realizing that a study of greater scope was needed in order to make generalizations regarding the sponsors' ability to implement their models in many locations, the Office of Education commissioned the Stallings/Kaskowitz study, which is summarized here. The study assessed the impact of the various classroom instructional processes used by sponsors on the growth and development of children, as well as the implementation of the Follow Through sponsors' programs in the classrooms.

The data presented in this report were collected in the spring of 1973 in thirty-six project locations. The sample represents approximately twenty first-grade and twenty third-grade classrooms for each of seven Follow Through sponsors, at five or more sites per sponsor.[2] Program implementation in the classroom was judged on the basis of two criteria: (1) the extent to which a

---

* Implementation means the ability of the sponsor to teach inservice teachers to use the materials and methods the sponsor has specified. The sponsor's staffs trained inservice teachers through the use of video tapes, workshops, demonstrations, discussions, observation sessions in model schools, and self-reports.

sponsor's classrooms were found to be uniform on selected implementation variables, and (2) the extent to which a sponsor's classrooms differed from the traditional Non-Follow Through classrooms on the same set of variables.

Classroom Implementation

Methodology Used in the Study of Implementation

The first step in the assessment of classroom implementation was to describe each educational model in detail. The model descriptions were prepared by The Standard Research Institute and reviewed by the sponsors and then revised according to the sponsor's specifications. With assistance from Follow Through sponsors, an observation instrument was developed to collect data that would describe each sponsor's educational program. The observation instrument recorded information regarding the materials used in the classroom, the activities that occurred, the grouping of adults and children, and the interactions that occurred between the adults and children.

After the observation instrument was developed, training materials were prepared and observers from each location were trained to at least a 70-percent reliability on all sections of the observation instrument.

Data were collected at each location using the observation instrument. From these data, variables were created to see whether or not critical components of each sponsor's model could be observed in the classrooms. For example, were children in models that tried to teach inservice teachers to provide individualized instruction receiving more such instruction than children in traditional classrooms? A list of variables was prepared by the staff that described representative elements of each model. Each sponsor was sent the list of variables and asked to rate each variable according to (1) its critical importance to her or his model, and (2) the frequency with which the variable was expected to occur in a conventional classroom. Thus, a list of variables was selected for each of the seven models. Admittedly, the critical list of variables describes a sponsor's model only in part and there is considerable overlap among the critical variables (see Table 4.1). Some of the important subtle processes of the programs, such as developing self-motivation in students or concepts of time and space, have not been assessed. Reducing a model of a list of variables can provide only a partial picture of implementation. (See the Appendix to this chapter for a description of the models.)

Since the Follow Through Programs are intended to be innovative and to represent alternatives to the conventional classroom, a pool of Non-Follow Through classrooms was used as the standard from which Follow Through classrooms were expected to differ in specified ways. The standards were established separately for first and third grades.

Table 4.1
List of critical variables selected by sponsors

No.	Description	Far West Labs	University of Arizona	Bank Street	University of Oregon	University of Kansas	High Scope	EDC
24	Child selection of seating and work groups	X	X	X			X	X
25	Games, toys, play equipment present	X	X	X			X	X
39	General equipment, materials present	X				X		X
65	Guessing games, table games, puzzles		X			X	X	
66	Numbers, math, arithmetic	X	X	X	X	X	X	X*
67	Reading, alphabet, language development	X	X	X	X	X	X	X*
70	Sewing, cooking, pounding		X				X	
71	Blocks, trucks						X	
74	Practical skills acquisition	X†	X	X				
83	Wide variety of activites, over one day	X	X	X			X	X
86	Teacher with one child	X		X			X	
87	Teacher with two children		X	X				
88	Teacher with small group			X	X	X	X	
92	Aide with one child	X						
94	Aide with small group		X	X	X	X	X	
114	One child independent		X					X
115	Two children independent			X				X
116	Small group of children independent	X		X				X
239	Math or science equipment/Academic Activities	X					X	X
240	Texts, workbooks/Academic Activities				X	X		

(cont'd)

*Third grade only.
†First grade only.

Table 4.1 (cont'd)
List of critical variables selected by sponsors

No.	Description	Far West Labs	University of Arizona	Bank Street	University of Oregon	University of Kansas	High Scope	EDC
343	Child to adult, all verbal except response	X		X				
344	Individual child verbal interactions with adult	X	X	X	X	X	X	X
350	Child questions to adults	X	X	X			X	X
363	Child group response to adult academic commands/requests or direct questions				X			
372	Child presenting information to a group			X			X	
375	Adult instructs an individual child	X						X
376	Adult instructs a group				X			
390	Adult task-related comments to children	X		X				X
394	All adult acknowledgment to children		X	X	X	X	X	
398	All adult praise to children				X	X		
412	Adult feedback to child response to adult academic commands/requests, questions				X	X		
420	Adults attentive to a small group	X			X		X	
421	Adults attentive to individual children	X	X	X		X	X	
423	Positive behavior, adults to children	X	X	X				
435	Total academic verbal interactions				X			
438	Adult communication or attention focus, one child	X		X		X	X	X
440	Adult communication or attention focus, small group				X			
444	Adult movement	X			X		X	
450	All child open-ended questions							X

No.	Description	Far West Labs	University of Arizona	Bank Street	University of Oregon	University of Kansas	High Scope	EDC
451	Adult academic commands/requests and direct questions to children	X			X			
452	Adult open-ended questions to children	X	X	X		X	X	X
453	Adult response to child's question with a question						X	X
454	Child's extended response to questions		X	X			X	
456	All child task-related comments	X	X					
457	All adult positive corrective feedback	X	X		X	X		
460	All child positive affect	X						X
469	All adult reinforcement with tokens					X		
509	Child self-instruction, academic				X*		X	X
510	Child self-instruction, objects			X			X	
513	Child task persistence			X		X		
514	Two children working together, using concrete objects						X	
515	Small group working together, using concrete objects			X				
516	Social interaction among children			X			X	X
574	Child movement	X	X				X	X
599	Child self-instruction, nonacademic	X						
	Total number of Critical Variables	28† 27*	21	27	16† 17*	17	29	20† 22*

*Third grade only.
†First grade only.

For each sponsor's classroom, an implementation score was computed fc
each variable of each sponsor. Table 4.2 illustrates the computation for on
variable, "Wide Variety of Activities," for one sponsor (Far West Laboratory
A total implementation score for each classroom was also computed.

To measure how well each Follow Through sponsor's model was impl‹
mented in the classrooms, a total score was computed for each Non-Follo‹
Through classroom using each sponsor's set of implementation variables. Th
average score of all Non-Follow Through classrooms was reported for eac
sponsor's set of variables. Comparisons were made separately for first an
third grades to show the differences between the Follow Through sponsor
classrooms and the Non-Follow Through classrooms.

Implementation Findings

Implementation was judged on two criteria: (1) Were the sponsors' classroom
different from the comparison Non-Follow Through classrooms? (2) Were th
sponsors' classrooms similar to each other in the frequency of specified pr‹
cesses used? In other words, do all four first grades in Salt Lake City have sin
ilar scores on the variables and do the four first grades in Berkeley have scor‹
similar to first grades in Salt Lake? (See Table 4.2.)

On the first criterion, all seven of the sponsors' implementation mea
scores for both grade levels differed significantly from the Non-Follo‹
Through classroom means. For the most part, on the second criterion th
twenty first grades and twenty third grades of each sponsor appeared remar‹
ably similar regardless of the site. There were some instances for some spo‹
sors where one site or one or two classrooms had implementation scores as lo‹
as, or, in one case, lower than Non-Follow Through. However, considerin
the diverse locations and the enormous task of making educational theor
come alive consistently in the classrooms, we conclude that the seven mode
have been implemented to a remarkable degree.

Classroom Processes and Child Outcomes

The study of implementation would be of little importance if we did not b‹
lieve that differing educational theory and practices affect children differentl‹

Like educators in general, Follow Through sponsors feel that the develo‹
ment of basic skills in reading and computing is important, but that it is als
desirable for children to develop such attributes as task persistence, attendir
ability, cooperation, inquiry behavior, and independence. While these attr
butes appear to be elusive, we have been able to operationally define and sy‹
tematically observe some of these behaviors.

Table 4.2
Wide variety of activities, over one day (variable 83)

Sites	First-grade classrooms with implementation scores of					Third-grade classrooms with implementation scores of				
	Poor	Fair	Good	Very good	Excellent	Poor	Fair	Good	Very good	Excellent
Berkeley, Calif.					4				1	3
Duluth, Minn.				3	1				1	3
Lebanon, N.H.					4					4
Salt Lake City, Utah					4			1	1	2
Tacoma, Wash.					4			2	1	1
Total Classrooms				3	17			3	4	13
Percentage of class-rooms				15%	85%			15%	20%	65%

Child Behavior

In a study based on 105 first-grade classrooms observed and tested in the spring of 1973, we are finding some interesting relationships between classroom processes used by the teacher and observable behaviors on the part of the children. These relationships have been adjusted to take account of entering ability. The classroom process data were collected on different days from the observed child behavior data. We do not know whether the findings are causal relations, but they do suggest hypotheses to test. The desirable child behaviors that will be discussed in this paper are independence, task persistence, cooperation, and question asking. Twenty-eight classroom process variables were correlated with these child behaviors.

In our study, *independence* is defined as a child or children engaged in a task without an adult. This type of independent behavior is more likely to be found in classrooms where teachers allow children to select their own seating and groups part of the time, where a wide variety of activities are available, and where an assortment of audiovisual and exploratory materials are available (see Table 4.3). The adults provide individual attention and make friendly comments to the children.

Fewer independent children are found in classrooms where textbooks and workbooks are used relatively more frequently. Fewer independent children are found in classrooms where adults ask relatively more direct questions regarding the subject matter. Fewer independent children are found in classrooms where adults praise children a lot (the variable describes praise in general, not for specific tasks or achievement).

The negative relationship between praise and independence is very high. This finding appears to support John Holt's description in *How Children Fail*[3] of the child who is dependent upon teacher's praise. Holt says such children are "teacher watchers"—they pitch their ears to what the teacher wants rather than behaving independently in relation to their own thoughts or tasks. This suggests that if teachers want to help children become independent in working on tasks, they should use praise sparingly and specifically.

However, praise does not affect all outcome measures in the same way. There is a positive correlation between praise for academic achievement and reading and math scores. A more thorough study of the relationship of praise to achievement in math showed that first-grade children in classrooms where the average entering ability was low had achievement scores in math that were more positively related to praise than did first-grade children in classrooms where the entering ability was higher. Third-grade children were less affected by praise.

The next dimension we will consider is task persistence. For this study, *task persistence* is defined as a child engaged in self-instruction over a desig-

Table 4.3
Partial correlations of instructional variables and child behaviors (Fall 1971 WRAT partialed out)

Instructional Variables	Independence		Task persistence		Cooperation		Child questions	
	Corre-lation	Signifi-cance level	Corre-lation	Signifi-cance level	Corre-lation	Signifi-cance level	Corre-lation	Signifi-cance level
Child/Adult ratio	.23	.02	.09		.02		−.15	
Children select groups and seats part of the time	.36	.001*	−.22	.03	.19	.05	.03	
Instructional materials used	−.01		.11		.09		−.07	
Audiovisual equipment used	.13		−.25	.01	.15		−.12	
General equipment and materials	.22	.02	−.08		.09		.005	
Total resource materials used	.13		−.23	.02	.18		.03	
Wide variety of activities occur concurrently	.22	.03	−.12		.15		.09	
Wide variety of activities occur during the day	.43	.001	−.36	.001	.32	.002	.14	
An adult with one child	.57	.001	−.16		.08		.14	
Use of TV	−.03		−.10		−.11		−.03	
Audiovisual equipment used in academic subjects	.24	.01	−.25	.01	−.01		−.04	
Exploratory materials used in academic subjects	.34	.001†	−.22	.03	.27	.006	−.11	
Math or science equipment used in academic subjects	−.18		.17		−.18		.11	

*.001 = 1 chance in 1000 that the relationship would occur by chance.
†.01 = 1 chance in 100 that the relationship would occur by chance.
Note: Number of classroom units used in the correlation computations = 102.

(cont'd)

Table 4.3 (cont'd)

Partial correlations of instructional variables and child behaviors (Fall 1971 WRAT partialed out)

Instructional Variables	Independence		Task persistence		Cooperation		Child questions	
	Corre-lation	Signifi-cance level	Corre-lation	Signifi-cance level	Corre-lation	Signifi-cance level	Corre-lation	Signifi-cance level
Textbook and workbooks used in academic subjects	−.33	.001	.31	.002	−.49	.001	−.04	
Puzzles and games used in academic subjects	.16		−.07		.09		−.07	
Adults asking children questions	−.17		.03		−.17		−.04	
Adult instructs an individual child	−.09		.23	.02	−.17		.22	.05
Adult comments to children	.22	.03	−.12		−.13		.36	.001
Adult task-related comments to children	.12		−.24	.02	.39	.001	−.16	
Adult acknowledges children	−.16		.15		−.11		.04	
Adult praises children	−.60	.001	.20	.05‡	−.21	.03	.02	
Adult speaks to one child	−.01	NS§	.13		−.06		.38	.001
Adult speaks to two children	.29	.003	−.13		.28	.004	−.03	
Adult speaks to a small group	−.15		.19	.05	.01		−.32	.001
Adult asks direct question about subject matter	−.41	.001	.07		−.28	.005	.03	
Adults ask open-ended thought-provoking questions	.16		−.12		.13		−.07	

‡.05 = 5 chances in 100 that the relationship would occur by chance.

§NS = Not significant

Note: Number of classroom units used in the correlation computations = 102.

ated period of time (a matter of a few minutes or more). If the child becomes ngaged in a conversation with someone else during the task, task persistence s no longer present, and the observer no longer codes task persistence. The ighest positive relationships indicate that task persistence occurs most often vhen textbooks and workbooks are used in the classroom. Where adults in-truct one child at a time, the children are also likely to be more task persis-ent. This may be because young children often have difficulty understanding roup instructions. However, in settings where adults work on a one-to-one asis, children can have a question answered or directions clarified and then ersist in the task at hand.

For this study, *cooperation* is defined as two or more children working ogether on a joint task. This kind of cooperation is more likely to be found in lassrooms where a wide variety of activities occur throughout the day, where xploratory materials are available, and where children can choose their own roupings. If the adults interact with two children, asking questions and mak-ng comments about the task, the children seem to be encouraged to join each ther in cooperative tasks. In classrooms where textbooks and workbooks which a child uses by himself or herself) are used a great deal, fewer children re coded as cooperating. (The negative correlation is strong.)

Educators have long recognized the value of a child's *asking questions* as a rimary means to gain information. Previous research indicates that question-sking is positively related to test scores.[4] In our study, we found that first-rade children asked more questions where there was a one-to-one relationship etween an adult and a child in the classroom, where adults responded to chil-dren's questions, and where adults made general conversational comments to hildren. Children asked fewer questions in classrooms where adults focused heir communication toward a small group.

Our observations indicate that the Educational Development Center's Open Education Program, Far West Laboratory's Responsive Educational Pro-ram, the University of Arizona's Tucson Early Education Model, and High/Scope's Cognitively Oriented Curriculum Model, all of which try to help hildren become independent and cooperative, have succeeded in their efforts. These Follow Through children are independent and do cooperate with each ther more often than do the children in comparison Non-Follow Through lassrooms. The children in the Bank Street College of Education Approach nd EDC's Open Education Program were observed to show more pleasure hrough laughter and smiles than do comparison children in Non-Follow Through classrooms. Children in classrooms using Far West's Responsive Edu-ational Program and University of Arizona's Tucson Early Education Model sk questions more often than do comparison children in Non-Follow Through lassrooms.

Test Scores

In a study of 105 first-grade and 58 third-grade classrooms in the fall of 197: we found that several classroom processes are related to achievement tes scores as tested on the Metropolitan Achievement Test in reading and mat (MAT). Test scores were adjusted to account for differences in scores childre received on the Wide Range Achievement Test when they first entere school.* Statistical tests were computed to see whether children in classroom with high test scores were taught in similar ways; that is, did their teachers us similar instructional processes.

In first-grade classrooms, we found that children with higher test score were most often taught in small groups of three to eight children. In thirc grade classrooms, children with higher test scores were taught in larger group of nine or more children.

Another finding indicated that children had higher test scores in clas: rooms where teachers more often used a stimulus-response-feedback inter action. In this kind of instructional process, the teacher provides a bit of infor mation and asks a question about the information; the child responds, and the teacher immediately lets the child know whether the response is right o wrong. If the child is wrong, the child is guided to the correct answer (positiv corrective feedback). If the child is correct, praise, a token, or some form c acknowledgment is given by the teacher to the child. This type of interaction i related to higher test scores in reading and math in both first and third grades.

Child self-instruction and task persistence are correlated with reading an math achievement. Also, in classes where social studies are taught, there is positive relationship with reading scores. Obviously, reading skills are used i social studies projects, but it is interesting to note that just the occurrence c social studies activities improves reading scores. In addition, the use of instruc tional aids such as programed materials, Cuisenaire rods, or Montessori mate rials is positively correlated with math scores.

Variables describing the average amount of time children spent in readin or math (either formal or informal) were highly correlated with math an reading achievement. A study of third-grade children's ability when the entered school indicated that the amount of time a child spent in math wa more closely related to achievement in classrooms where the children's enter ing school ability was lower than in classrooms where the children's enterin school ability was higher. This finding suggests that third-grade teacher should allocate more time to children who had lower scores when they entere school than to those who had higher scores. The relationship of praise t

---

* These are called adjusted gain scores.

achievement in math was similar. This type of interaction treatment study could be useful in planning educational programs to enhance the learning of children with differing abilities.

University of Oregon and University of Kansas, both structured models that instructed teachers to use the processes described above, have the highest scores of all sponsors in first-grade reading, and University of Kansas has the highest score in first-grade math. In third grade, the University of Oregon has the highest scores in both reading and math.

In general, a low absence rate, high independence, and high scores on Raven's Coloured Progressive Matrices (a test of nonverbal perceptual problem solving) tend to be associated with the more flexible classroom where a wide variety of materials are used, many different activities occur, and children are allowed to select their own groups and seating part of the time. In these more flexible classrooms, adults interact with children on a one-to-one basis, questions are more open ended, and children show more verbal initiative. Far West, University of Arizona, Bank Street, High/Scope, and Educational Development Committee use these processes. For the most part, children in these model classrooms have higher scores on the Raven's, lower absence rates, and show more independence than do children in either University of Kansas or University of Oregon, which are classified as structured models.

The Intellectual Achievement Responsibility Success Scale shows a positive correlation with variables describing the more open classrooms. Our results indicate that children from the more flexible classrooms take responsibility for their own success but not for their failure. Children from the more highly structured classrooms take responsibility for their own failure, but attribute their success to their teacher's competence or other forces outside themselves.

Child Outcome Scores Explained by Entering Ability and Classroom Processes

Whether or not classroom procedures affect the growth and development of children has been seriously questioned by other researchers such as Coleman, Jencks, Herrnstein, Moynihan, and Mosteller. Their research has indicated that a child's entering aptitude is of primary importance and, in fact, governs what the child will achieve in school. The study reported here, however, found that observed classroom procedures contributed as much to the explanation of test score differences as did the initial ability of children. Table 4.4 presents findings from a stepwise regression where the Wide Range Achievement Test score was entered into the regression first. The third and seventh columns report that part of the differences in test scores is explained by what the teacher does in the classroom; these are called the classroom process variables.

Table 4.4
Summary statistics for the stepwise regression analyses

Outcome Variable	First grade (N=105)				Third grade (N=58)			
	R^2 WRAT variables	R^2 WRAT, Process variables	Process variables (unique)	Number of process variables (included in regression)*	R^2 WRAT	R^2 WRAT process variables	Process variables (unique)	Number of process variables (included in regression)*
Behavioral Outcome Variables								
Child questions	.00	.28	.28	2	.00	.29	.29	3
Self-esteem	.00	.48	.48	5	.01	.42	.41	6
Child independence	.00	.67	.67	5	.01	.41	.40	3
Task persistence	.00	.44	.44	9	.06	.61	.55	6
Cooperation	.00	.32	.32	2	.10	.61	.51	5
Verbal initiative	.00	.22	.22	3	.00	.38	.38	2
Days Absent	.01	.67	.66	14	.07	.69	.62	6
Test Outcome Variables								
MAT math	.32	.74	.42	10	.17	.81	.64	8
MAT reading	.50	.73	.23	8	.42	.79	.37	7
Raven's	—	—	—	—	.41	.86	.45	9
IAR—success	—	—	—	—	.18	.57	.39	4
IAR—failure	—	—	—	—	.04	.83	.79	11

* These columns contain the number of process variables that entered the stepwise regression with an "F-to-enter" that was significant at .05.

In both first and third grades, child behavioral outcomes were only slightly explained by entering aptitude. As might be expected, these behaviors were much more related to classroom processes.

Very little of the absence rate was explained by entering ability, in either first or third grade. Approximately 60 percent of the variance was explained by the instructional procedures used in the classroom, suggesting that what occurs in classrooms is related to whether or not the child stays away from school.

The achievement of children in math at the end of first grade can be attributed in part to their ability as it was measured when they entered school, but even more so by the instructional practices used by their teachers. In first grade, entering ability accounts for approximately 40 percent of the achievement (Table 4.4). By the third grade, less of the achievement can be attributed to entering school ability and more to classroom practices.

One of the most important findings centers around the Raven's test of nonverbal reasoning or preceptive problem solving (considered to be a culture-fair test of fluid intelligence). The abilities required to function well on this test have not been considered to be influenced by environment. This study found that ability to perform well on the Raven's test was related to the classroom environment and strongly suggests that children who, for a period of three years, have been in classrooms that use a wide variety of activities and provide a wide variety of manipulative materials have learned to see the relationship between parts and wholes. At any rate, they learn to see spatial relationships similar to those tested on the Raven's.

Summary and Conclusions

Our evaluation suggests that it is possible to find out what a teacher can do to bring about desired child behaviors. In the more academically oriented classrooms, where there is a high rate of drill, practice, and praise and where the children are more frequently engaged in reading or math activities, the gain scores on reading and math are higher. These children also take more responsibility for their failure as tested on the Intellectual Achievement Responsibility Scale. These findings are supported by the fact that the sponsors that use these processes in their classrooms (University of Oregon and University of Kansas) also have higher scores on these tests.

In the more open, interdisciplinary classrooms, where a wide variety of activities are occurring, where a wide variety of materials are available, and where children can select their own groupings part of the time and engage in activities without adults, children have higher scores on the Raven's perceptual problem-solving test. They are also absent less often, and take more responsibility for their success as measured on the Intellectual Responsibility

Scale. They are more independent, cooperate more often, and ask more questions.

Classroom instructional processes (what teachers did) predicted as much or more of the outcome score variances as did the entering school test scores of children. On the basis of these findings, we conclude that what occurs within a classroom does contribute to achievement in basic skills, good attendance, and desired child behaviors.

Appendix A

1. Responsive Educational Model—Far West Laboratory

The Responsive Educational Program model advocates structuring learning activities so that they are self-rewarding (autotelic), and providing an environment that is responsive to each child's needs. The child's culture and the child's interests are the cornerstones upon which the curriculum is built. According to the autotelic principle, children learn best in an environment where they can try out things that interest them, and in which they can risk, guess, ask questions, and make discoveries, without serious negative psychological consequences. Autotelic activities include experiences and learning activities that are viewed as helping a child to develop a skill, learn a concept, and acquire self-direction and inner controls.

In a Far West Laboratory classroom, children are free to explore and to choose activities within a carefully controlled environment that contains learning centers and a variety of games, activities, and experiences. The children can search for solutions to their problems in their own way, using a variety of resources. Rather than being directive, the adults pose questions and guide the children to the discovery of solutions that may fit together and lead in turn to still other discoveries. The children's intrinsic satisfaction and pleasure in the experience are considered to be their reward, rather than extrinsic rewards.

The assumption is that no single theory of learning can account for all the ways in which children learn. It is considered essential that a variety of educational alternatives be available to build on whatever background, cultural influence, or life style the child brings to school.

Either individual children or small groups of children can be found in a variety of learning centers. Teachers, aides, or volunteers may work with a small group or with individual children. Concrete objects are often used for instructional purposes. In order to promote child inquiry, adults are most likely to ask leading open-ended questions or to respond to a child's question with another question.

2. Tucson Early Education Model (TEEM)—University of Arizona

Using children's characteristics when they begin school as a base, the TEEM model attempts to develop a foundation for their future learning. The goal is to increase the children's competence by improving their skills in four general curriculum areas: (1) development of language competence; (2) development of an intellectual base (ability to attend, recall, organize, and evaluate); (3) development of a motivational base (attitudes of productive involvement such as a liking for school and for learning, task persistence, and expectation of success); and (4) development of societal arts and skills (reading and math skills, social skills of cooperation, ability to plan). These skills are to be developed in a functional setting where concepts are illustrated by the use of practical examples from the children's home and school environments. Thus, the use of the home, neighborhood, and community as instructional resources is central to the model.

The classroom is organized around a variety of behavioral settings and learning centers. Children are allowed to make choices regarding their activities and seating arrangements. Small groups of children are able to learn from each other and are given individual attention from adults. Teachers are expected to be models of desired behavior. The sponsor of TEEM believes that the child's acquisition of language and other skills is affected by such modeling on the part of adults. Children are encouraged to ask questions and adults respond with liberal quantities of praise, support, attention, and affection. Every effort is made to ensure that the child will come to regard school as significant, desirable, and rewarding.

3. Bank Street College of Education Approach

The teacher in a Bank Street classroom creates a learning environment that is both challenging and supportive. There are opportunities for varied experiences and many options for learning: teachers meet with the whole class to share experiences and to plan the day's activities. They work primarily with individual children or small groups. Even in a group activity they always have the individual children in mind. When they are not actively engaged in a group activity, they move about the room analyzing children's work at various learning centers, stopping to elicit ideas from individuals or groups of children, exchanging comments about the task, helping children extend and build upon their ideas, or acknowledging their progress in specific terms.

The assistant, who is a paraprofessional, is a cooperative member of the teaching team, and participates in various learning activities that have been planned jointly with the teacher. The role of the assistant is very similar to that of the teacher in that both work with children on a one-to-one basis or in small groups in order to stimulate and extend learning.

The children in Bank Street classrooms are expected to take an active role in their learning. They can choose learning activities and materials. They can also participate in large- and small-group experiences planned by or with adults, such as discussions, story telling, or use of Cuisenaire rods. However most of the children's activities do not require adult direction but are enhanced by adult response, support, recognition, and extension. Independent activities may be engaged in by the children individually or cooperatively with other children. In general, academic experiences (reading, writing, computing) are integrated functionally into classroom activities such as cooking, experimenting with science equipment, and making things (for example, creative stories, woodwork). However, texts and workbooks are used occasionally. Children are encouraged to use language throughout the day. They question and exchange comments with their peers and the adults in the classroom, and these questions are viewed as revealing their ability to think, to reason, and to express themselves with positive affect. The program emphasis is on having the child experience work at first hand.

For the most part, Bank Street sites do not differ very much from each other in the degree of implementation. The greatest difference is seen in the third grade, where Tuskegee and Brattleboro have scores of 73 and Philadelphia has a score of 64. The variance among sites is not, however, greater than the variance within sites. The greatest within-site variation is found in Fall River first grades and Tuskegee third grades. Overall the Bank Street classrooms do differ significantly from non-Follow Through classrooms (with the exception of Philadelphia third grades).

A study of observer accuracy for Bank Street indicates that in general the codes that form the variables used in this section were acceptably reliable. There is one exception. The third-grade observer from Fall River had difficulty coding direct questions from the videotape. This is reflected in the fact that all Fall River third grades are in the first quintile on a variable that uses this code.

The reader is reminded that a sponsor's implementation is evaluated in two ways: (1) Do sponsor's classrooms differ from the traditional classroom? and (2) Are a given sponsor's classrooms similar to each other in level of implementation? The classrooms differ five points from non-Follow Through in seventeen out of nineteen first grades and thirteen out of nineteen third grades. Those instances of low classroom implementation scores are scattered over several sites. An analysis of variance indicated that the difference between sites is not greater than the difference within sites. Fall River first grades and Tuskegee third grades evidenced the most variance within sites.

4. Englemann-Becker Model for Direct Instruction, University of Oregon

The Englemann-Becker model is a highly structured academic program based on the premise that with proper instruction and consistent reinforcement all children can master the skills necessary to bring them up to the achievement level of national norms for their age group.

The model uses programed reading, math, language, and science materials. Highly specific methods are used to teach concepts and skills required for mastering sequenced tasks oriented toward an increasing level of competence.

Desired behaviors are systematically reinforced by praise and enthusiastic acknowledgment. Teachers and students share the pleasure of each other's achievements. Unproductive or antisocial behavior is ignored or stopped by a short reprimand. Ignoring is intended to withdraw from the behavior the attention that often reinforces it. When this is true, ignoring will eventually extinguish the behavior.

The classroom is usually staffed with two or three adults (regular teacher and one or two full-time aides recruited from the Follow Through parent community) for every twenty-five to thirty children. Each adult has been carefully trained. In most cases the adults teach a single subject. Working very closely with a small or large group of children, each teacher and aide use the programed materials in combination with predefined teaching strategies. A task is presented by the teacher. Demonstration is usually given and performance of the task by the children is tested. When the children respond the teacher provides immediate feedback. She or he proceeds only when each child is successful with a given instructional unit. When the children have completed their lessons with one adult, they proceed to their next subject with a different adult.

5. Behavior Analysis Approach—University of Kansas

The University of Kansas Behavior Analysis Approach aims at teaching children basic skills by means of systematic positive reinforcement of desired behavior. The model uses a token exchange system to provide an immediate reward to the child for successfully completing a learning task. Earned tokens can be exchanged later for special activities, such as participation in a spelling bee or a game of musical chairs, work on a puzzle, or play with blocks and trucks. Instruction (work time) and special activity (spend time) alternate throughout the day, with the amount of time spent on instruction increasing as the amount of reinforcement needed to sustain motivation decreases.

To encourage the child to move from external rewards to self-motivated behavior, more tokens are given during the initial stages of learning a task and progressively fewer are given as the child gains skills and takes pleasure in the skill. Similarly, fewer tokens are given as the child progresses through the grades.

The program emphasizes individualized instruction based on sequenced learning materials. The curriculum materials include a description of the behavior a child should be capable of at the end of a learning sequence, and clearly provide criteria for judging a correct response.

Small groups formed for reading instruction are directed by the teacher. A full-time trained aide provides math instruction. Spelling and handwriting are taught by another aide. Individual tutoring is provided by parent aides. Although children in this model are in small groups, they receive adult attention on a one-to-one basis.

The curriculum materials also provide for periodic testing and monitoring of achievement gains. A system of careful record keeping allows the teacher to keep a close watch on each child's progress and to tailor the curriculum to each child's needs.

6. Cognitively Oriented Curriculum Model—High/Scope

Derived from the theories of Piaget and developed through eight years of research with disadvantaged children, the Cognitively Oriented Curriculum model provides teachers in the early elementary grades with a theoretical framework that embraces cognitive goals, a teaching strategy, and suggested materials.

Five cognitive areas are emphasized: classification, number, causality, time, and space. The curriculum contains a carefully sequenced set of goals that enable the teacher to focus on the development of specific thought processes perceived as essential to children's mental growth.

In the cognitive curriculum, the teaching of basic skills is incorporated into the daily routine and is an integral part of the "plan, work, and evaluate" instructional sequence. There are a variety of learning centers from which children can choose the activities they wish to pursue. Each day, the children make a plan for their activities, follow their plan, represent or evaluate their activity in some way, and discuss what they have done in a group setting. The development of a child's reading, writing, and computation skills is expected to be a natural outgrowth of experiencing events, recording the events experienced, and transmitting these experiences to others.

More specifically, during the planning period, the children verbalize and then describe in writing what they are going to do during work time. Sometimes they make a list of the things they are going to use. The teacher helps to clarify and extend their thoughts with appropriate questions. During the work period, the children carry out their plans. They may involve themselves directly with reading, writing, or math activities by reading in the quiet area or writing a story in the book-making area; or they may involve themselves indirectly in such things as games, construction, and dramatic play. Writing and drawing during "representation" time requires the children to think about what they have done and to record these thoughts in some way; thus, reading and writing skills are developed. Language skills are emphasized during evaluation time when the children verbalize the thoughts they have recorded as part of their representations.

The cognitive approach is based on the sponsor's conviction that children must initiate their own learning. In order to promote such child initiative, specific instructional processes are required of High/Scope teachers: (1) instruction should be conducted with individual children and small groups; (2) children should engage actively with learning materials; (3) teachers should be good listeners; (4) discussions should be designed to encourage speculation and evaluation; (5) self-direction should be encouraged; and (6) verbal interaction among children should be encouraged.

7. Educational Development Center Open Education Program

The EDC Follow Through approach is a program designed to help communities generate their own resources to implement open education. EDC believes that learning is facilitated by a child's active participation in the learning process, that learning is optimized in a setting that provides a range of materials and problems to investigate. The program is based on the belief that children learn in many different ways and therefore should be given a variety of opportunities and experiences. Traditional academic skills are important, but they are more usefully and permanently learned when children have many opportunities to develop them in flexible, self-directed ways that allow learning to become a part of their lifestyles outside as well as in the classroom.

Interweaving of subject matter is essential to the open classroom. Children are expected to be purposefully mobile and independent, choosing activities out of their own interests. Thus, classrooms are often divided into several interest areas for activities in construction, science, social studies, reading, math, art, and music. Any or all of these interest areas may be used simultaneously by children during the day. An interdisciplinary or curriculum core approach is often used to teach reading, writing, and computation through a project, such as setting up and operating a store. Essentially, the intent of this approach is to encourage the development of: (1) problem-solving skills; (2) the ability to express oneself both creatively and functionally; (3) the ability to respect one's own thoughts and feelings; and (4) the ability to take responsibility for one's own learning.

Notes and References

1. Jane Stallings and David Kaskowitz, *An Assessment of Program Implementation in Project Follow Through* (Menlo Park, Ca: Stanford Research Institute, 1975).

2. The sponsors were distributed as follows: Far West Laboratory for Educational Research and Development (5 sites), University of Arizona (6 sites), Bank Street College of Education (5 sites), University of Oregon (5 sites), University of Kansas (5 sites), High/Scope (5 sites), Education Development Center (5 sites). They were chosen for observation because they met the criterion of having five or more sites being implemented.

3. John Holt, *How Children Fail* (New York: Pitman Publishing, 1964).

4. J. Stallings, *Follow Through Program Classroom Observation Evaluation 1971-1972*; and J. Stallings, J.P. Baker, and G.T. Steinmetz, *Interim Evaluation of the National Follow Through Program 1969-1971*, Appendix B Classroom Observation Evaluation 1970-1971.

Suggested Readings

Dunkin, M.J., and B.J. Biddle. *The Study of Teaching*. New York: Holt, Rinehart & Winston, 1974.

Good, T. *et al. Teachers Do Make a Difference*. New York: Holt, Rinehart & Winston, 1974.

Hall, G.E. *The Effects of "Change" on Teachers and Professors—Theory, Research, and Implications for Decision Makers*. Austin, Texas: Research & Development Center for Teacher Education, the University of Texas, 1975.

Joyce, B., and Marsha Weil. *Models of Teaching*. Englewood Cliffs, N.J.: Prentice-Hall, 1972.

Rist, R.C. *The Urban School: A Factory for Failure*. Cambridge, Mass: M.I.T. Press, 1973.

Soar, R.S. and R.M. Soar. "An Empirical Analysis of Selected Follow Through Programs: An Example of a Process Approach to Evaluation." Chapter II. In Gordon, I.J. (Ed.). *Early Childhood Education*. Chicago: National Society for the Study of Education, 1972.

Spaulding, R.L., and M.R. Papageorgiou. "Effects of Early Educational Intervention in the Lives of Disadvantaged Children, Final Report." Project Number 1-I-124. National Center for Educational Research and Development, U.S. Department of Health, Education and Welfare, June 1972.

Stallings, J.A. "Implementation and Child Effects of Teaching Practices in Follow Through Classrooms," *Monographs of the Society for Research in Child Development*, Ser. No. 163, 1975, Vol. 40, Nos. 7–8.

Stallings, J.A. "A Study of Implementation in Seven Follow Through Educational Models and How Instructional Processes Relate to Child Outcomes." *Journal of Teacher Education*, Spring 1976, American Association of Colleges for Teacher Education.

Tikunoff, W.J., D. Berliner, and R. Rist. *An Ethnographic Study of Forty Classrooms*. Technical Report No. 75-10-5. San Francisco: Far West Laboratory for Educational Research, 1975.

Wiley, D.E. "Another Hour, Another Day: Quantity of Schooling, a Potent Path for Policy." *Studies of Educative Processes*, No. 3. Chicago: University of Chicago, July 1973.

Thomas E. Curtis

Middle school grades

5

In previous chapters, Dr. Gallagher dealt with early childhood education and Dr. Stallings with elementary education. In this chapter, Dr. Curtis focuses his attention on the middle school grades.* The importance of these grades to the development of the child, and the various skills needed by the teacher to effectively work with middle-grade children, have been carefully delineated by Dr. Curtis.

---

* Some material from this chapter has been derived from Thomas E. Curtis and Wilma W. Bidwell, *Curriculum and Instruction for Emerging Adolescents* (Reading, Mass: Addison-Wesley), 1977.

Thomas E. Curtis

Dr. Curtis has been influential in the middle school movement since its inception. Included in his publications are *Curriculum and Instruction for Emerging Adolescents, The Middle School* (as editor), and many journal articles. He has served as consultant in school districts throughout the nation in addition to presenting speeches on middle school education to national educational organizations during the last decade. His work at the State University of New York at Albany includes inservice education for middle school teachers.

A largely neglected area in teacher education is that of the preparation of teachers specifically for middle schools or junior high schools. Most college students interested in teaching as a career elect either elementary or secondary teaching rather than grades 5 through 9. Problems exist for those expressing an interest in middle school teaching because most colleges do not offer a systematic series of undergraduate courses leading toward certification in this area. A significant percentage of colleges do not offer a course in education for emerging adolescents. In a majority of states no separate licensure is available for these specific grades; they are included in the certificates for the elementary and secondary grades.

Since most prospective teachers are not familiar with the advantages of teaching in the middle school they do not elect to take courses in middle school teaching even when they are offered, and do not elect to teach in middle schools as a first choice upon graduation. Hence, it is not unusual that some research studies indicate that some middle school teachers trained under these circumstances are not always happy with their lot, and would opt to go into secondary or elementary school if given an alternative.

To a long-time teacher in the middle school, accustomed to associating with active and enthusiastic children of this age, this situation seems puzzling. The only solution that springs readily to mind is the general lack of knowledge on the part of prospective teachers concerning both the purposes of middle school education and pupil characteristics at this age. Hence, the purpose of this chapter is to clarify for you, as a prospective teacher in the middle school, the following topics:

1. Characteristics of middle school education
2. Characteristics of pupils
3. Organization for teaching
4. Teaching functions
5. Teacher characteristics

With this information, as well as more opportunities to view the middle school setting, more prospective teachers might elect to teach in middle schools than is currently the case. Middle school education offers not only a great challenge to a teacher, but also great reward in the satisfaction of helping children emerge into a healthy adolescence.

Characteristics of a Middle School

The middle school is a transitional school whose programs should be designed to help pupils cope with personal and educational development needs during emerging adolescence. It is transitional because it serves an articulation function between elementary and senior high school. It is successful to the extent that it emphasizes curriculum and instructional practices rather than simple changes in administrative organization.

A well-organized middle school should serve three functions in the educational continuum of grades K–12. These are:

1. Establishment of an educational transition from elementary to secondary school philosophies
2. Development of a cultural transition from childhood to later adolescence
3. Recognition of and appropriate consideration for the extreme variabilities within and among the emerging adolescent group

Cultural transition from childhood to adolescence constitutes a series of steps, which move from a parent- and family-centered subculture, through a teacher-centered subculture, into an attitude toward life influenced by age-mates. The development from dependence on others to a condition of relative independence is an important part of this progression. Part of this growth includes the development of a value system that will enable adolescents to make decisions based on their own uniquely personal values rather than those of others, either adults or children.

The educational changes that occur as one progresses from elementary to secondary schools is evident to everyone. Elementary schools emphasize basic skills (reading, writing, and so forth) and social and emotional needs of children. Secondary schools place more emphasis on academic and subject matter acquisition in preparation for college and on the adult responsibilities of later adolescence. The middle school should serve as a transition between these two types of schooling, presenting an opportunity for children to learn how to learn, utilizing the basic skills acquired in the elementary school; to solve problems; and to utilize their newfound ability to conceptualize. Thus such purposes as the development of thought processes and the development of individual self-evaluation are emphasized.

At no time, with the exception of the first few months of life, is there more variance within and among an age group than is found among the emerging adolescent group. These differences make the development of alternative paths for individual purposes extremely important. The primary functions of a middle school should be based on the assumption of complete personalization of purposes,* of criteria for achievement, and of instructional procedures for the emerging adolescent.

---

* Personalization of purposes in this context refers to diagnosis and prescription based on personal purposes of individual pupils. Thus, one person may desire a career-oriented experience, whereas another may prefer an academic emphasis, while yet another is interested in aesthetic pursuits. Each set of purposes should be met.

In order to achieve these purposes the programs in middle schools should stress not only intellectual but also physical and emotional goals. In the area of physical development certain areas of concern are generally accepted. For example, the typical physical education instructor works toward the development of the individual physique of each pupil and stresses the pupil's acceptance of that body. Other areas of concern to all teachers are recognition and acceptance of an appropriate sex role and arrangement for adequate health diagnoses as well as evaluation of physical ability for each pupil. A crucial issue for emerging adolescents is that the concept and perception of sex first enters their lives in a practical way at this age. Until this age awareness of sex has an academic, unreal form. Suddenly, with the sexual maturing of puberty, this knowledge becomes very real and extremely important. A recognition of differences between boys and girls, and an acceptance of a more mature sex role, becomes vital. Both girls and boys develop a natural interest in the opposite sex. A compassionate understanding of this attitude on the part of the teacher can make this a more satisfying period of life for the uncertain emerging adolescent.

Emotionally, emerging adolescents become aware of themselves as independent and individual entities for the first time. This recognition of independence requires a concomitant degree of concern for social responsibilities, bringing ethics into consideration for the first time. At the same time comes a new sense of individuality and awareness, with more emphasis on leisure and service activities. As emerging adolescents look around them with more discriminating eyes, more thought is also given to the development of an aesthetic sense.

Programs in the middle school should not, because of this emphasis on physical and emotional concerns, devalue in any way the development of intellectual effort. Intellectual rigor is necessary within any school framework. However, differentiation should be made between content absorption and the dynamic sense of learning acquired in a true educational situation. For example, emerging adolescents should be learning to evaluate their own progress; they should be learning how to learn, using both skills and modes of learning as well as creativity and logic. They should be developing unique personal intellectual interests that will enable them to branch out into more meaningful experiences as they proceed to high school and college. They should have an opportunity for intellectual enjoyment at this period of their lives, in addition to developing a knowledge of content to serve as a base for future study.

To summarize, the primary purposes of the middle school should be to personalize the education of each individual pupil according to his or her own unique purposes, needs, desires, standards, and abilities to understand. If these goals are met, the middle school becomes an important element of the ladder from kindergarten through college.

Characteristics of Emerging Adolescents

Because the basic rationale for the organization of a middle school is concern for personal and educational development of emerging adolescents, it is necessary to investigate the characteristics of those individuals. When they enter the middle school most of them are children physically, emotionally, and intellectually. When they leave the middle school most have achieved puberty and are in the early or later adolescent stage. A major problem facing the middle school teacher is that children achieve sexual maturity at different ages. Some few girls may have reached sexual maturity prior to entrance to the fifth grade, whereas a small percentage of boys will not have reached puberty at the time of entrance into high school. The differences between prepubertal and postpubertal boys and girls are so radical that teachers should give considerable attention to this phenomenon. Girls ordinarily reach this stage approximately a year and a half earlier than boys (age twelve for girls, thirteen and a half for boys). In addition, girls and boys who achieve puberty earlier are generally more popular with members of both their own and the opposite sex. As might be expected, late maturers find this situation discomfiting.

Sudden growth spurts are common at this stage, ordinarily occurring just prior to puberty. However, some aspects of this sudden growth can create problems for a middle school youngster since clumsiness and weariness are usually found as a concomitant, tending to create problems both in the teacher's view of the emerging adolescent and in that individual's self-perception.

Physical growth at puberty can be divided into two different but equally important phases: the development of glands and organs having to do with sexual maturity; and the development of other internal organs, such as heart and lungs, which are associated with general physical growth. The development of various glands and the production of new hormones creating the beginning of sexual adulthood can create a stressful phenomenon that must be taken into account by teachers of middle school children. Increasing interest in the opposite sex occurs relatively early in the middle school for girls and is relatively common among boys by the eigth grade. This interest, in some cases, may be the most important single concern in the lives of these youngsters during this period. For girls the development of secondary sexual characteristics and body contours becomes extremely important. Both boys and girls are concerned with acne and complexion. Boys, particularly late maturers, are concerned about the apparent greater maturity of girls.

A corresponding development in physical maturation occurs. Internal organs grow in size at a rapid rate. Bones and muscles grow rapidly but at varying times and speeds. Large motor coordination occurs before small muscle coordination. The resulting clumsiness is a natural part of life for boys and girls of this age but is a source of embarrassment to them and of discomfiture to the teacher who is not aware of the problem. At the same time that the body is growing rapidly, basic metabolic rate* declines markedly. Such change creates a rather common problem of weariness for children at this age, and restlessness and inattention occur because of this weariness. A further confounding variable is that after a certain degree of weariness occurs the child begins to operate on nervous energy, thus compounding the problem. Teachers who do not understand this problem may think that restlessness is a reflection on their teaching abilities, but this is ordinarily not the case.

Relatively little is known about intellectual development at puberty. Two major ideas will be presented here, neither of which has been authenticated by large-scale and longitudinal types of research. Both seem to have strong bases for support predicated on observation and theory. First is the presence of a learning plateau at the onset of puberty. Researchers have theorized from comparisons of achievement tests and IQ tests that learning ability tends to rise in relatively direct correlation with age until the period of puberty, at which time it begins to level off for a few years, after which it begins to return to the direct correlation of earlier childhood. This lessening in growth of learning ability immediately around the age of puberty cannot be explained for sure, but it does indicate that a teacher might reasonably expect lower academic achievement from pupils in the middle school.

Several theories have been presented for the learning plateau idea, and, while no direct relationship between intellectual change and physical puberty can be proved, a correlation does seem to be indicated. One theory that would explain this plateau is that of Piaget, who has indicated a *developmental theory* for the intellect. He maintained that there is a shift in cognitive abilities of pupils during the years of childhood through early adolescence. According to this theory, at or about the age of puberty the mind is able to shift from concrete, logical thinking to a formal, logical operation. Thus, the individual changes from an acquirer and cataloger of facts such as multiplication tables to an analyzer, interpreter, and synthesizer of the data that have been gathered. If the theories of Piaget are accepted the intellectual plateau at the onset of puberty might be explained by the fact that the individual mind is moving from the concrete to the formal stages, and thus moves forward less rapidly in those areas most commonly measured by achievement tests. A further complicating factor in the question of intellectual growth at puberty is the above-mentioned variation of ages at which puberty is reached. Those who reach puberty earlier seem to excel more at academic tasks than children of the same age who mature at a later age.

---

* The rate at which heat is given off by the body at complete rest.

Development at puberty is such that the person who thinks as a child at entrance to the middle school should in the space of three or four years be thinking in relatively adult terms due to the newfound ability to perceive abstractions and to conceptualize. These newfound abilities foster several emotional frameworks for the thought patterns of children at this age. Thus, idealism develops to a greater extent at this age than any other, since for the first time the emerging adolescent is able to perceive not only what is, but what might be. While such idealism is a delightful characteristic, and one to be encouraged, certain problems may develop unless the teacher is prepared to cope with them at their inception. For example, the idealism of the emerging adolescent is ordinarily more extreme than might be expected because it is not as yet tinged with realism—with the frustrations and disappointments that represent the reality of life with which the pupil will later come to grips. Thus idealism, unless tempered by judicious but kindly reality brought into focus by the teacher, may create a frustrated individual.

Enthusiasm is also evident at this age. It is in many cases unfocused, (or focused in a direction not desired by the teacher), and one of the major functions of a middle school teacher is to focus this enthusiasm. Like idealism, enthusiasm needs to be tempered with realism, since many middle school pupils with few failure experiences will naturally become disappointed when their enthusiasm proves unrealistic. However, as a basic emotional force, enthusiasm must be encouraged in order to most effectively bring out the personal and educational potential of the emerging adolescent.

Another aspect of emotional development at puberty is the desire for independence, whether in social activities, classroom activities, or others. Lack of experience may cause this desire to be expressed in ways not always acceptable to teachers. However, every child must progress from dependence on parents to dependence on the teacher, then dependence on peers, and finally, hopefully, to independence. In order for independence to occur it must be encouraged at all levels, but particularly in the middle school where its initial symptoms are especially evident. Independence can be achieved only by fostering. Certainly, the child striving for independence whose inexperience leads him or her to act in socially unacceptable ways is difficult to handle. But the price is worthwhile, since it is essential to encourage this independence if the pupil is to develop independence as an adult.

One of the more interesting phenomena tied to the desire for independence is a corresponding search for security on the part of the emerging adolescent. These two competing desires create an ambivalence, and the child may move from one extreme of wanting complete independence to a position of desire for security within a very short period of time. The teacher expecting a degree of consistency in this area is certain to be disappointed. Emerging adoles-

ents are confusing creatures to both the teacher and themselves as they seek
rom moment to moment either dependence or independence.

If any one characteristic can be highlighted within the emotional framework of emerging adolescence in the middle school, that characteristic is vari-
bility. The prepubescent girl may be totally dependent, physically weak, and
cademically less able than expected. A postpubescent boy will certainly be
more physically capable, emotionally mature, and probably more academ-
cally able than his less-mature age-mates. This intense variability will require
rom the teacher a greater flexibility in both personal and classroom interac-
ion than would be expected either in elementary or high school. The teacher
who is full of enthusiasm, flexible, and interested in the personal development
f individuals should find the characteristics of the emerging adolescent a con-
nuous challenge and delight.

Organization for Teaching

The primary purpose of any administrative organization in a school is to facili-
ate the instruction by teachers and/or the learning by students. In order to
nalyze the various forms of organization commonly found in a middle
chool, we will review the three major functions of the middle school. Five
ypes of organization will be investigated to ascertain the extent to which these
unctions are realized within them. The three functions, as previously men-
oned, are establishment of an educational transition from elementary to
econdary school philosophies, development of a cultural transition from
hildhood to adolescence, and recognition of and concern for the great varia-
ility found among and within emerging adolescents. The five types of class-
ooms we will investigate in terms of these three functions are:

1. Self-contained
2. Departmentalized
3. Nongraded
4. Core
5. Interdisciplinary

The *self-contained classroom* is ordinarily found in elementary organiza-
ions where grades are divided into K–6 or K–8. Within this setting, the upper
rades of the elementary school (5–8) may utilize the same self-contained
rganization as the primary grades. In this framework the teacher is ordinarily
xpected to teach the so-called major subjects; that is, language arts, social
tudies, arithmetic, and science. Special teachers in music, art, physical educa-
ion, and other such subjects may visit the classroom on a regular schedule, or
lse pupils may be excused at certain periods of the day to go to those rooms.

This particular organization is currently found in a relatively small percentag of classroom organizations for emerging adolescents, but the possibility exist that a teacher might be asked to teach several subjects to a single group of stu dents.

In reviewing the functions a middle school should perform, it woul appear that the self-contained classroom would not serve well in the cultura transition from childhood to adolescence since it seems to offer few opportuni ties for the many and varied activities that should be broadening the emergin, adolescent's cultural framework. The educational transition from elementar to secondary education philosophies also seems to be hampered because th organization and the instructional practices facilitated by the self-containe classroom seem more oriented toward elementary education, thus leaving large transitional gap between eighth and ninth grade. The concern for th variability of pupils could probably be satisfied to some extent since on teacher would have responsibility for approximately thirty pupils for a majo part of the school day, and thus would have an opportunity to know pupil well and to give more personalized concern to individual needs. However, spe cialized equipment and resources that might aid in the learning process, sucl as resource center materials, science laboratories, and physical education facil ities, would probably not be as readily available in this setting as in othe organizational frameworks.

The teacher in the self-contained classroom needs to try particularly har to develop a large number of resources for enrichment of the learning experi ence; to present opportunities for relatively sophisticated social and cultura experiences with larger, more varied groups of individuals; to cooperate witl any available special teachers; and especially to approach interdisciplinar studies so that children may see the correlation between various subjects Middle school teachers in self-contained classrooms will find satisfaction fron the opportunity to work more closely with a smaller group of youngsters, in cluding the opportunity to know each individual more fully as a person, whil placing less emphasis upon subject matter than might be found in some of th other organizations.

The *departmentalized classroom* will ordinarily be found in smalle school districts utilizing a K–6/7–12 administrative system or in junior hig schools utilizing a traditional educational approach. It is probably the mos common organization found in emerging adolescent education today. In thi setting the teacher is a subject matter specialist working with groups of chil dren as they move from classroom to classroom.

In terms of the three functions of the middle school, the educational tran sition from elementary to secondary school philosophies does not seem to b effectively consummated with this system because the system is so strongl oriented toward secondary school. This leaves a transitional gap between th self-contained sixth-grade classroom and the seventh-grade departmentalized classroom. This system also leaves something to be desired in terms of cultural transition because it tends to introduce secondary school cultural traditions, for example, dances, interscholastic athletics, music contests, and so forth, at a time in the life of the pupil when such social traditions are relatively inappropriate. Finally, emphasis on subject matter, which is a part of the philosophy of the departmentalized classroom, gives less attention to differentiation in needs, purposes, and abilities of emerging adolescents, since a class norm is ordinarily considered rather than individual development. Teachers beginning their careers in departmentalized classrooms are expected to be familiar with the subject matter of their specialization, and to have knowledge of the level of achievement to be expected from a majority of pupils in the grade being taught. Less attention is given to correlation between subject matters in this organization than others considered in this section.

The *nongraded classroom* is a relatively new and rare setting for education in the middle school. Two frameworks have been utilized in the organization of nongraded systems. One is the continuous progress approach, which is ordinarily used for sequential subjects such as arithmetic or reading, and the other is homogeneous grouping, which is commonly utilized for older groups of youngsters who are at varying levels of conceptualization ability. The fundamental premise of nongrading is that grade structure should be abolished and that the children, regardless of their ages, should be placed among youngsters who are capable of doing the same type and level of work. This system has become popular in educational theory within the last decade, but is being utilized in a relatively small number of middle schools. Its greatest use is in elementary schools.

In terms of the three functions of the middle school, the nongraded school's transitional function between elementary and secondary school both educationally and culturally is not as effective as might be wished since most elementary and secondary schools are not nongraded in nature. In those schools where nongradedness is present in the elementary school it can be highly recommended as a middle school practice, since it does strongly support the third function, that of concern for the wide variation in abilities and purposes of emerging adolescents. In fact, nongradedness is probably the strongest of the five organizations in this particular function. The Association for Supervision and Curriculum Development has recommended that all middle schools should be nongraded, and this may be the movement of the future. Teachers currently concerned with teaching in the middle school should be aware of the principles, practices, and implications of nongrading but should recognize its relative rarity on the current middle school scene.

The fourth organization to be considered is the *core classroom*. This framework varies tremendously depending upon the purposes of the administration and faculty of the particular school where it is being practiced. It may range from a situation in which a teacher teaches social studies and language arts, correlating them where possible, to a more radical approach where the teacher and the pupils together determine problems of society upon which mutual agreement has been reached, utilizing subject matter as a tool to assist in the solution of those problems. Such an organization presents an opportunity for one teacher to be with a single class of students for more than a period and less than a day, thus serving as a compromise in the time element between the self-contained classroom and the departmentalized classroom. The subject matter, ordinarily based upon problems, is also concerned with content midway between the subject-centered approach of the high school and the child-centered approach of the elementary school.

For these reasons the core classroom can serve as one of the more effective systems for serving as both a cultural and educational transition between elementary and high school. Because of the core classroom's emphasis on the social concerns and the general education needs of all, regard for the variation among and between emerging adolescents is not as strong as might be possible in other settings. The organization is arranged in such a way that special attention could be given to individualization, but the philosophy, based upon small-group interaction, militates against it to some degree.

The core classroom, then, seems strong in two of the three functions of the middle school, and could be organized to be satisfactory in the third. As such, it could be strongly recommended in a middle school. Teachers, in order to be successful in this framework, must be aware of the problems facing society today, concerned with the social problems of individuals in their class, aware of ways to utilize subject matter to solve or ameliorate social problems, knowledgeable about correlational aspects of various subjects, and concerned with the social as well as intellectual development of their pupils.

Interdisciplinary team teaching is ordinarily composed of an organization of some predetermined number of teachers who agree to work together to plan, teach, and evaluate a common set of students. The most usual arrangement is the teaming of language arts, social studies, arithmetic, and science teachers. The planning, teaching, and evaluating done by these four teachers is intended to constitute the strongest aspects of subject matter teaching while giving fullest opportunity to correlational aspects of knowledge. In addition, four teachers working with the same 100 to 120 students can form the equivalent of a school within a school, with the teachers responsible for these children for a significant portion of the day. This presents an opportunity for teachers to know students better than they would in a larger enrollment setting.

The transition between elementary and secondary school philosophies is effectively carried out in this system because each teacher is a subject-matter specialist, thus relating strongly to secondary ideas, and at the same time works in close coordination with other teachers to develop the child-centered approach most appropriate in the elementary school. The cultural transition from childhood to adolescence is also achieved relatively effectively because possibilities occur for meeting more children in this setting than in a self-contained classroom, but without the complexities of a high school with a thousand-pupil enrollment. Activities within a team are ordinarily more informal and less competitive, partly because of the size of the group and partly because of the philosophy of the team process.

Teachers planning to instruct in an interdisciplinary team organization should be knowledgeable in their subject matter; able to work with other professionals in planning, teaching, and evaluating; concerned with the overall intellectual, emotional, and physical development of the child; and flexible, since varying activities will be taking place at various times.

Table 5.1 summarizes the five organizational settings and evaluates their potential for achieving middle school functions. Organization is only for the facilitation of instruction; good instructors can work around a system while poor instructors are unable to work through a system. Hence, this table can serve only as a general guide.

Table 5.1
Evaluation of classroom organization in terms of the functions of a middle school

	Educational transition	Cultural transition	Variability of pupils
Self-contained	Poor	Poor	Good
Departmentalized	Poor	Poor	Poor
Nongraded	Average	Poor	Excellent
Core	Good	Good	Average
Interdisciplinary	Excellent	Good	Good

From Table 5.1 it is clear that no one organization is ideal for answering problems involved in the functioning of a middle school. Therefore the teachers' own purposes should determine to some extent the organization of a classroom. For example, if great concern is to be given to variability and arrangements for dealing with it among emerging adolescents, nongraded techniques might prove most useful. However, a teacher using these techniques should recognize that they are not so effective in the transition from elementary to secondary school philosophies or from childhood to adolescent cultural activities. The same would hold true for other types of objectives. For example, the educational transition from elementary to secondary school might best be served by the interdisciplinary approach, while the core classroom might serve equally as effectively as interdisciplinary teaming in approaching the cultural transition from childhood to adolescence.

In summary, you will find the departmentalized classroom (which, because of its closeness in philosophy and practice to the high-school approach, is rather poor in its approaches to educational practice in the middle school) to be probably the most common classroom organization to be found at this grade level. Interdisciplinary teaming and self-contained classrooms are probably next in proportion of use, and are relatively equal in terms of the numbers of schools utilizing them. Since the self-contained classroom is so closely aligned with elementary practices it cannot be so readily recommended as the interdisciplinary team approach, which theoretically would seem to be the best of the five organizations. The other two organizations, nongraded and core classroom, are both more effective in certain middle school functions than either departmentalized or self-contained, but are rarely found in middle school practice at this time; the nongraded being not yet completely accepted, and the core classroom having passed its greatest popularity. It should be noted again that the purposes of the school and teacher should be the primary considerations in determining the organization of a classroom. Each may serve a different function in some way more effectively than other organizations, thus rendering any particular generalized evaluation not completely valid.

Instructional Functions

In every classroom a teacher will perform certain instructional functions. The purpose of this section is to indicate how functions of a middle school teacher might vary from those of a person teaching in either elementary or secondary schools. It will be segmented into subdivisions, focusing upon the role of the teacher as a:

1. Manager
2. Model
3. Planner
4. Diagnostician
5. Curriculum guide
6. Learning facilitator

Every social organization has a leader or leaders, whether they be appointed, elected, or informal. In the classroom, the teacher has been appointed

as leader by the school board and/or principal. One of a teacher's most important functions is to *manage* the classroom and the pupils within it. This does
not indicate a dictatorial control, but rather a democratic form of management
in which all members of the group achieve some degree of autonomy, that
degree being the one most appropriate to their stage of growth.

Such mundane matters as controlling the amount of warmth and light and
the degree of cleanliness in the classroom are an expected and little-mentioned,
although extremely important, aspect of the teacher's role. More often considered—and the major emphasis here—is the teacher's role in maintaining a
viable social structure to accomplish the purposes of the classroom, that is, the
most effective development of each member of the class. In order to accomplish this a teacher must consider the developmental characteristics of emerging adolescents mentioned above. Arrangements must be made for maintaining some degree of order while still encouraging physical movement around
the classroom. Enthusiasm and liveliness on the part of some students must be
channeled into meaningful activities while other pupils need to be aroused
from apathy. The extreme variability of developmental characteristics among
emerging adolescents creates a need for the teacher to manage the classroom in
terms of individuals, or small groups, rather than the entire classroom. Few
occasions will be found in which all pupils should be pursuing similar activities.

The middle school teacher's role will be more similar to that of an elementary classroom teacher, who works with individuals in their learning processes, rather than that of the secondary school teacher, who works with an
entire group in the acquisition of subject matter. The question of discipline, as
such, will concern the teacher only to the extent that the natural enthusiasm of
the emerging adolescent has not been focused in the direction the teacher
thinks necessary. When this occurs the teacher should consider whether the
direction is correct, or whether similar objectives could be achieved through
moving in directions desired by pupils.

A second teacher role is that of a *model* for emerging adolescents. The
idealism of youngsters at this age makes them particularly apt to view the im-
perfections of adults with a jaundiced eye. In the elementary school these im-
perfections are not seen so clearly; in secondary schools they are accepted
more readily. It is in middle school grades that pupils first see that teachers
have human faults, but they are as yet unable to accept this fact completely. A
teacher should strive to achieve those personal characteristics that can be most
appreciated by emerging adolescents so that they may have an adult model to
copy. Some of these characteristics are flexibility, enthusiasm, humor, and
firmness in the right. These characteristics need not be "preached" to middle
school pupils, but rather practiced by the teacher in every way possible. Chil-

dren seeing these characteristics will be more likely to accept both the characteristics and the teacher as being worthy.

Teachers should be sufficiently knowledgeable concerning subject matter they are expected to teach to be able to *plan* the objectives for the course work to be taught. Many teachers utilize the content of texts, workbooks, and syllabi as goals rather than developing a series of objectives that, with the aid of these sources, would serve as a basis for classroom efforts. To accomplish these objectives teachers must have a strong knowledge of the structure of their subject matter, the portion that is to be emphasized within certain grades, and the specific goals to be utilized as evidence of achievement. Whether stated in behavioral terms or not, these goals should be specific enough that some measurement of their achievement can be made. This particular teacher ability is one that is too often gained only through experience rather than preservice courses. Prospective middle school teachers should place a strong emphasis upon this ability prior to student teaching experiences.

In addition to developing specific objectives, teachers must be able to determine the level of progress of each individual pupil in the achievement of those objectives. Such a *diagnosis* must be more specific than required in the past. They should be able to state not only a grade for the pupil, but the fundamental concepts and skills the pupil lacks. This specific diagnosis presents teachers with an opportunity to conduct remedial efforts to help the student achieve the set objectives. Sequences in planning will create a series of objectives, the achievement of one of which will lead to the next. The teacher's task in this type of learning is to determine the level at which a student is located. In nonsequential learning the teacher has a more difficult diagnostic task, but should still be prepared to speak to the level at which the pupil is located in his or her understanding of a concept. This enables the teacher to lead the pupil to the next deeper level of thought process in the subject. As an example, a pupil should be able to understand the abstraction "the Dark Ages" before being asked to conceptualize feudalism, since the second is a more explicit aspect of the first. Thus, planning of subject matter without diagnosis of individual learners within a specific framework is meaningless.

Another task of a middle school teacher is to be a *curriculum guide*. In this context, curriculum is defined as all of the learning experiences the pupil has within the framework of the school. Thus, after the teacher has determined the objectives of the course and the criteria that will be utilized in measuring achievement, she or he must then determine what experiences each individual should have in order to achieve those objectives. This matter is complicated by the fact that different pupils learn more effectively by different means. Thus, one pupil may learn best by individual reading, another by small-group discussion, another by film, another by large-group lecture, and others by different means. In developing curriculum experiences a teacher must understand individual pupils well enough to predict which learning style might be most effective for each pupil in the achievement of a specific objective. This is more essential in the middle school than in elementary or secondary school due to the greater variability found there. The primary consideration is the development of an education most appropriate for each individual adolescent rather than the establishment of a norm to be achieved by a majority of the pupils in the class. Above all, a middle school teacher should realize that curricular experiences are not the chief purpose of the school, but rather the achievement of the broad range of objectives established for that school. Thus, the learning of a particular subject matter is valuable only insofar as it aids in the achievement of the objectives set forth for a pupil in the intellectual, physical, and socio-emotional areas.

The last function of the instructor to be considered is that of *learning facilitator*. Teachers do not merely inform pupils of certain facts. They facilitate learning as the pupils move toward the achievement of the objectives set for a unit and/or course. This learning facilitation may take several directions. For example, teachers may work with the pupils on needed basic skills, library utilization, creative thinking, critical thinking, taking lecture notes, and many other learning methodologies. Such areas as learning to participate in group activities, learning to work alone, and so forth are important parts of the learning process. In elementary school a pupil is expected to learn basic skills and to learn from the information presented by the teacher. By secondary school, teachers hope that pupils will be able to learn independently. Somewhere in the middle school the objective should be to help them move from dependent to independent learner status. The teacher's role as a learning facilitator, that is, as someone who helps the pupils develop their independent learning stance, becomes just as important if not more so than his or her role as the presenter of information about certain specific content. Thus, a teacher who aids a pupil in finding material and developing thinking skills, who encourages academic independence, is highly prized in a middle school. Schools that have utilized such approaches toward learning have expressed gratification in the achievement accomplished by pupils. Their administrators report that not only do pupils learn how to learn, but in addition they actually learn more subject matter through the years than do those whose schools have placed a stress upon the accumulation of information.

In summary, the six roles of the teacher in the middle school are those that might also be expected to be found in the elementary and secondary school. However, they are more important in the middle school due to the unique characteristics of emerging adolescents. The teacher not willing to become an expert in each of these six areas should probably be wary of going into middle school education. The teacher willing to accept the task of attempting to achieve excellence in all of these areas will become that rare and valuable person, a good middle school teacher.

Teacher Characteristics

What should be the characteristics of an effective teacher in a good middle school? Rather than attempt an encyclopedic listing, which might end as a meaningless catalogue of the characteristics of any "good" person, the author telephoned several colleagues, who are principals of some of the better middle schools in his geographic area. His question to them was, "What do you look for in a beginning teacher who applies for work in your school?" Interestingly, they responded with the same qualities the author would have suggested, but gave more authenticity to the answer.

While the different criteria were listed in varying orders, general agreement seemed to be both unanimous and strong. The first characteristic sought seems to be a general feeling of energy, excitement about children, and other qualities that would indicate a concern for children rather than subject matter. The energy is needed to cope with the unbounding enthusiasm and idealism of emerging adolescents. The excitement about this age was considered important, so that this position would not serve as a steppingstone to either elementary or high school teaching. The total quality of child-centeredness was stressed by the principals as being aboslutely essential on the part of any middle school teacher.

The aspect of child-centeredness was reinforced by the second criterion on most of the lists, which was a knowledge of psychology—both learning theories and emerging adolescent psychology. The principals stated that beginning teachers should know what to expect from the youth with whom they work, whether in terms of personal characteristics or in terms of how learning takes place. Without such knowledge the best-placed energy, excitement, and concern would seem to have little effect.

Third on the list of criteria of the principals was flexibility in learning situations, with the accent on activities and individualized learning. One principal noted particularly that he would be wary of a teacher applicant who expressed preference for lecture approaches. Such flexibility is necessary if learning basic skills and learning how to learn are to take precedence over mere acquisition of knowledge. Acquaintance with various individualized activities, be they units, programed books, workbooks, learning activity packages, or others, is essential knowledge that should be developed during the training of teachers planning to participate in middle school education. The principals emphasized the necessity for a good academic background, in depth in the teaching area, but particularly in breadth to aid in interdisciplinary team teaching, which all

hought was the best current approach for middle schools. General consensus
eemed to rest upon the premise that a broad academic background would
orm a base that was necessary, but that this should be expected of all teachers.
Hence, their concern, after having surveyed the academic background of pro-
pective teachers, would be based upon the questions of child-centeredness,
knowledge of psychology, and flexibility in learning situations.

As we discussed previously, the middle school offers both distinctive
problems and opportunities for the teacher who desires to work in such an environment. The importance of the middle school is receiving more and more
ecognition, and the teacher of the future will undoubtedly find that some of
he most challenging opportunities in education are available to individuals
who wish to work with this age group.

Suggested Readings

Alexander, William M., *et al. The Emergent Middle School*, 2d ed. New York: Holt,
Rinehart & Winston, 1969.

Bondi, Joseph, *Developing Middle Schools: A Guidebook*. New York: MSS Information Corporation, 1972.

Bossing, Nelson L., and Roscoe V. Cramer. *The Junior High School*. Boston: Houghton Mifflin, 1965.

Curtis, Thomas E. (Ed.). *The Middle School*. Albany, New York: Center for Curriculum Research and Services, State University of New York at Albany, 1968.

Eichhorn, Donald H. *The Middle School*. New York: The Center for Applied Research
in Education, 1966.

Gruhn, William T., and Harl R. Douglass. *The Modern Junior High School*, 3d ed.
New York: Ronald, 1971.

Hansen, John, and Arthur Hearn. *The Middle School Program*. Chicago: Rand Mc-
Nally, 1971.

Howard, Alvin W., and George C. Stoumbis.· *The Junior High and Middle School:
Issues and Practices*. Scranton, Pa.: Intext Educational Publishers, 1970.

Leeper, Robert R. (Ed.). *Middle School in the Making: Readings from Educational
Leadership*. Washington, D.C.: Association for Supervision and Curriculum
Development, 1974.

Overly, Donald E., *et. al. Middle School: Humanizing Education for Youth*. Worth-
ington, Ohio: Charles A. Jones, 1972.

Van Til, William, Gordon F. Vars, and John H. Lounsbury. *Modern Education for the
Junior High School Years*, 2d ed. Indianapolis, Ind.: Bobbs-Merrill, 1967.

William V. Burgess

Adolescent development in the secondary school

6

Dr. Burgess' chapter is a natural extension of the preceding chapter. Dr. Burgess concentrates on those developmental traits that typify the adolescent and those strategies that the successful teacher needs to utilize in working with students in the secondary schools.

William V. Burgess

Dr. Burgess is Associate Professor of Education at the University of San Francisco. He is a former high-school teacher, principal, and District Superintendent of Schools in Illinois. At USF, he was for two years the Dean of Summer Session/Intersession. From 1970 until 1975 he served as instructor and project coordinator of the San Francisco "Law in a Free Society" program, a K–12 curriculum in law-related civic education

Virtually every teacher who enters a secondary school classroom for the first time enters with some trepidation. There is just cause for that feeling. Quite apart from the state of excitement that develops over the first meeting with any class, the secondary teacher knows that in this room full of adolescents, things are different than in other classrooms.

The teacher knows the secondary school classroom will be different from other classrooms because they are made up of people who are different from any other segment in our society. And not only are adolescents quite distinctive in their differences from the rest of our society; each is different from other adolescents as well.

One indicator of that distinctiveness is the number of separate words and phrases teachers and parents use to describe adolescents. The terms "adolescent" or "teenager" are as neutral in their meaning as any term used to describe this age group, but even they have extra meanings to many people. We are likely to hear such adjectives as "rebellious," "awkward," "hot-tempered," "clumsy," "squeaky-voiced," or "pimply-faced" used in connection with the more neutral terms of "adolescent" or "teen-ager."

The teenagers' own fascination with words with special meanings and with slang expressions led to the widespread usage of one of the most descriptive phrases ever to be applied to that age group. "You crazy, mixed-up kid," a popular remark of the 1950s, has special meaning when used in connection with any discussion of adolescents.

Adolescents *are* mixed up. They stand between childhood and maturity with some of the traits of each. What is more, some adolescents exhibit a different mix of these traits than do others. Girls, for instance, may show more biological maturation than do boys of the same age, yet the boys may possess greater physical strength than the girls. An adolescent may be incredibly bright and fully developed intellectually but without the life experience needed to acquire the social skills necessary to deliver that newly formed intellectual power. One fifteen-year-old boy could be fully matured physically while one of his classmates could be just beginning to show signs of adult development.

As a group, adolescents can be very diverse in their intellectual, emotional, social, and physical development. For the teacher, that diversity presents an equally wide range of opportunities, challenges, delights, and problems. Because of this diversity, most teachers face the secondary school classroom with more than the usual level of alertness. There is a need for careful consideration of teaching activities in order to allow for the range of abilities and interests. There is a need for flexibility in order to seize the opportunity of that "teachable moment" when one student has expressed curiosity and the class interest is at the peak of its ability to learn and its responsiveness to teaching.

Adolescent Development

The adolescent is defined variously as a person between thirteen and nineteen years old, or between puberty and maturity, or between the end of childhood and the beginnings of adulthood. In education, we typically set the lower limit of adolescence at the beginning of the seventh grade (or about age thirteen) and the upper limit at the end of the twelfth grade (or about age eighteen). This upper limit of adolescence now corresponds closely with the lower limit of legal adulthood and society is thus assured that the person is legally fully responsible for his or her decisions, emotional responses, physical actions, or social behaviors.

There is no comparable lower limit to mark the onset of adolescence with such clear definition. Some psychological studies have placed it as early as age ten. Puberty may be attained by some girls as early as age ten, but this keystone in development may also be delayed for several years beyond the age of ten by many boys. Because physical strength and size are allied with sexual development, they also vary widely and provide little indication of the true beginnings of adolescence. Since social behaviors are so much a part of cultural traditions, we must look to the customs of the land in identifying the onset of adolescent social behaviors.

In the United States, we customarily mark the beginning of adolescence with the beginning of secondary education. This definition is certainly not precise because it allows for exceptions according to local school district plans of organization. In many rural areas, for example, the schools are organized on two levels, K–8 and 9–12. This would imply that adolescence begins with the ninth grade. Of course it is not really true, since many of these pupils have responsibilities for full-fledged adult tasks on the family farms. But the definition of adolescence we are using here is no worse than any others because they all allow for exceptions of an unusual nature. With all the separate factors of intellectual development, emotional behavior, social skills, and physical growth patterns under consideration, the entry into the seventh grade and the simultaneous onset of adolescence is a reasonable coincidence.

As was indicated earlier, the adolescent is a "mixed-up kid," so our description of adolescent development must necessarily be a mixed-up description. None of the four factors under consideration—intellect, emotion, social behavior, or physical growth—proceed hand in hand, one with the other, at the same rate throughout the course of development. Intellect is the first of these to show relative stability, so it will be the first to come under discussion.

Intellectual Development

Just as parents and teachers have observed progressively more complex physical skills developing in children as the children grow older, so have psychologists observed and measured progressively more complex intellectual patterns as children develop. Some ideas that come to small children with great difficulty (or not at all) are developed with great ease by older students. There appears to be a necessity for the human mind to go through certain stages of lower complexity in order for the intellect to deal satisfactorily with the higher complexities. One of our everyday expressions, "Its just a phase," came to us from the work of G. Stanley Hall, a psychologist who was studying the sequence of events in human intellectual development.

Currently, the foremost proponent of a series of developmental stages, or hierarchy, is Jean Piaget, the Swiss psychologist. Piaget has defined intellectual development according to the following stages:

1. Sensorimotor period (0–2 years)
2. Concrete operations period (2–11 years)
3. Formal operations period (11–15 years)

Obviously, the adolescent in our secondary schools has already completed phases 1 and 2 and has entered into the final period of intellectual development. It is in this period of development that logical relationships are formed and the student is able to propose hypotheses about events in the abstract—the student no longer needs to manipulate the actual object in order to make decisions about the object's properties. The student is aware of gaps in the learning series and in the core of experience and realizes that because of these gaps there are difficulties that will be encountered. As this extension of probability occurs, the student's thinking also extends into the realm of possible solutions to the difficulties; that is, hypotheses are formed that require propositional logic.

It would be incorrect to say that we reach our intellectual peak in adolescence. It is correct, however, to say that there is less gain in mental ability after adolescence, for in adolescence the tools of intellect are fully formed and in later years we simply polish and sharpen those intellectual tools. In other words, intelligence or mental ability is no more a constant than is height or weight. Each factor in human development is subject to change over time and intellect will continue to grow, although at a slower rate, so long as the tools of intellect are kept in use. Figure 6.1 demonstrates this rate of intellectual growth.

In Fig. 6.1, the rapid rise in intelligence test scores from childhood through adolescence is clearly demonstrated, as is the slower rate of projected growth in later years. The line does not continue because there was no measure of intelligence taken after age eighteen in this study. We see that intellectual growth is almost complete, however, and other studies have shown that intellectual growth can be maintained for many years.

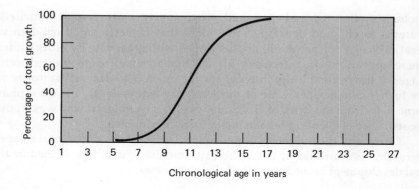

Fig. 6.1 Age changes in intelligence test scores [After Dearborn and Rothney, *Predicting the Child's Development* (Cambridge, Mass.: Sci-Art Publications), 1941].

As we view the graph in Fig. 6.1 and review the statements made earlier concerning Piaget's interpretation of the learning stages, it would appear that in the adolescent years we should expect to find the greatest production of ideas for new and unique solutions to problems. Adolescents are able to consider the several possibilities for a solution, have a good understanding of the relationships between objects and propositions, and are certainly capable of taking a fresh look at many different concepts. Each of these elements has been determined to be necessary for creative thinking.

Very seldom do high levels of creative production occur during the adolescent period of intellectual development, however. The interactions of other factors that continue to operate during adolescence undoubtedly affect the process of creative thinking. High school students have so many concerns with their bodies, their social relations, and the torrent of confusion that surrounds them that there is little opportunity for a creative idea to incubate. The environmental and social pressures are too strong and too immediate to allow for the contemplation required for the creative process or for the acceptance of unusual ideas generated by the creative adolescent.

Emotional Development

So many powerful factors impinge on the adolescent that it is no wonder the period is filled with emotional turmoil for most teenagers. The wonder is not that they experience confusion, but that they retain their resilience and general good nature in the face of such confusion.

The period from ages thirteen to eighteen is filled with extremes of emotion. When asked for an opinion on something, the adolescent will often say "Its okay" but just as often give the reply "I hate that." The switch from one extreme to the other can be rapid. Each new piece of information an adolescent receives on a topic seems to be given equal weight in the teenage mind, causing the balance of opinion to tilt wildly as each new piece is added. In early adolescence especially, controversies are hard to accommodate. Expected to exercise judgment on a matter, the adolescent often reacts with a strong opinion that conflicts with the ability to give a reasoned response. The strong statement with an emotional basis is generally an expression of the adolescent's need for independence. By taking an extreme position on an issue, the adolescent demonstrates the ability to stand alone.

This need to demonstrate a lack of dependence accounts for much of the emotional conflict between adolescents and their teachers or parents. The result is apparently foolish behavior in the eyes of the adult. The foolish behavior creates concern among parents and teachers, leading them to express a desire to help and to try to take an active role in helping the adolescent over the difficulty. The very act of helping leads the teenager to question his or her own ability to be independent, sets in motion another series of actions designed to test that ability, and creates anew the round of silly behaviors.

Tension builds to such extremes after a few rounds that no further communication is possible and we have what is called the "generation gap." If a parent suggests something, the son or daughter does the exact opposite. If a teacher threatens, the student accepts the dare and a discipline problem develops simply because the adolescent *must* prove the capacity to stand alone.

The turning away from parents and other adults in the primary relationship extends to such elemental matters as the choice of friends and religion. The surest way for a mother to prevent any romance between her teenage daughter and any boy is for the mother to suggest that boy as a possible partner. When Mother says, "Why don't you go out with Tom? I think he is a nice boy," Tom has just received the kiss of death so far as Susy is concerned.

Nor is it uncommon in these stressful times for teenagers to turn to religion for satisfaction of some of their problems. If parents push it, however, the adolescent may choose not to participate as fully as expected or may choose to participate in another faith.

These choices are not often made on theological grounds in the case of religion nor necessarily on the basis of mutual attraction in the case of friendships. The choices are made most often on the basis of the adolescents' need to demonstrate an independence from the adult authority they have known all through childhood. They want to show that they can stand alone.

Not that they in fact do stand alone. The teenager in conflict with one teacher will turn to another teacher for guidance. The teenager in conflict with a parent will turn to an uncle or an aunt or a neighbor for a helping hand. Parents are constantly amazed that their Johnny or Jennie who won't lift a finger to help out at home without an argument will go next door and give the neighbors the benefit of their services on a regular, volunteer basis. Teachers comparing notes in the faculty room commonly find that one teacher's diligent student is another teacher's classroom terror.

The sources of emotional confusion are many. Parents and teachers, as well as persons the teenagers have never met, are potential sources of emotional turmoil. Rock singers, movie stars, and other glamorous entertainers are among the latter. These people generate awe and envy in the adolescent. With the typical teenager's concern over body development, the professional athlete or TV star is a real source of fantasy life for an adolescent. The movie star's lavish display of wealth when most teenagers are dependent upon parents for income is a real source of envy. Teenagers' bodies betray them by either growing too fast in some places (nose, hands, feet) or not fast enough in others (breasts, shoulders), or their bodies will have warts, pimples, and dandruff while the movie star's body will have none of the defects and all of the assets. The teenager is too young to hold a steady job that will allow economic independence and is too old to accept money outright without some loss of pride.

It is a cliché among high school coaches that they lose many potential male athletes at around age sixteen as the boys turn their attention away from sports. At sixteen, they are old enough to get a job to earn money to buy a car so they can get a girl to spend money on. The adolescent's need to be independent and to respond to the biological and social pressures is apparent in that little cliché.

The sex life of the teenager is also one of the sources of emotional conflict. The body is rapidly changing as the sex hormones induce the procreative urges that societal taboos prohibit. Consequently, the sexual relationships of most adolescents are fantasized for the first few years of biological maturity. A popular weekly magazine reported a poll in which

> ...*the first sexual experience of American men occurred at age 17 or younger for 42 per cent of those polled. It occurred between the ages of 18 and 20 for another 34 per cent, and at age 21 or older for the remaining 24 per cent. The median age at first sexual intercourse for men is 18. For women, it is 20.*
>
> *The first sexual experience for women, according to the poll, occurred at age 17 or younger for 22 per cent of the females. Another 40 per cent engaged in a first sexual experience between 18 and 20, and 38 per cent waited until they were 21 or older.* [1]

Teenagers' sex lives contain everyday problems of emotional conflict quite apart from those generated by their fantasies involving rock singers and movie stars (after all, these are attainable in fantasy and *nobody* is attainable under existing societal taboos).

Girls outgrow the boys of their age group and turn to older boys for attention. The combination of the need for independence from parents and the need for sexual attention from an older person represents the potency behind the "teenage crush." The same adults to whom adolescents turn for counsel and advice become the object of sexual attraction. Teachers, then, are prime targets for crushes. The frequency with which this occurs undoubtedly accounts for the strength of the sanctions against teacher-student dating in the secondary school.

Boys vary so widely in individual maturation rates that many experience severe mental disturbances at being left behind biologically. In the same gym class, sexually experienced boys share conversation with the sexual fantasizers and also with those who still have not the faintest idea about what the conversation means. According to Sullivan, "in certain instances, at least, these operations are very costly to the personality when finally the puberty change and the phases of adolescence begin."[2] Those who are able to go through the motions of sexual development more by bravado than by experience with hormonal influences still know there is baby fat or a skinny torso behind all the bold talk. Until the biological change has personal meaning for them, these boys are likely to be very unhappy with themselves.

Adolescents are often unhappy and confused. They do not always understand the roles assigned them nor the conflicts in the roles they do perceive. They have a strong sense for what is right and realize that it does not correspond to what actually happens. They sometimes feel abused by being halfway between childhood and adulthood, yet delight in having friends who are partners in the problem. They are moody and morose, even rebellious at times, yet have valued and pleasing personalities in their own group. That peer group to which most teenagers belong gives them the strength and resilience needed to meet the confusion of the everyday contradictions in the progress from youth to maturity. Without the knowledge and understanding of sympathetic parents and teachers and without the strong support *of the teenagers'* best friends, the problems are overwhelming.

Social Development

In adolescent society, the power of the peer group is unequalled. The statutes, religious tenets, and adult sanctions all yield to the influence of the peer group on teenagers. The peer group has no written rules yet every member follows the rules. The peer group has its own language, fashion, and code of conduct and uses these to give the adolescent support and protection from the adult environment while the member is learning the language, fashion, and code of conduct of the adult society.

It is in the peer group that the adolescent makes trial efforts toward the development of adult competence in carrying on conversation, behaving toward others, and accepting sex roles and responsibilities. As teenagers talk to each other in their special language, a code no adult can fully decipher since it changes so quickly, it is apparent that the content of the conversation is not as important as the process of conversing. The need to talk to someone who will listen is a high-level need for adolescents. Since most adults think teen talk is silly, the peer group assumes the responsibility for the therapy of conversation. It is in the peer group that the adolescent reveals fears and desires, loves and hates, angers and pleasures.

The social skills of organizing for the accomplishment of group tasks are learned in the peer group. Adolescents learn to be leaders and followers, for their value to the peer group is based upon their ability to fulfill responsibilities within the group, not simply to dominate the group. The most popular figure in the entire student body may not be given leadership roles by the peer group when the task demands another talent. The talents of leadership and the talents of followership, arranging work and cleaning up after work, are each given utility value within the peer group. Acceptance into the peer group is based on the contributions of various competencies and recognition of the competencies is distributed throughout the group. One factor does seem to stand out as a component of leadership in most of the typical teenage peer groups. The person with the strongest heterosexual behaviors is most often in a favored position. In any event, behavior that is too far afield from the group norm will be brought into line by ridicule or by studied indifference so that the nonconformist either changes or leaves the group.

The peer group in adolescence is usually made up of an equal number of boys and girls, since by this time they have begun to pair off in the formation of heterosexual relationships. In the peer group, girls will have one or two intimate friends and boys will have four or five more casual friends. The rank order of those friends can change quickly, though, since the adolescent emotion is rarely stable on any issue. In a survey taken in upstate New York, 10 percent of the students had dropped their "best friend" from a list of three favorites after only two weeks.[3]

A few individuals are always on the fringes of the peer group and there are some high school students who belong to no group at all. The highly creative student often does not belong to a group because that student will not yield to the pressures to conform and often demonstrates character traits that are not true to the accepted behavioral stereotype for the sex role. Otherwise, mental ability seems to have little bearing on peer group membership, the ability to contribute to the group being more important than academic achievement. The "grade grind" is usually not fully accepted into the group—grades are an adult sanction and as such suppress the adolescent's independence. Nor are students with offensive personal hygiene readily accepted into the peer group. There are various other reasons for nonacceptance into the peer group, some of which are built around snobbery. Students rejected for this reason from one group do find another group to belong to in most cases.

Wattenberg[4] has identified four types of peer groups:

1. Friendships—a peer group of two people who are best friends, usually most evident in early adolescence
2. Informal aggregations—a peer group of people who live near each other, enjoy the same activities, or represent a clique within a larger group
3. Organized youth groups—under adult jurisdiction and influence, a peer group that develops out of religious activities or club work whose chief function is to give girls and boys group support while they learn social skills in a parent-approved setting.
4. Gangs—a peer group with a heavily ritualized code of conduct, meeting places, and narrowly defined activities.[4]

The school system is most representative of the third type of peer group mentioned above. Although it serves the societal function of promoting learning, like all other adult organizations it takes second place to the peer group in the development of learning or behavioral styles. In some instances, the peer group has shown that it can provide more effective teachers of disadvantaged learners than the schools.[5] And the code of behavior of the peer group supersedes the rules of the school—a student will endure all the punishment the school has to offer rather than "fink out" on a friend.

In review, some of the reasons for the strength of the peer group are as follows:

1. It provides a safe place to discuss the emotional torment of adolescence. Students who have no peer group to talk to generally require another form of therapy, sooner or later.
2. It provides an avenue of independence. Within the peer group, adolescents count for who they really are, not for who they might become in adult eyes.
3. It provides the strength of numbers. The adolescent is not really alone and need not fear the flight from dependence into the freedom of a world where there is no previous experience to provide guidance.
4. It provides fun and recreation. In the peer group the adolescent finds others with similar interests and attitudes. The peer group is a happy place that nurtures a sense of love, belonging, and self-esteem.

Physical Development

In previous sections the body and its adolescent changes have been mentioned as part of the discussion of other factors. We have already learned that there is a rapid growth spurt among girls early in adolescence followed by a similar growth spurt among boys a couple of years later. The biological maturation (puberty) and development of the sex characteristics common to adults is also obvious and has been previously mentioned. The fact that rapid growth is accompanied by an unequal distribution of that growth (hands, feet, ears, and nose seem to grow faster than the rest of the body) and that this contributes to the adolescent's self-embarrassment and emotional turmoil has also been mentioned. What remains to be said are some of the less obvious statements about adolescent physical growth.

First of all, the unequal growth rate is not confined to the external body features. The heart, for example, has been observed by some physcans to be less fully developed in proportion to body size among adolescents than are the other life-support organs. The nervous system grows so rapidly that it is almost fully developed by age two. The lymphatic tissues (adenoids, tonsils, and so forth) also grow much more rapidly than do the muscular or skeletal tissues. In fact, the tonsils and adenoids may grow beyond normal adult size during youth and early adolescence, shrinking to normal size when the body matures. During this period of disproportionate enlargement, the adenoids and tonsils create partial obstruction of the nasal air passage.

The possibility that the heart of a junior high student does not develop as rapidly as the rest of the body could help explain some of the apparent listlessness and "moping around" observed in this age group. The young athlete may be more easily overextended than body size alone would indicate. Similarly, the slack-jawed mouth-breathing of an adolescent may be due to more than careless personal habits. It could be that the body's demands for oxygen exceed the capacity of its clogged intake system.

Secondly, growing up takes an incredible amount of energy. To supply this energy, kids eat a lot—most of it fad foods and empty calories picked up in snack bars and fast-food places that do not offer a balanced meal. In spite of the enormous intake of food, in fact, it has been estimated that only one teenager in ten has a diet that is completely nutritious and adequately balanced to support optimum health. Many of the worries that teenagers have over their bodily appearance can be traced to poor diet.

Finally, although girls reach puberty at an earlier age than boys, the male sex drive peaks earlier. Kinsey reported this in his 1948 study and it seems to be reconfirmed in the 1975 survey reported earlier in this chapter. In the most recent report, 42 percent of males had their first sexual experience before age seventeen while only 22 percent of the females had their first sexual experience before age seventeen. As cultural standards change, these differences may also change, but for the present we must recognize that physical maturity and sex drive do not coincide in the adolescent.

This final point is one further example of the confusion and conflict that adolescents experience while adapting their changing bodies to environmental and social pressures. This period of physical and sexual confusion is well portrayed in the Turner cartoon shown in Fig. 6.2. The hunger of the young couple for each other is exceeded only by the young man's hunger for food.

In summary, by the end of adolescence mental ability is at its peak and physical development is complete. The late adolescent and early adult are practically indistinguishable on these points. Creative thinking ability is on the increase, the bursts of emotion are coming under control, and the lack of experience is the last hurdle before full social development.

CARNIVAL   **by Dick Turner**

"Who are we to fight nature, Janie? Let's go see what's in the refrigerator!"

Figure 6.2
Reprinted by permission of Newspaper Enterprise Association.

Teachers and the Secondary School

Teachers who know and understand adolescents can make a contribution to the completion of this transition from childhood to adulthood. Teachers who care and are available to listen to adolescent conversation will provide for some of the tension reduction necessary in adolescent emotional states.

Teachers who help to develop school curriculum and school policy can also help by doing the following:

1. Providing for learning experiences that present the adolescent with opportunities to test hypotheses against the data of the real world
2. Providing a range of educational activities that allow for the wide variations in mental ability, emotional stability, social aptitude, and physical capacities
3. Recognizing the value of the peer group and using it effectively within the school system for the benefit of the group and the individuals within the group
4. Relying on what we know about adolescents in the development of secondary school curriculum. A curriculum designed for adult needs will have little effect upon adolescents.

Teachers do have real cause for concern when they enter the secondary classroom if they are uninformed about their students. The assumption that a high school teacher need only teach history or mathematics is false. Those teachers who manage to teach students about themselves as well as teach the subject lessons are much more certain to have their teaching effectiveness fully realized. Teaching is not easy. It is a lot more pleasant, however, when the teacher knows—and cares—about the students.

Notes and References

1. *Parade* (Nov. 7, 1975), p. 4.
2. H. S. Sullivan, *The Interpersonal Theory of Psychiatry* (New York: W. W. Norton, 1953), p. 259.
3. J. E. Horrocks and G. C. Thompson, "A Study of the Friendship Fluctuation of Rural Boys & Girls," *Journal of Genetic Psychology* 69 (1946), 189–198.
4. W. H. Wattenberg, *The Adolescent Years* (New York: Harcourt Brace Jovanovich, 1973).
5. T. J. Vriend, "High-Performing Inner-City Adolescents Assist Low-Performing Peers in Counseling Groups," *Personnel and Guidance Journal* 7 (1969), 897–904.

Suggested Readings

Anastasi, Anne. *Differential Psychology*, 3d ed. New York: Macmillan, 1958.

Biehler, Robert F. "Age-Level Characteristics," Ch. 4 in *Psychology Applied to Teaching*, 2d ed. Boston: Houghton Mifflin, 1974.

Cole, Luella, and Irma N. Hall. *Psychology of Adolescence*, 7th ed. New York: Holt, Rinehart & Winston, 1970.

Erikson, Erik. *Identity: Youth and Crisis.* New York: Norton, 1968.

Friedenberg, Edgar Z. *The Vanishing Adolescent.* Boston: Beacon Press, 1964.

Goodman, Paul. *Growing Up Absurd.* New York: Vintage Books, 1956.

Money, John, and Anke A. Erhardt. *Man and Woman, Boy and Girl.* Baltimore: Johns Hopkins University Press, 1973.

Phillips, John L., Jr. *The Origins of Intellect: Piaget's Theory.* San Francisco: W.H. Freeman, 1969.

Sexton, Patricia. *The Feminized Male.* New York: Random House, 1969.

Stone, Joseph L., and Joseph Church. *Childhood and Adolescence,* 3d ed. New York: Random House, 1972.

Tiger, Lionel, and Robin Fox. *The Imperial Animal.* New York: Holt, Rinehart & Winston, 1971.

Torrance, E. Paul. *Guiding Creative Talent.* Englewood Cliffs, N.J.: Prentice-Hall, 1962.

Michael O'Neill

Private elementary and secondary education in the United States

7

When we think about elementary and secondary education in the United States, we all too often think only about the public schools. Actually, of course, private elementary and secondary schools enroll millions of children and are an extremely important part of the educational process here in the United States. Father O'Neill has written a definitive chapter concerning these schools. The implications of Chapter 1 as well as of Chapters 8, 9, and 10 are often made concrete and tangible by activities that take place outside of the public schools and can best be understood against the background Father O'Neill has presented.

Michael O'Neill

Father O'Neill is currently the Director of the Institute for Catholic Educa
tional Leadership at the University of San Francisco. From 1967 through
May of 1976, he was Superintendent of Education for the Diocese of
Spokane in Washington. Father O'Neill received a doctorate in Education
from Harvard University in 1967, and was a Teaching Fellow in Education at Harvard from 1965 to 1967. He is the author of two books and of
numerous articles and reviews.

Historical Overview

In his seminal essay on the historiography of American education, Harvard historian Bernard Bailyn argued that much of the writing on American educational history has assumed, quite incorrectly, that public education as we now know it began to take shape shortly after the Pilgrims landed. The writers of this history, Bailyn said, were usually not trained historians but rather "educational missionaries" who wanted to prove that "the past was simply the present writ small."

> *Public education as it was in the late nineteenth century, and is now, had not grown from known seventeenth-century seeds; it was a new and unexpected genus whose ultimate character could not have been predicted and whose emergence had troubled well-disposed, high-minded people. The modern conception of public education, the very idea of a clean line of separation between "private" and "public," was unknown before the end of the eighteenth century.* [1]

Bailyn and many historians since have shown that the history of education can be adequately understood only when one looks not just at schools and colleges but also at other educative agencies, such as family, church, work, and the local community itself. In the mid-nineteenth century, schools and colleges emerged as the dominant agencies within the process of education in American society, but it is important to recall that for the first two centuries of its history American education was primarily "private," taking place through the nuclear family, larger kinship groups, tutors employed by families or small groups of families, apprenticeship programs and other work experiences, the church,[2] newspapers, town hall meetings, and occasionally travel and military experience. Further, many of the schools that did exist during the seventeenth and eighteenth centuries were what we would now call "private schools,"[3] but this term is just as misleading as the term "public school" when applied to the early history of this country.

The origin of private schools in the modern sense of the word took place in the early and middle nineteenth century, at the same time that public education in the modern sense really began, and principally for the same reason: the massive influx of immigrants. The loosely knit and largely informal education of earlier days was simply not able to meet the needs caused by immigration. Public schools were quickly developed to educate and tame the immigrants' children. But these schools inevitably, and largely unconsciously, reflected the prevailing views and values of the dominant group in the society, Anglo-American Protestants. These views were, to put it mildly, not always sympathetic to Jews, blacks, Catholics, Irish, Italians, Poles, Slovenians, Orientals, and other groups. Some of these newly arrived and understandably threatened groups saw the Anglo-American Protestant public schools as threats to much of what they held dear—their religion, their language, their culture and customs, often their very names. Millions of Americans today have names different from those of their immigrant ancestors because these strangers in the land were instructed that their names were not "American" and therefore should be changed, in much the same way that whites used to convey to blacks the message that only if they ironed their hair straight would they be attractive.

Especially suspicious were the Irish Catholic immigrants who arrived in increasing numbers during the 1830s and particularly during and after the great Irish famine of 1846–1851. For centuries the Irish had been crushed by English imperialism, and had lived under the English-imposed Penal Codes, which denied the Irish most forms of education, professional work, travel, political rights, and freedom of religion. Edmund Burke had called the codes a policy "as well-fitted for the oppression, impoverishment and degradation of a people, and the debasement in them of human nature itself, as ever proceeded from the perverted ingenuity of man."

Many Irish who came to America to escape famine and this English tyranny were the products of anti-Irish schools established in 1831 when England imposed compulsory elementary education in Ireland but strictly prohibited the learning of Irish language, literature, history and legends. Yet upon arriving here the Irish were expected to embrace the very same superior Protestant tradition in the name of which so many of their people had been slandered, patronized, colonized, slaughtered, and enslaved.[4]

The private schools in the United States grew primarily out of a protest movement. Within recent years many American historians and sociologists have demonstrated how effectively schools can teach children to feel inferior because of racial, social, economic, or ethnic differences. The nineteenth-century melting-pot philosophy was a well-intentioned but crude and often cruel effort to clean up and organize America after the hordes of messy immigrants had arrived. Many of the immigrants saw the public school movement as a systematic attempt to remake them in a white Anglo-American Protestant mold.

It is no accident that the largest group of American private schools was at that time and still is Catholic, since most of the newly arrived immigrants (Irish, Italians, Poles, Southeastern Europeans, and many Germans) were Catholic. To be at the same time Irish and Catholic or Polish and Catholic or Italian and Catholic was to be doubly condemned in the dominant American value system of the nineteenth and early twentieth centuries. The resistance movement among the immigrants and their sons and daughters took place through a variety of institutions, one of the most formidable and visible of which was the countercultural "protestant" non-public schools, most of them Catholic.

Most American private schools are church related. It is ironic that private schools are now associated with religion whereas public schools are not. In the first two centuries of our country's history virtually all schools of any type were clearly religious in orientation. Even during the great public school movement of the nineteenth century, nobody ever intended to make the public schools secularist or atheist or even really neutral. Horace Mann and others simply wanted the public schools to express good, solid, nondenominational Christianity.[5] That pleasant thought did not work and never would work because to Catholics the "nondenominational" Christianity was clearly Protestant Christianity, with the King James Bible, hymns written by Martin Luther, textbooks hostile toward Catholics, and so on.[6] To dissident Protestant groups, Jews, and other non-Christian religionists, neither the mainline Protestant nor the Catholic approach was acceptable.

As time went on, in spite of the original intentions of Horace Mann and other founders of the public school movement, American public schools inevitably and inexorably became so "pure" of religious influence that even Christmas celebrations or moments of silent prayer became suspect if not unconstitutional. American education, which in its beginnings and for at least two centuries was predominantly "private" and religious, is now predominantly "public" and a-religious, with only the church-related private schools carrying on the much older tradition of integration of education, religion, and morality.

General Categories and Statistics

Table 7.1 shows the major groups of private elementary and secondary schools in the United States. The largest group by far is that of Catholic schools, which account for over 80 percent of the students enrolled in private schools of any type.[7] Figure 7.1, from the report of the President's Panel on Nonpublic Education, gives another breakdown.[8] Church-related schools in general account for 93 percent of private-school students. Nondenominational schools make up a statistically small but otherwise important and influential group within private education.

Due to their size and relative visibility we will discuss Catholic schools in more detail in the next section. The following are brief descriptions of the other subgroups within American private education.[9]

The Lutheran schools are concentrated in the midwestern section of the country. There are several different groups of Lutheran schools, the largest of which is made up of the Lutheran Church–Missouri Synod schools with 1,268 schools and over 166,000 students. Other groups of Lutheran schools are those of the Wisconsin Evangelical Lutheran Synod, the American Lutheran Church, the Lutheran Church in America, and the Church of the Lutheran Confession.

Table 7.1
Nonpublic school enrollments by religious affiliation, 1970–1971

Roman Catholic	4,134,299
Lutheran	200,914
Seventh-Day Adventist	53,527
Jewish	65,335
Protestant Episcopal	73,393
Christian Reformed	29,486
Baptist	35,098
Friends (Quaker)	13,784
Methodist	10,760
Presbyterian	7,489
Other	52,299
Total church related	4,676,384
Not church related	467,674
Total nonpublic	5,144,058

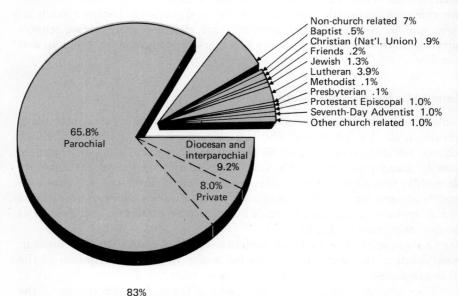

Non-church related 7%
Baptist .5%
Christian (Nat'l. Union) .9%
Friends .2%
Jewish 1.3%
Lutheran 3.9%
Methodist .1%
Presbyterian .1%
Protestant Episcopal 1.0%
Seventh-Day Adventist 1.0%
Other church related 1.0%

65.8%
Parochial

Diocesan and
interparochial
9.2%

8.0%
Private

83%
Roman Catholic

Fig. 7.1 Nonpublic school enrollment distribution [From *Nonpublic Education and the Public Good: The President's Panel on Nonpublic Education* (Washington, D.C.: Government Printing Office, 1972), p. 7.]

In 1974–1975, the 1,750 Lutheran schools in North America enrolled approximately 216,000 students.

Lutheran education in America dates from before the Revolution. One of the first Lutheran schools in the country, St. Matthews in Manhattan, opened in 1749. According to Donald A. Vetter, director of the American Lutheran Church elementary schools, Lutheran-school students are drawn from all socioeconomic levels and tend to be less rather than more affluent as well as similar to the general population in the spread of academic aptitude. Over 10 percent of the students are black, with a substantial number of Spanish-speaking children.[10]

The Seventh Day Adventist Church began in the mid-nineteenth century in the United States, with roots in the general reform movement in the country at that time.[11] Few people would associate the conservative and deeply religious Seventh Day Adventists with today's "health foods nuts," but the SDA church stood strongly for the reform and cleansing of all aspects of American life, not the least of which was the food Americans ate. The headquarters of the SDA church for many years was Battle Creek, Michigan, and both Kellogg and Post dry cereal companies originated with and are still heavily influenced by Seventh Day Adventist religionists.

Seventh Day Adventist schools are heavily subsidized by local congregations and stress hard work both academic and physical. Many SDA schools include work as part of their curriculum, with furniture factories, farms, and so forth, available for the student-workers. While the work programs enable the students to pay all or a substantial part of their tuition, their principal purpose is to develop in the students character, steady work habits, and thrift.

The schools are also characterized by their stress on health. SDA believers do not consume alcohol, tobacco, meat, or coffee, and put great stress on fresh air and water, sunlight, exercise, and proper diet. Their schools are typically located away from congested and polluted cities, in open, clear-air situations. In spite of the stress on exercise and sports, competition and hard body-contact sports are discouraged.

Beginning with the first SDA academy established in 1872, the Adventists now operate elementary and secondary schools and colleges throughout the world. Of the 5,000 elementary and secondary schools, about 1,100 are located in the "North American Division," with over 50,000 students in United States schools. Adventists elementary schools are usually very small, sometimes enrolling only twenty to thirty students. High schools and colleges include many boarding operations.

A very high percentage (often over 90 percent at the elementary level) of Seventh Day Adventist children attend SDA schools. Catholic and Lutheran schools, by contrast, draw 33 percent or fewer of the children of Catholic and Lutheran families.

The Christian Reformed schools (National Union of Christian Schools) had their origin in 1857, when a group of orthodox Calvinist congregations in Michigan seceded from the more liberal Reformed Church in America, the descendant of the original Dutch Reformed Church. The Christian Reformed group maintains 145 elementary and 66 secondary schools in the United States, with about 30,000 students. The NUCS schools generally resemble the moderate conservatism of the Missouri Synod Lutheran schools. Most Christian Reformed schools are coeducational day schools with strong roots in the Dutch Reformed Church and Calvinist theology. The Christian Reformed schools are heavily concentrated in the state of Michigan.

Episcopal schools, which tend to resemble the upper-class, nondenominational "independent" schools more than they do Lutheran, Christian, and most Catholic schools, form one of the oldest groups of schools in the United States, having their roots in the early seventeenth-century settlements on the shores of the Chesapeake Bay. However, Episcopal schools began to thrive only after the Revolution and the establishment of the Protestant Episcopal Church in 1789, which broke away from the parent Church of England. One of the most famous Episcopal schools is Groton, which includes among its graduates Franklin Delano Roosevelt and many other renowned American leaders. Episcopal elementary and secondary schools enroll about 75,000 students.

The Society of Friends (Quaker) schools are very small in number—65 schools enrolling 14,500 students—but have an importance and influence that goes far beyond their size. One of the first Quaker schools was the William Penn Charter School in Philadelphia, which began in 1689. Over half the Quaker schools today are within fifty miles of Philadelphia.

Quaker schools were among the very earliest in this country. The strong Quaker commitment to racial equality, service to the poor, and pacifism have long characterized these schools. Quaker schools provided some of the earliest examples of school racial integration in the United States, and were among the first to educate girls as well as boys. Poor students were admitted free; families who could afford tuition were expected to pay it.

Quaker schools, like Episcopal schools, now tend to be affiliated more with the nondenominational independent schools than with the mainline Protestant and Catholic schools.

Baptist schools, heavily concentrated in the South, enroll 35,000 students. Baptist schools tend to be conservative on religious and social issues. Part of the growth of Baptist education resulted from the increasing secularism of public education during the late nineteenth and twentieth centuries.

Methodist schools, which number 34 and enroll fewer than 10,000 students, are also concentrated in the South. They form a relatively minor apostolate within the large, evangelistic Methodist churches of the United States.

Presbyterians were strongly committed to church-related education before the Civil War. They largely withdrew from this effort later, however as a
result of the disruption caused by the war, conflict within the Church over the
slavery issue, the rapidly spreading public school ideology, the influence of re-
vivalism (with its emphasis on emotional personal conversion, and appeal to
the heart rather than the head), and the emergence of Presbyterians as an
upper-middle-class group with access to good suburban public schools and
prestigious independent schools. Presbyterian schools today enroll only about
7,500 students.

Besides these major Protestant groups there are a number of smaller and
usually more separatist Christian school groups, such as the Amish, Mennon-
ite, Hutterite, Moravian, and Christian Scientists. The 1974 *Wisconsin* v.
Yoder decision of the United States Supreme Court, upholding Amish parents'
right to refuse to send their children to public high schools, is regarded by
many as a historic decision of the Court on religious freedom and education.

American Judaism represents a wide divergence of opinion with respect to
private education. The great majority of American Jews attend public schools
and colleges and strongly support public education. Some American Jews are
concerned that private, particularly church-related, schools will divert resources from the public schools and strongly resist any proposals for government aid to such schools. On the other hand, the Orthodox branch of Judaism
has in recent years set up many Hebrew day schools. This has been almost entirely a phenomenon of the last three decades. Although Jews have lived in
America since the early colonial days their numbers were small until immigration from Europe and Russia in the latter part of the nineteenth century, stem-
ming from political upheaval, pogroms, and other causes. In 1854 there were
only seven Jewish schools in the country and in 1940 there were still only
thirty, all of them Orthodox. The Conservative and Reform groups had no
schools. There are currently three hundred Hebrew schools in the country,
thirty of them under Conservative auspices, the rest Orthodox.

Hebrew schools are characterized by a bilingual approach to education, a
very long school day, and high standards of academic achievement. The typical Hebrew day school offers all the secular subjects taught in public schools as
well as the Hebrew language and special programs in Jewish religion, history,
and culture. Normally the day is divided between the Hebrew studies and the
"English studies." Like many private schools, Hebrew schools are much
smaller than public schools, with an average enrollment of about 250 students.
Hebrew schools prior to 1940 admitted only boys. Currently girls also are involved, but often in separate classes.

The issue of government aid for private schools has dramatically shown
the disagreement within the Jewish community about private education. Jew-

ish school groups are strongly in favor of such aid, while the American Jewish Committee and the American Jewish Congress strongly oppose such aid.

The newest of the religiously affiliated schools are the Black Muslim schools. About a dozen such schools enrolling a total of perhaps five thousand students are located in large cities such as Detroit, Chicago, New York, Los Angeles, Washington, and Atlanta. The schools are strongly oriented toward discipline, academic achievement, and black pride.

One of the smaller but most important groups of private schools is made up of the nondenominational, "independent" schools. The varied characteristics of these schools are described by Kraushaar:

> *The independent schools nationwide exhibit even greater heterogeneity than the religiously affiliated ones. There are obvious external differences among them such as boarding and day schools; schools in rural, in suburban or urban settings, or ranches, in the desert, in the mountains, by the sea or on northern ski slopes; schools for boys or for girls and coeducational schools. Subtler but significant differences concern the clientele the school is designed to serve. There are schools for students of high, middling and low aptitudes, and for a deliberate mixture of these; racially integrated and segrated schools; schools for the handicapped, the psychologically disturbed; schools for the rich and privileged and for the poor and disadvantaged; schools for the well-motivated and for problem children. These schools differ also as to their educational philosophy and goals. There are college preparatory schools, military schools, tutoring schools, laboratory and demonstration schools, conventional schools and progressive experimental schools, schools specializing in foreign languages, in world-mindedness, in community involvement, in music or fine arts, in choir singing, in athletics, in character building, in work-study programs, in no-nonsense discipline or in an informal, permissive, first-name atmosphere. They are governed in a variety of ways—some by the benevolent dictatorship of the headmaster backed up by the trustees, others by a more democratic rule of the head working in tandem with trustees and faculty, students, and parents working it out together in community "town-meetings."* [12]

The largest and by far most influential independent schools are schools like Phillips Exeter, Phillips Andover, and Choate, which charge high tuition, have low student-faculty ratios, cater to academically superior students from upper-middle and upper classes, and put great stress on academic excellence. Many of the nation's political leaders, corporation executives, foundation heads, and community leaders are graduates from and now members on the boards of trustees of these independent schools. Admired by some as imaginative and highly effective, criticized by others as elitist,[13] these independent chools have in spite of their small numbers had a major impact on American fe. Some would even argue that these schools have influenced more of the top eadership of American political, economic, and social life than have all the ther private schools put together.

These independent prep schools tend to be concentrated in the northeast nd more generally Atlantic seaboard states and stem back to the earliest days f the republic. For instance, Andover was founded in 1778, Exeter in 1781, Deerfield in 1797, and Lawrenceville in 1810. Although many independent chools are now coeducational, the boys' prep schools grew up alongside but eparate from the "female seminaries," or girls' boarding schools such as Greenfield Hill Academy (1785), Troy Female Seminary (now known as Emma Villard) (1821), Mount Holyoke Seminary (1836), and Hartford Female Seminary (1828).

The prestige independent schools around the country tend to be similar to ach other, largely following the New England academy model of Exeter and Andover. Other independent schools exhibit an almost dizzying variety—progressive schools, university lab schools, ethical culture schools, Harlem storeront academies, Mississippi free schools, Montessori schools, schools modled after A.S. Neill's Summerhill School in England, black community chools (to be distinguished from the Black Muslim schools), military schools, reudian and other psychologically oriented schools, free schools,[14] and so n.[15]

After legal segregation in Southern schools was ended by the 1954 Brown ecision, a number of private, all-white "segregation academies" opened in the outheastern states. Still, even in the states of the deep South, 94 percent of the tudents are in public schools. Nationally, 10.1 percent of private school students are minority-group students, as compared with 20.9 percent of public chool students.

Catholic Elementary and Secondary Schools

n 1974–1975 there were 10,095 Catholic elementary and secondary schools in ne country, enrolling 3,492,000 students, nearly three-fourths of these in the lementary grades (K–8). Catholic schools differ from other private schools ot only in numbers but in geographical distribution. While Lutheran schools re concentrated in the Midwest, Christian Reformed schools in Michigan, ewish schools in New York, Quaker schools in Philadelphia, elite prep chools in New England, Baptist and Methodist schools in the South, and Seventh Day Adventist schools in scattered small towns and rural areas, Catholic chools are found in every region in the country. However, they of course folw the distribution of Catholic population, which for historical reasons primarily connected with immigration is concentrated in the large metropolitan population centers. In cities such as Philadelphia, Boston, New York, Cleveland, Detroit, and Chicago, Catholic schools constitute between 20 percent and 30 percent of the total school population. This is, however, less true of southern and western cities (for example, Seattle, Portland, Phoenix, Atlanta, Dallas, Denver)[16] and suburban, small-town and rural areas. In 1974–1975, 32.8 percent of Catholic school students were in urban areas other than inner city, 15.5 percent in inner-city schools, 31.8 percent in suburban schools, and 19.9 percent in small-town or rural schools. The percentage of enrollment in inner-city schools increased from 11.3 percent in 1970–1971 to 15.5 percent in 1974–1975.[17]

The typical Catholic grade school is affiliated with one parish, which contributes from general parish funds 50–75 percent of the school's operating revenue. The rest of the income derives from tuition, fees, and local fund-raising. In a few cases, usually inner-city schools, there is also a subsidy from the diocese or archdiocese.[18] Many but by no means all parishes have a parochial elementary school or co-sponsor a school with one or more other parishes. Many parishes also give a regular contribution or subsidy to nearby Catholic high schools.

Patterns of control and accountability differ somewhat from parish to parish. The pastor is appointed by the bishop and is responsible for all aspects of the parish including the parish elementary school (a few parishes also have high schools), but in recent decades the professionalization of Catholic educators and the increasing involvement of parishioners in decision making through parish school boards has led to some shift in influence. The principal of the school is usually a nun, appointed for that purpose by a religious community of sisters. About half the teachers in the school are nuns, and the other half are lay teachers. Most of the lay teachers are female. The principal of the school serves several different masters (the relationship among whom is murky and sometimes a bit strained, but on the whole positive): her superiors in the religious community, the pastor, the diocesan superintendent, and the local parish school board (if there is one). There are many variations on this theme and the power structure will differ from school to school depending on the personalities involved, but this is a generally recognizable picture of the decision making structure of most Catholic elementary schools.

A Catholic school principal, like most private school principals, has far more authority and responsibility than a public school principal. For instance, she hires and fires teachers (at least lay teachers), prepares the school budget and is executive officer to the parish school board, which sets policies, authorizes the budget, determines tuition and fees, and in most cases decides lay teachers' salaries and fringe benefits. The principal makes most of the decisions about the school's curriculum and other aspects of its program. Although each diocese has a diocesan superintendent of schools who exercises some authority over the parish schools (the amount and types of authority differ greatly from diocese to diocese), Catholic schools are far more autonomous on the local level than are public schools. The diocesan school office is a mixture of educational service agency and administrative authority, with more emphasis on the service agency aspect.

A parallel and sometimes more important set of directions and services comes from the religious teaching community. The community appoints the principal, occasionally but not often with significant input from the diocesan superintendent, pastor, and parish school board. The community, with input from the principal and from individual sister teachers, decides which sister teachers will go to what schools to teach what grades and subjects. In recent years and especially since the Second Vatican Council, individual teaching sisters have more and more freedom to determine where they will go and what they will teach or indeed if they will teach at all.

There are hundreds of different religious communities, male and female, in the United States. One wag has said that the only thing the Holy Spirit doesn't know is how many communities of nuns there are. In a medium-size diocese there will be at least twenty to thirty different religious communities teaching in the Catholic elementary and secondary schools of the diocese.

Nearly all elementary schools are either parish or interparish schools. In 1974–1975 only 0.9 percent of elementary students were in diocesan elementary schools and 3.7 percent were in Catholic private schools (schools owned and operated by a religious community rather than by a parish or a diocese).[19]

Catholic high schools fall into several categories. In 1974–1975, 18.5 percent of the secondary students attended parish-sponsored high schools, another 13.1 percent attended high schools co-sponsored by two or more parishes, 28.4 percent attended diocesan high schools, and 40 percent attended private (religious community) high schools. The phenomenon of the parish high school is gradually disappearing from the American Catholic scene as high school education becomes more specialized and more economical to conduct in larger institutions. For instance, the number of students in parish high schools went down from 23.2 percent in 1970–1971 to 18.5 percent in 1974–1975, while interparochial, diocesan, and private high schools all increased their percentage of total enrollment.

Parish and interparish high schools, like parish grade schools, get a substantial proportion of their income from the sponsoring parish(es). They may also receive a smaller subsidy from the diocese. Diocesan high schools typically receive a larger percentage of their income from the diocese and/or parishes in that area (the distinction between an interparochial high school and a diocesan high school is not always easy to make). Private high schools typically get no subsidy from parishes and little from dioceses. Nearly all of their income is from tuition, fees, and fund raising. However, even the parish, interparish, and diocesan high schools must rely more on tuition, fees, and fund raising than do elementary schools.

Because of their administrative distance from pastors and their funding sources, Catholic high schools tend to be significantly more autonomous in decision making than Catholic elementary schools. Catholic private schools, elementary and secondary, are not under the day-to-day jurisdiction of either pastor, superintendent, or bishop, but do exist in the diocese at the pleasure of the bishop and must follow his general policies, particularly with regard to the teaching of religion.

Catholic schools stem from the earliest days of American settlement. As mentioned earlier, the first school in the present confines of the United States was a Catholic school established in St. Augustine, Florida in 1605. Catholic schools were an integral part of the Spanish and French settlements in the Southeast, the Southwest, and the Mississippi valley. They also existed off and on in Maryland, depending on the fluctuations in Catholic acceptability there.

The history of anti-Catholic prejudice in America has been well documented by historians but is not generally known by most Americans. Catholics were prevented in many colonies from having their own schools or even their own churches. After the Constitution and the Bill of Rights, Catholics had more freedom, but anti-Catholic feeling was still very strong, especially during the peak periods of immigration. Paradoxically, as we have seen, anti-Catholic feeling ultimately led to the widespread establishment of Catholic schools. At the beginning of the Civil War there were two hundred Catholic schools in the country; by 1900 there were about five thousand. In 1884, largely in response to cresting anti-Catholic prejudice and the fear that public schools were a subtle means of indoctrination, the American Catholic bishops in the Third Plenary Council of Baltimore decreed that "near every church a parish school, where one does not yet exist, is to be built and maintained *in perpetuum* within two years of the promulgation of this council, unless the bishop should decide that because of serious difficulties a delay may be granted." The decree, like many papal and episcopal decrees, was often observed in the breach. (In 1884, 37 percent of American Catholic parishes operated schools; in 1891, 44 percent; and by 1900 the figure was down to 36 percent again.) Nevertheless, from 1884 until only recently the official Catholic ideal was "every Catholic child in a Catholic school."

Catholic school enrollment steadily increased as the general Catholic population increased through immigration and large families. In 1964, the peak enrollment year, there were 5.6 million students in 13,250 Catholic elementary and secondary schools.

Since 1964 the number of schools and students has been declining steadily. In the decade between 1964–1965 and 1974–1975, Catholic schools lost 2.1 million students, a drop of over 37 percent. Catholic educators, church officials, and sociologists have studied this phenomenon and suggested a variety of causes. Certainly one contributing factor is the drastic decline in the Catholic birth rate since 1957. The number of infant baptisms (roughly, the number of children born to Catholic families) in 1957 was 1,284,534, and in 1974 was 876,306—a drop of 32 percent. Since the first year of birth-rate decline was 1958, it is probably no accident that the enrollment decline began after 1964 as fewer and fewer Catholic children were available for first-grade classes. Another factor is that as the Catholic populace slowly ascended the socioeconomic ladder and moved out toward the suburbs, Catholic schools were not built in the suburbs to accommodate the new Catholic population there. Still another factor is the sharp increase in Catholic school tuition charges, due primarily to the declining number of teaching sisters (who work for subsistence wages), the consequent increase in the number of lay teachers, and the improvement of both religious and lay salaries, as well as cost increases in every other area of school expenditure. Regardless of efforts to keep tuition as low as possible and offer tuition scholarships to needy students, Catholic schools became too expensive for some Catholic families.

Catholics still debate how seriously this financial argument should be taken. For one thing, elementary tuition and fees are still extremely low—an average of $105 per student per year in 1972–1973, the last year for which national figures are available. Also, sociologists have demonstrated that Catholics are making considerably more money than they used to, even taking inflation into account. In fact, one recent study indicated that Irish Catholics (traditionally the group most likely to send their children to Catholic schools) rank number one in income among Christian groups in the United States. Some Catholic educators question whether there is as much genuine financial inability as there is a change in values and priorities among some Catholic parents.

However, Catholic high school tuition is now higher than before, and is prohibitive for some families. The average 1972–1973 tuition and fees income was $373 per student per year in parish and diocesan high schools and $700 per student per year in private high schools. Since 1972–1973, both figures have certainly increased substantially and in 1975–1976 would be around $500 and $900 respectively, if not higher. Also, many Catholic families experience the problem of the *cumulative* effect of tuition and other costs; a family with, for instance, two children in Catholic grade school and two children in Catholic high school might easily face a total bill of almost $2,000 per year for tuition, fees, books, uniforms, and transportation.

Another possible cause for the enrollment decline is that some Catholic parents and students no longer believe Catholic education is sufficiently important to them. Reports in the Catholic and secular media have often suggested in the last ten years that this is the principal if not the only reason for

Catholic school enrollment decline, and writings like Mary Perkins Ryan's *Are Parochial Schools the Answer?*[20] were seen by some as signs of a dramatic shift of opinion among American Catholics. However, careful study of Catholic attitudes has not given any significant support to this view. Andrew M. Greeley of the National Opinion Research Center in Chicago conducted two nationwide surveys, one in 1963 and one in 1974, which included a study of Catholics' attitudes toward Catholic schools.[21] Greeley found little if any support for the thesis that there has been an attitude shift of Catholic lay people away from the Catholic schools. In fact, following a decade in which several significant measures of Catholic involvement (Mass attendance, reception of the sacraments, church membership, attitudes toward church authority, religious vocations, and so forth) showed a sharp decline, the level of stated support for Catholic schooling remained very consistent and very high. Also, when Catholic parents with children in public schools were asked why the children were not in Catholic schools, the answer most frequently given in both 1963 and 1974 was simply that there was no Catholic school available. The second most frequently mentioned answer in the 1974 study referred to the cost problem. Greeley concluded that the nonavailability factor (either because of location or because of finance) was by far the most important reason for the smaller percentage of Catholics now sending their children to parochial schools. He also concluded that there were few if any signs of serious disaffection with the schools.

The two Greeley reports and several other research studies have investigated at some length what effects Catholic schools have on the students' religious beliefs, attitudes, and practices; academic achievement; future economic and social status; tolerance; civic participation; and general attitudes toward life.[22] The studies indicate that Catholic schools have moderate but significant positive effects on religious knowledge, values, and behavior; economic achievement; racial tolerance; and participation in the society. Catholic school Catholics score significantly ahead of public school Catholics in all the above areas. Comparative studies of Catholic and public school academic achievement have shown Catholic school students scoring as well as or better than their public school counterparts.

As Greeley and others have noted, the statistics of these studies are quite clear and undebatable; but their policy implications are certainly debatable and have in fact been widely argued. Some members of the Catholic Church have said that Catholic schools do not have enough effect to merit the large financial and personnel investment in them; others have argued that, in view of the relatively small effect produced by schools generally and the doubtful effect of alternative church programs for religious formation,[23] Catholic schools are well worth the effort and should be continued and even expanded.

Ironically, the Greeley data strongly suggest that the "consumers" (Catholic families) are just as positive toward Catholic schools as they have ever been, while the "producers"—bishops, pastors, some religious community educators—have begun quietly to move away from their former strong support of Catholic education.

The decade from 1964 to 1974 was a time of great identity crisis and self-doubt within Catholic education and the church generally. The Second Vatican Council produced a climate in which many traditional elements of Catholicism (meatless Fridays, Lenten fasting, birth control practices, the language of Mass and the sacraments, life styles and clothing of nuns and priests) were changing dramatically. Catholic schools were certainly as traditional a part of Catholicism as anything else, and naturally Catholics began to raise questions about whether the schools should go also. Mary Perkins Ryan's book *Are Parochial Schools the Answer?* though hardly a profound critique of Catholic education, did come at just the time when Catholics were beginning to ask the same question, and thus had somewhat of a bombshell effect.

There are signs within the last few years that the decade of panic and confusion within Catholic education is coming to an end and giving way to more calmness, security, and a renewed sense of mission. The enrollment decline has begun to level off in spite of the continuing decline in the Catholic birth rate, the continuing migration of Catholics to suburbs, and the continuing rise in Catholic school tuition costs. Catholic educators, for years on the defensive, began in the 1970s to go on the offensive, improving their public relations efforts, aggressively recruiting students, and taking a strong stand for government aid to private schools. Whether this new mood of optimism will prevail over the countervailing forces of cost increases, decline in religious staff, and the apparently continuing erosion of support from top church administrators, is a question that will be answered as this largest of all private school systems in the history of the world enters the late 1970s and the 1980s.

Constitutional-Legal Issues

As we have seen, the distinction between "public" and "private" schools in American life is a relatively recent one. Some question the validity of the terms even now. Until the 1954 Brown decision of the United States Supreme Court, the better southern "public" schools were carefully reserved for white students. Due to the extreme residential segregation of nearly all large American cities, the public schools in the central areas are filled with low-income, minority group students while wealthy suburbs a few miles away have public schools with students coming almost exclusively from rich white families. The per-pupil expenditures in wealthy suburban districts are often twice as much as in inner-city schools. Some have asked what "public" means when applied to the schools of the exclusive suburbs, which are in effect open only to students who come from white families making at least $30,000 a year.

On the other hand, the "private" schools of the United States spend billions of dollars each year to educate nearly 5,000,000 future American citizens in reading, writing, mathematics, science, history, civics, and many other subjects thought valuable to the preservation and development of the society. Many of these schools also teach religious and moral values. The founding fathers of the country and most Americans since have believed that religion and morality are critically important to the strength and stability of our culture. Further, even though some people for whatever reasons like to regard American private education as a refuge for wealthy white racists, the actual fact is that American private elementary and secondary schools serve hundreds of thousands of students from lower-middle-class and poverty areas, including many minority group students. For instance, the Catholic schools in the central areas of New York, Chicago, Detroit, St. Louis, Los Angeles, and other American cities are regarded by many ghetto residents as far superior to the public schools in those areas. While these Catholic schools labor under severe economic pressures, they rarely have empty classrooms, and in many cases well over half the students belong to religions other than Catholic, and a higher percentage still are nonwhite.

On these grounds many proponents of private education have urged that the state and federal governments recognize that private schools are in fact "public" in much of what they do, and that the state should recognize this public service in private education just as it recognizes and financially aids private hospitals, nursing homes, maternity homes, children's homes, and other social and health service institutions. They argue that if it is constitutional to pay the salary of a Catholic priest for saying Mass and hearing confessions in a penitentiary or in the military service, if it is constitutional to pay a Jewish veteran's tuition to rabbinical school under the G.I. Bill, it certainly should be constitutional for the government to pay part of a private school science teacher's salary or buy the science books or build the labs or pay that part of a student's tuition that is related to the science course.

The courts, however, have generally rejected this line of argument. During the 1960s and early 1970s a variety of state aid programs for private schools were enacted by legislatures throughout the country.[24] The courts, above all the United States Supreme Court, have struck down partial payment of teachers' salaries, direct grants to the schools, state income tax credit for tuition paid to private schools, some forms of materials and equipment assistance, and auxiliary educational services such as counseling, remedial reading, and speech therapy. The Court has affirmed the constitutionality of state laws that provide for free loan of nonreligious text books to private as well as public school students, free school bus transportation for private as well as public school students, and tax exemption for nonprofit private schools. The Court's decisions on the private school issue have aroused considerable feeling on both sides. Some have acclaimed them as safeguards to religious liberty; others have bitterly criticized them as narrow, secularistic, and even prejudiced.

Several major constitutional-legal questions remain to be clarified by the Court. For instance, the educational voucher idea, first proposed by Adam Smith in *The Wealth of Nations* (1776) and more recently advocated by conservative economist Milton Friedman and liberal social critic Christopher Jencks, would give a voucher or chit to every school-age pupil. Students could attend any state-approved school (private or public), presenting the voucher to the school of their choice. The school could then cash in the voucher and use the money to operate.

The voucher idea is quite simple—letting education operate by free market competition and free consumer choice. It has been tested in Alum Rock, California, and an independent Rand Corporation evaluation concluded that the Alum Rock experiment was highly successful. But the voucher is strongly opposed by all public school associations, particularly the teacher unions, as well as by the American Civil Liberties Union. The Courts have not yet ruled on the constitutionality of the voucher idea.

Also still at issue is the constitutionality of Title I (Elementary and Secondary Education Act of 1965) and other federally funded programs, and the constitutionality of some newer state aid programs. Currently in Congress is a proposal that tuition paid to private schools be declared tax deductible.[25] There will in all probability continue to be court action on these and other private school aid issues in the years to come, but many feel that the decisions handed down between the Everson (1947) and *Meek* v. *Pittenger* (1975) decisions have answered most of the major questions about the constitutionality of private school aid, and have answered them negatively.

Private Schools as Educational Alternatives

The history of education in the United States is marked with a far greater variety than most Americans imagine. Much education, formation, and training always has taken place and still takes place in nonschool contexts (family, church, news media, peer group, military service, work, travel, libraries, parks, museums, and so on). Even in that segment of education that takes place in formal institutions like schools, a great deal of the educational effort in American history has been in private school settings. As we have seen, the sharp distinction now made between private and public would have made little sense to the colonists of the seventeenth and eighteenth centuries. The distinction did not become a seriously accepted part of American life until about the time of the Civil War. To forget this history, to be oblivious to the wealth of education still around us, is to take a narrow and uncreative view of the possibilities of American education in the present and future.

Furthermore, if we take the trouble to study the history and present reality of education in other societies, we will find many models other than the model of American public education.

It is, to say the least, not at all clear from the history of education in our country and others that a single educational system is the best solution to the perennial problem of education in human society.[26] In fact, as can easily be seen from the history of education in some countries and perhaps in parts of our own country, having one single state-controlled educational system *can* lead to bureaucratic sluggishness, unresponsiveness to the needs of students and parents, and vulnerability to the influence of power-hungry politicians. The American creed of public education is that it is "of, by, and for the people," but it would be interesting to ask the average resident of Harlem whether the nearby private storefront academy is less "of, by, and for the people" than the board and administration of the New York public schools, which enroll over 1,000,000 students.

There may be aspects of private education that should lead Americans to rethink their basic assumptions about education rather than operate as if putting more money into public schools will solve all problems. For instance, in private schools more educational decisions are made at the classroom and school level. Private schools have a great deal of professional autonomy in hiring teachers, choosing textbooks and materials, deciding budget priorities, and trying new approaches. There are risks in this arrangement, but it can and usually does lead to greater responsiveness to student needs than when all such decisions are made in a distant central administrative office.

Parents have direct effect on the private school decision-making process. Because most of the important decisions are made by the school's board, the principal, and the staff, parents can go directly to these people when they want to see something changed (or continued). In most public school systems, the size and complexity of the system often discourage parents from even trying to make their wishes known.

In some ways the most important characteristic of a private school is, paradoxically, that it does not have to be there, it does not have to exist. Any time there is a group of school-age children the existence of a public school is mandated by the state and the parents must send their children to that school. This is not the case with private education. The parents and students do not have to go there, and the teachers do not have to teach there. Stated more positively, this means that the people who staff private schools, and the families who use them, are there because of personal choice and conviction—often at personal financial sacrifice. This sets up a bond of freedom and commitment at adds greatly to the strength, cohesiveness, spirit, and flexibility of private schools. It takes a certain resourcefulness, desire, and self-sacrifice to choose private schools when free public schools are available. Private school educators, students, and parents often form strong educational communities in which everybody has to work hard and sacrifice for the same common goals. Many Americans think that private schools have fewer discipline problems than public schools because they dump all their problem students into the public schools. This is simply not borne out by the facts. Studies of the IQ, socioeconomic status, family background, and other characteristics of private school students have found them generally similar to public school students—slightly higher in these measures but not enough to make much difference in disciplinary incidence. Nor would even cursory visits to private and public schools support the view that the two are significantly different in their disciplinary practices. The simplest explanation of the difference in disciplinary problems is that people are in private schools because they freely choose to be, and people who freely choose something and make significant personal sacrifices to back up that choice are not likely to treat lightly what they have chosen, much less destroy it by disruptive and violent behavior.

There has been a trend in some public school districts recently toward providing more opportunities for choice (such as open enrollment, in which students can enroll in any school in the city regardless of place of residence), but these changes are at least offset in some cities by the phenomenon of mandatory busing. The issue of free choice in education is a vital one and perhaps will not be fully solved until and unless the society is ready to consider such controversial ideas as the voucher system and the value of compulsory school attendance laws.

The principal reason for the existence of most private schools is religious formation. While some social theorists continue to believe that any sort of religious activity is socially destructive, most Americans still hold what was axiomatic to the founding fathers, that it is very beneficial to the society that citizens believe in and live by religious principles. Private educators would certainly not advocate the introduction of religious instruction into public schools. One has only to remember that it was the Catholics, Jews, and non-mainline Protestants who bitterly opposed the religious indoctrination of the mainline Protestant public schools of the nineteenth century. But it might be well for the society to consider whether public schools could not cooperate in other ways with families desiring some integration of education and religion. Public school programs could be scheduled so that part of the day could be turned over to religious groups who, with their own personnel and at their own expense (including rental of the buildings for that time period), could offer religious education programs to any students wishing to take them, with options (for example, study periods) available for students who did not so

wish. Other possibilities of cooperation could be devised by sincere and creative policy makers. Such forms of cooperation would not in any way spen-
public tax dollars for private religious purposes and would simply allow th
kind of common-sense cooperation between societal agencies and all religiou
groups that has, after all, characterized American society from its earliest ori
gins. This would probably prove to be a far more satisfactory answer to th
relationship of education to value systems than including pallid courses abou
values or "the Bible as literature" within the public school curriculum. As pri
vate educators have always contended and as sociologists are more and mor
ready to admit, there is no such thing as value-free education whether "public
or "private." Public schools are strongly laden with many different values
Most of these are acceptable to virtually all Americans (for example, values o
honesty, fairness, and hard work), but some are not. For instance, millions o
public school teachers have for decades taught about the Revolutionary War
the Civil War, the First World War and the Second World War (and some
Korea and Vietnam) in such a way as to convey clearly the notion that "wha
we did was the right thing to do, the American thing to do, and what Go(
really wanted us to do—fight the British, fight the South, fight Kaiser Bill
fight Adolph Hitler and the Japs." What happens to the values of Quaker another pacifist students in such classrooms? After Vietnam we are a little mor-
willing to admit the possibility that American war policy is not *ipso facto* th-
hand of God guiding our manifest destiny. But can anyone seriously argue tha
this attitude toward American wars did not prevail in millions of public schoo
classrooms for many years?

As citizens of the United States and the world we face many critical mora
and religious questions. The public school is simply not equipped to deal witl
all of them. Most public schools studiously avoid certain issues for fear of controversy and legal entanglement. A woman once invited George Bernard Shav
to a dinner, requesting that he refrain from discussing religion and politics
Shaw wrote back to decline the invitation, explaining, "Madam, there is nothing else worth discussing." Private schools have kept alive the concept tha
value questions, morality, and religious formation are for many people essen
tial elements in education. The public schools cannot adequately handle thes-
issues but they should at the very least not try to come up with pallid substi
tutes but rather cooperate with agencies that can handle them.

Private schools have their problems and doubtless have made at least a
many mistakes as public schools throughout their long history of educationa
service to this country. Private educators have much to learn from publi
schools but public educators also have much to learn from private schools
The society in general needs most of all to learn that education is and mus
continue to be full of variety and alternative responses to the needs of th
many individuals who make up our society.

Notes and References

1. Bernard Bailyn, *Education in the Forming of American Society* (Chapel Hill: University of North Carolina Press, 1960), p. 11.

2. While we remember with a shudder the extraordinarily long, complex and hell-bent sermons of the Puritan divines, we should also remember that their erudition and preaching played an important role in the general education of the people. Much of early American education was motivated by the idea that young people had to be able to read the Bible—and those long-winded sermons.

3. For instance, the first school within the present confines of the United States was founded by Spanish Franciscan priests in St. Augustine, Florida, in 1605.

4. William Greenbaum, "America in Search of a New Ideal: An Essay on the Rise of Pluralism," *Harvard Educational Review*, **XLIV**, 3 (August 1974), p. 417.

5. See Jonathan Messerli, *Horace Mann: A Biography* (New York: Knopf, 1972).

6. See Marie Leonore Fell, *The Foundations of Nativism in American Textbooks, 1783–1860* (Washington, D.C.: Catholic University of America Press, 1941). The two best general studies of Protestant reaction to Catholic immigration are Ray Allen Billington, *The Protestant Crusade, 1800–1860* (N.Y.: Macmillan, 1938); and John Higham, *Strangers in the Land: Patterns of American Nativism 1860–1925* (New York: Atheneum, 1963).

7. *Statistics of Nonpublic Elementary and Secondary Schools, 1970–71* (Washington, D.C.: U.S. Government Printing Office, 1973). It is difficult to obtain recent, accurate figures on private schooling from the U.S. Office of Education. Different private school groups keep their own statistics, which are usually somewhat different from USOE's and probably more accurate. For instance, the National Catholic Educational Association statistical report on 1970–71 showed 4,367,323 students in Catholic elementary and secondary schools. See *A Report on U.S. Catholic Schools, 1970–71* (Washington, D.C.: NCEA, 1971), p. 10.

8. *Nonpublic Education and the Public Good* (Washington, D.C.: U.S. Government Printing Office, 1972), p. 7.

9. For a fuller description see Otto F. Kraushaar, *American Nonpublic Schools: Patterns for Diversity* (Baltimore: John Hopkins University Press, 1972). Our section borrows liberally from this excellent study.

10. *Outlook*, newsletter of the Council for American Private Education (November 1975).

11. Some of the church founders, for instance, were deeply involved in the New England abolitionist movement.

12. Kraushaar, *American Nonpublic Schools*, p. 54.

13. See C. Wright Mills, *The Power Elite* (New York: Oxford University Press, 1959), pp. 64–65; and E. Digby Baltzell, *The Protestant Establishment* (New York: Random House, 1964). For a different view see James McLachlan, *American Boarding Schools* (New York: Scribner's, 1970).

14. For a good recent summary of the free school movement see Allen Graubard "The Free School Movement," *Harvard Educational Review*, **XLII**, 3 (Augus 1972), pp. 351–373. Graubard notes the enormous difficulty of keeping track c how many free schools there are and how many students they enroll since almos by definition free schools dislike involvement in such record keeping. Also, man free schools close after one or two or three years of existence, and by the time th statisticians learn about their existence, they are no longer in existence. He est mates the total number of free schools as between 350 and 400, and their total er rollment as between 11,500 and 13,000 for the 1970–1971 school year.

15. For a brief description of the "infinite variety" of these schools, see Kraushaar *American Nonpublic Schools*, pp. 74–88. These schools include some of the mos creative recent developments in American education, and merit much more atter tion than they have received.

16. Some exceptions to the exceptions: New Orleans and San Francisco, which ar heavily Catholic. In general, see *Nonpublic Schools in Large Cities, 1970–7* (Washington, D.C.: U.S. Government Printing Office, 1974).

17. The best recent statistical information on Catholic elementary and secondar schools in the United States is found in the publications of the National Catholi Educational Association: *A Statistical Report on Catholic Elementary and Secor dary Schools for the Years 1967–68 to 1969–70* (1970), *A Report on U.S. Catholi Schools, 1970–71* (1971), *U.S. Catholic Schools 1971–72* (1972), *U.S. Catholi Schools 1972–73* (1973), *U.S. Catholic Schools 1973–74* (1974), and the reports c the Curriculum Information Center in Denver, Colorado, which now include th NCEA information: *Ganley's Catholic Schools in America, 1974* (1974), *NCE, Ganley's Catholic Schools in America, 1975* (1975).

18. A Catholic diocese is a geographical subdivision of the church and usually cover several counties. A parish is a geographical subdivision of a diocese. An archdio cese is best understood simply as a larger diocese. The number of parishes withi a diocese or archdiocese could range from twenty to five hundred.

19. Legally and technically all parish assets, including the school and everything con nected with it, are the property of the diocese or more exactly the "corporatio sole"—the occupant of the position of bishop of the diocese. However, man financial and administrative decisions are in effect delegated to pastors and/o parish councils with the result that there is a great deal of autonomy at the loca parish level, far more than exists in the subunits of other corporate structures.

20. New York: Holt, Rinehart and Winston, 1964.

21. Andrew M. Greeley and Peter H. Rossi, *The Education of Catholic American* (Chicago: Aldine, 1966); and Andrew M. Greeley, William C. McCready, an Kathleen McCourt, *Catholic Schools in a Declining Church* (Kansas City: Shee and Ward, 1976).

22. For summaries of much of this research see Michael O'Neill, *How Good Ar Catholic Schools?* (Washington, D.C.: NCEA, 1968); and Michael O'Neill, *Net Schools in a New Church* (Collegeville, Minn.: St. John University Press, 1971) pp. 14–73.

3. The Greeley studies could find little evidence that Catholic after-school and Sunday-school religious education programs had any lasting effect.
4. For a concise summary of the many aid programs operating in the fifty states see *State and Federal Laws Relating to Nonpublic Schools* (U.S. Office of Education, 1975).
5. Donations to private schools are tax deductible, but tuition is not.
6. For a history and critique of the single-model approach, see David B. Tyack, *The One Best System: A History of American Urban Education* (Cambridge, Mass.: Harvard University Press, 1974).

Suggested Readings

Erickson, Donald A. *Public Controls for Nonpublic Schools.* Chicago: University of Chicago Press, 1969.

Greeley, Andrew M., William C. McCready, and Kathleen McCourt. *Catholic Schools in a Declining Church.* Kansas City: Sheed and Ward, 1976.

Greeley, Andrew M., and Peter H. Rossi. *The Education of Catholic Americans.* (Chicago: Aldine, 1966.

Johnstone, Ronald L. *The Effectiveness of Lutheran Elementary and Secondary Schools as Agencies of Christian Education.* St. Louis: Concordia, 1966.

Kramer, William A. (Ed.). *Eight Critiques of the Johnstone Study on the Effectiveness of Lutheran Schools.* St. Louis: Board of Parish Education, The Lutheran Church—Missouri Synod, 1967.

Kraushaar, Otto F. *American Non-public Schools: Patterns of Diversity.* Baltimore: John Hopkins University Press, 1972.

Nonpublic Education and the Public Good. Washington, D.C.: U.S. Government Printing Office, 1972.

State and Federal Laws Relating to Nonpublic Schools. U.S. Office of Education, 1975.

Mario D. Fantini

Alternatives and choice in the public schools

8

Dr. Fantini's chapter articulates very clearly both the causes of and a possible solution to our lack of responsiveness in elementary and secondary education today. This chapter shows how the requirements of minority, bilingual, and other students with special needs can be accommodated within the framework of the public school system.

Mario D. Fantini

Dr. Fantini is presently Professor and Dean of Education at the State University of New York at New Paltz. He is an active speaker, author, and coauthor of many books and articles. In late 1964 and early 1965, Dr. Fantini served as a consultant to the Fund for the Advancement of Education of the Ford Foundation. In May 1965, he joined the regular staff of the Ford Foundation as Program Officer. Additionally, in May 1967, Dr. Fantini was appointed Executive Secretary of Mayor Lindsay's Panel on Decentralization of the New York City Schools, and became Staff Director of the Bundy Report.

Can our public schools be regenerated without dismantling them or the people within them? Can a constructive and viable plan of educational reform be implemented that will provide each school user with a learning environment that he or she wants and needs; liberate the strengths and talents of teachers and other professional educators; increase parent and citizen participation and satisfaction in our schools; not add to the current costs of education, but make fuller utilization of existing resources; and be acceptable to most citizens, school boards, teacher organizations, and so forth? Is there a way in which our schools can respond to such real common parental concerns as the following?

> *"My sixteen-year-old daughter is bright but completely turned off by high school. She has the ability to go to college, but with her present attitude I'll be happy if she just finishes high school. What can I do?"*

> *"My son, who is no slouch, sees no reason why he should continue high school when he feels like a number in a big factory. I know he has talent but he is not applying himself. How can I deal with this?"*

> *"My daughter has a talent in art. She would like to really advance in this field, but she feels that her school is not giving her the kind of education she needs. I can't afford a private school. What can I do to help her?"*

Do the answers to this list of questions sound impossible?

Consider a public high school of 1,500 students and 80 teachers in middle America. The school building is new, and most of the students are college bound. While this high school has one principal, one football team, one newspaper, one diploma, and so on, it is actually organized as five educationally different subschools, each much smaller in size. This school-within-a-school format provides each parent, student, and teacher with a direct choice from the following range of five optional forms of education:

1. *Traditional*—in which a teacher specializing in an academic field teaches each course in 55-minute periods (10 teachers and 300 students)

2. *Flexible*—in which teachers are provided a more flexible schedule through minicourses, modules, and so forth (17 teachers and 400 students)

3. *Individualized*—in which teaching methods are designed to meet the style of learning of the student, including wide use of experiences outside the school (12 teachers and 300 students)

4. *Fine arts oriented*—in which teachers create an artistic environment, utilizing the arts as the medium for academic and social development (9 teachers and 130 students)

5. *Career oriented*—in which the goal is to enable all learners to develop their talents and to relate such talents to their roles as workers (21 teachers and 175 students)

These choices followed a period of cooperative planning involving par ents, students, teachers, and administrators.

Is this a fictitious school? Not at all. Quincy Senior High School II i located in Quincy, Illinois, and has become the focus of considerable nationa attention for its "education by choice" approach that began in 1972. Th Quincy "alternatives" program is one of many surfacing in our public school today.

What seems to be a rather simple notion—offering parents, students, an teachers choices from among a range of legitimate educational alternatives o options—may become the major pattern for solving many of our nagging pub lic school problems in the decades ahead. This trend toward educational diver sity has grown out of several decades of frustration in which we tried to mak a monolithic public school system work for everybody. We were preoccupie with improving a single model of education. At every level of public educa tion, nursery through secondary, the notion of offering greater variety an choice through such organizational schemes as "schools within schools" an separate alternative schools is gaining wider acceptance. A Gallup poll con ducted in 1973 showed that the great majority of parents and teachers thin that alternative schools are a good idea.

This concept is deceptively simple. We have known for some time tha children learn in different ways; that teachers teach in different ways; tha there are different types of education that place varying responsibility upo students for what they learn and how, when, and where; and that dependin, on their values, parents have preferences as to the type of education their chi dren receive. The new trick is to find better matches between student an teacher and student and program by offering the family more choices. Wh among us, whether parent, teacher, or student, has not experienced the conse quences of a mismatch or had a new program imposed on them? This has ofte led to faculty and community dissatisfaction. We now know that there is n single agreed-upon path to quality education.

Optional patterns of education can now be found in some of the nation' most prestigious school districts, such as Newton, Massachusetts; Webste Groves, Missouri; Beverly Hills, California; Mamaroneck and Great Neck New York; and Bethesda, Maryland, to mention a few. Some of our bigges school systems are also into options, including among others Los Angeles Portland, Seattle, Racine, San Antonio, Dallas, Cincinnati, Kansas City Phoenix, Denver, and Philadelphia.

Prior to this new exploration of options within our public schools, th only available alternatives were to be found in our private schools. Divers independent schools from Montessori to college preparatory, free to military religious to secular, ethnic to multicultural, have provided choices—usually t those who could afford it. For the masses, however, the only choice was rather uniform public school system. The new alternatives are not to be confused with the old "tracks," such as vocational education or special programs for dropouts, unwed mothers, and the like. Present-day options offer students, regardless of background, a more personalized educational environment.

What are these options like? So far they seem to fall within certain basic categories that reveal their distinctive features.

Standard. The overwhelming majority of schools throughout the country retain the usual pattern of schooling, with its self-contained classrooms and graded K–12 curriculum structure.

Basic skill oriented. Some alternatives want to focus more heavily on directed programs in the fundamental 3 Rs. For example, Pasadena has a Fundamental Alternative School.

Flexible. While retaining the basic curriculum, these schools offer more elastic schedules for students and teachers through such devices as upgrading, team teaching, minicourses, and so forth. Taft Interdisciplinary School, for example, is a subunit of Taft Junior High in San Diego. Teachers in English, social studies, and science, for instance, form an interdisciplinary team for the 160 students in this program.

Open. Emphasis is on self-direction, with the student deciding when and how he or she learns. Teachers become facilitators and advisers. For example, the St. Paul Open School is organized around seven major learning areas: art, music-drama, humanities, math-science, industrial arts, home economics, and physical education. Students plan their own schedules. Shanti, located in an old railroad station in Hartford, Connecticut, offers an individually tailored program for each of its 95 regional high school students.

Talent based. The unifying curriculum element here is student talent. While the other academic subjects are also offered, they are integrated with the student's career aspirations. The Houston Public Schools have a High School for Performing and Visual Arts and a High School for Health Professions, which is located on the campus of the Baylor Medical College. Cleveland has a High School for Aviation Sciences, which is located at the Airport.

Schools without walls. The community and its resources become the major laboratory for learning. Museums, hospitals, government agencies, business, industry, television studios, and so on become "classrooms." The Chicago Public High School for Metropolitan Studies (METRO) is a school without walls in which the city is the classroom. The current enrollment of 350 students in grades 9–12 is conducted by a staff of 27 teachers and over 30 cooperating personnel who are members of the Chicago community. Students at METRO can choose a course in animal and human behavior taught by experts at the Lincoln Park Zoo, or TV production at NBC. Several other major city school districts have schools without walls, including New York (City as School) and Philadelphia (Parkway).

Multiculture. These schools promote cultural pluralism by having a diverse student body and/or a curriculum that gives full play to ethnic and racial heritages, including multilingual education. Agora is a subschool of Berkeley's Community High. The student body of about 120 students is composed of one-third black, one-third Chicano, and one-third white. The culture of each group is reflected in the curriculum. The Brown School in Louisville is an alternative program that operates in a former downtown hotel. With an enrollment of 400 students, grades 3 and 12, the Brown School has a multicultural flavor to it and serves as a voluntary model of integrated education.

The smaller size of alternative schools permits a degree of individualization and parental involvement not usually found in larger conventional schools. For instance, many of these schools have "town meetings" in which the entire school community participates.

Despite their growth, are alternative schools really succeeding? Are they overrated and merely a passing fad? While it is too soon to give any definitive results, on balance one can report—so far so good. Certainly it is difficult to ignore the many personal testimonies of those who are associated with the new schools. For example, during the first graduation exercises of the School Without Walls in Philadelphia, being held on the steps of that city's famous Art Museum, a parent with tears in her eyes explained to a group of visitors, "If it were not for this school, my daughter would have dropped out. Now she's graduating and going on to college." Or consider Eileen, a senior at Ramapo High's School Within a School (SWAS), who made a decision to take fifteen courses this year, including a philosophy seminar in the morning, poetry in the afternoon, and law and politics in the evening. Eileen feels that the alternative school gives her an opportunity to orchestrate her own education. "Now I feel like a whole person with confidence," she says, and she hopes to enter a small prominent New England college next fall. Or take Greg, a senior at Shanti, whose personalized program helped develop his talent in communicative arts, and who will be assuming an important position in Cable TV after graduation. These cases are becoming typical to alternative schooling.

On a broader basis, there seems to be no problem with the graduates of alternative schools being admitted to college. In fact, most of the graduates of alternative high schools intend to continue their education in college.

Successful alternative schools have been characterized by careful planning that involves school administrators, parents, teachers, and students; by an emphasis on quality; by clarification of program objectives and methods; by retention of standard education as a legitimate option; and by application of guidelines, including continuous evaluation and reporting. Above all, it is crucial to make clear that alternatives are not dumping grounds for so-called difficult students.

We have learned some other important lessons from our experiences thus far. Some programs have overstated what they could actually deliver or have based their appeals on some ill-defined notion of "freedom." In these cases, high expectations of students, parents, and teachers soon turned to frustration and a downgrading of the option itself. One teacher who was involved in a so-called free school put it this way: "Of what benefit is a school that says anything is acceptable?"

Some students have admitted that their initial choice was motivated, in part, by which option appeared easiest. However, if each option is equally valid educationally, then such a criterion is not of great concern. However, if alternative programs are not worked out carefully and become dumping grounds for the "discontented," or settings in which each does one's "own thing," then this aspect of being easy can become a real problem for professionals, parents, and students alike.

Parents considering optional forms of education need to ask certain basic questions: Are these options equally valid educationally? Will the quality of education be maintained in each alternative? Will my child be able to go to college after attending the alternative school? Parents and students as educational consumers have a right to have these and related questions answered by school officials. They should feel that any choice of a program different from the usual will not be inferior or result in problems later.

Throughout the country, parent, student, and teacher groups are forming around the theme of alternative education. This has posed some problems for school boards and administrators that have not yet given consideration to the new trend. With sensitive leadership, the idea of alternatives can bring diverse parties together. Thus, whether conservative or liberal, professional or parent, there is something for each. On the other hand, ill-defined alternatives can lead to confusion and conflict. For example, advocates of one philosophy of education or another may attempt to impose their own concepts at the expense of another.

Students especially need to weigh which of the educational patterns best fits their learning style. Some students prefer a nondirective environment; others a teacher-directed approach. The personalities of certain students are suited to more open, self-directive learning, while others need a quieter, more sequential context. Student awareness of these and other differences among educational environments is important if choices are to work.

The individuals involved need to establish the ground rules that can help guide alternative public schools in responsible ways. These include the following:

1. Alternatives must include a broad, common set of educational objectives, not just limited objectives. Alternative public schools are responsible to the public for comprehensive intellectual and attitudinal goals that cannot be compromised. These include basic skills, learning-to-learn skills, talent development, preparation for the basic societal roles (citizen, consumer, worker), and self-concept development.

2. Alternatives do not practice exclusivity.

3. Alternatives do not cost more money than existing per-student expenditures; they are based on a reutilization of existing resources.

4. Since public school alternatives seem to be educationally, economically, and politically feasible, provision for such a planning period should be made from local, state, and federal resources.

National directories on public education alternatives are available at the Schools of Education of both the University of Indiana at Bloomington and the University of Massachusetts at Amherst, and at the Center for New Schools in Chicago.

We should see an expansion of alternative education in the future. This can result in a broadening of free *public* education into a framework that offers a variety of sound educational options, including many that were formerly considered the province of private schools—and all by choice.

Neil V. Sullivan

The ultimate hope

9

This chapter by Dr. Neil Sullivan indicates to us how the school can be used not just as a place of instruction for youngsters but rather as the focal point for the entire community. It is an interesting alternative and fits in well with the presentation in Chapter 8. Many of the problems mentioned in Chapters 12 and 13 could be solved if such an approach were adopted.

Neil V. Sullivan

Dr. Sullivan is Chairman of the Department of Educational Administration at California State University, Long Beach. Formerly the Commissioner of Education for the Commonwealth of Massachusetts, he has taught at Harvard University, Stanford University, Boston University, the University of New Hampshire, and the University of Maine. He was formerly Superintendent of Schools in New York, Maine, Virginia, and California.

As I travel this country from coast to coast, meet with urban school administrators from Boston to Detroit to Denver to San Francisco, and listen to elected officials, one message comes through both loud and clear—"our secondary schools are in a shambles." Everywhere I go, citizens, parents, and students are demanding a new model and I heartily agree.

The thrust of my argument is that we must make the school a *public* instrument, used by all in both formal and informal situations, and make *the community* (all of its businesses and industries) *the school.* Prior to World War I, the schools, by and large, were used as community centers. However, as our cities became larger and larger, community living became complicated and led to a situation that isolated staff from students and the school from the community. Although the schools received the financial support of the community, they tended to ignore almost completely the problems of the community at large. The communities, nevertheless, kept on growing, and the school and the community paid little attention to one another.

The school calendar was built around an agricultural lifestyle—we scheduled classes so that our schools would be closed during the planting and harvesting periods. Our economy was dependent on the availability of children and young adults to work in the fields and the schools regulated their hours and weeks around this principle. However, World War I and the industrial revolution of the early twenties, followed by technological developments, changed our economic thrust from agricultural to industrial. Now we did not need inexperienced hands, and the work week was reduced to forty hours. The school, however, paid no attention to the change in our economic system and our lifestyle. We still operated our schools as we did in the nineteenth century—five hours a day, five days a week, one hundred and eighty days a year.

The community had taxed itself heavily to provide a facility that was being used 25 percent of the time by a small percentage of the total population—those from ages six to eighteen.

As the years rolled on, parents and taxpayers looked at the rising costs of public education and began to ask pertinent questions. In answering these questions, educators realized they had to reach back to the community for support. There appeared more and more frequent reports to parents, periodical bulletins, official communications by school superintendents, school surveys, master plan committees, budget reports, and radio and television editorials. The word was out—our school staffs and facilities were being misused and underutilized. At the same time, the dropout rate increased, student and teacher strikes increased, and delinquency and crime increased in both the city and the school.

I believe that education is a continuing lifetime pursuit and a shared responsibility of home, school, church, and community—that schools must be a center of the community endeavor to improve the quality of living and learning for all citizens, both young and old.

Before offering suggestions on model programs for community schools, I think it necessary to pause to assess the situation in our schools today.

The school system that exists in most communities today continues to be structured for the middle class. Administrators are almost without exception white Anglo-Saxons, and they are quite insensitive to the needs of minority children. The typical classroom teacher comes from the same middle class and has been educated in a system that prepared him or her for teaching middle-class children. The curriculum, the program of studies, and the school calendar are built to satisfy middle-class needs. How to change all of this so that every citizen has a fair shake is the challenge.

The change that must occur will come about only when we establish goals and standards that are "fair to all concerned." If we agree that the goal is "to make the school the nerve center for all community activities and to meet the needs of all the people," then middle-class teachers and administrators must make way for equal numbers of teachers and administrators with minority backgrounds.

A major reason why the system has remained unchanged is that people, particularly poor people, were never encouraged to visit school and were not brought in to participate in policy decisions. They were, in fact, excluded.

Will the change that I am insisting on occur voluntarily? My response is a resounding no. It will occur, however.

The impetus that was needed came first in Massachusetts in 1971, when I recommended to the State Board of Education that all communities receiving federal aid under the Elementary-Secondary Education Act of 1964 be required to have Parent Advisory Committees elected by the parents of poor children. The State Board's unanimous approval (over strong opposition from the establishment) had an immediate statewide effect. For the first time in a single state, elected officials (local school committees) were required to meet and consult with numbers of the minority.

The State Board followed up this action in 1972 in even more dramatic style. They mandated that every local school system consult with a community-wide parent advisory committee and work with them in implementing statewide goals and objectives.

The state legislature got the message and in the spring of 1972 passed legislation requiring local school committees to meet monthly with a student-elected committee from each high school.

I mention these events because I firmly believe that the best way to change the system is by a "bottoms-up" movement. For many years minority people were encouraged to change the system from the top—they were encouraged to run for office and, once elected, use their vote to bring about change. In a few situations this has worked, but across the country it has failed miserably.

I suggest that we must have strong state leadership (education is a state responsibility) and that state boards of education adopt guidelines and issue mandates requiring local compliance.

Why do I feel so strongly about mandatory parent involvement and making the school the nerve center of the community? Because it is our last hope and maybe our last chance if our society is to survive.

Something must pull us back together again. For decades we felt that the home would do this for us. In some cases it has, but the escalating divorce rate, and the increasing number of working mothers, commuting fathers, and children turned off by parents resulted in less home influence. Many concluded that the church could handle the situation, providing the coordination and leadership. But the church, like the home, has had its problems and is in no position to be the driving, motivating force needed in a badly shaken, deteriorating society.

The "bottoms up" movement can, and will, reshape the system in the image of the total community. Instead of having one or two minority members on a nine-member committee we will have hundreds of parents, students, staff, and people from the community at large making decisions at the community school level. They will decide on how long the school will be open, and they will help in its supervision and operation. When this occurs the community will start to discipline itself. The school will not be stoned or burned or ransacked because it will be the people's school—their home—and will meet their individual and group needs.

I believe that in a society of constantly shifting values, community schools can serve as the focal point to bring about the changes needed to help all citizens fulfill their needs, to challenge them, and to help them achieve their wants. I further believe that total citizen involvement in the community school will increase our ability to achieve these goals. Our educational leaders must stop planning things *for* people and start working out programs *with* people. We must turn to minority groups, those oppressed, and ask the question, Where did the system fail? Once we identify the cause of the failure we involve *all* of the partners in suggesting ways and means to overcome the problem.

The basic function of the community school is to offer every child and adult an opportunity to have those living and learning experiences that will enable them to behave as a responsible, considerate, contributing, self-sustaining members of society. If we accept this tenet, the community school must consider the social order in which the children and adults now live and the one in which they are likely to live. The community school must, therefore, provide for *three kinds* of learning: first, learning concerned with individual learning;

second, learning concerned with group living; and third, learning that will provide individuals with saleable skills, in a competitive labor market.

The areas of individual living and learning experiences include those attitudes, abilities, and skills that ensure satisfactory human relationships and acceptance of civic responsibility. Individuals should develop the ability to get along well with others—to grow from self-centered persons into intelligent members of society so that they will discharge responsibilities commensurate with maturity and capacity.

The last and probably most important area, which deals with the schools' responsibility for providing individuals with marketable skills, is the greatest of all challenges facing the community school. Our rapidly changing industrial system requires constant retraining, at all ages, for the ever-changing challenges of a technological revolution. The community school must be equipped with the facilities and the staff to provide new learning experiences on a round-the-clock basis, and to retrain all citizens, regardless of age, with new abilities and skills that will insure them economic efficiency and self-realization. This training must be career oriented and provide formal learning plus the work and study habits needed to capitalize on the basic skills already attained by the individual.

The community school philosophy is not really a new one—the concept itself has been accepted by a few educators for the past twenty-five years. However, the application of the philosophy has been limited to just a few districts, the best known being the program at Flint, Michigan, and, more recently, one in Worcester, Massachusetts.

Years ago, school leaders were concerned primarily with the academic instruction of children. This, by and large, has not changed with the passing of years. Our response to Sputnik was "more of the same" with greater emphasis on the teaching of foreign languages and on mathematics and science. Today, teachers are finally becoming more conscious of the importance of individuals to themselves and of their present and potential contributions to society. This widens the scope of interest and necessarily involves adults in the community.

The traditional school continues to emphasize the three Rs; the attitude is subject-matter centered, not child or person centered, and at the end of the school day, the school buildings are closed. However, today we are moving away from the traditional approach and have shown a strong desire to build our programs around social services, recreation, civic involvement, and careers. With this change, and with the advent of adults into the school picture (schools are for people of all ages), the community school becomes the center for educational, recreational, and social activities for all ages. Instruction is not only as important as ever, it becomes more vital as actual learning situations are planned by *parents, students, and teachers cooperatively.* The participating partners now discover that there is too much to be learned, too much to do, and that it cannot all be squeezed into a six-hour day, a five-day week, and a nine-month year.

We must keep in mind that if we are to rise to the challenges of the last quarter of the twentieth century and meet the needs of all of our people, we can no longer conceive of the "school" as four brick walls located on a few acres of land. Instead we must conceive of a school that has no walls, no limited acreage. The school is the entire community; it includes all of the libraries, the museums, the churches, the Young Men's and Young Women's Christian Associations, and the community and state universities in the area (both private and public). All of our resources (those of labor and industry included), human and material, must be included as part of the community schools' resources and used in a massive effort to meet the challenge. The solutions to our human problems (reducing crime, educating all our people for purposeful living, and so on) should, and must, be our end, and history will judge us in that light. All of our technology, all of our facilities, must be made available. We must shape and provide for all a comprehensive education that will carry all of us (not some of us) from birth to death. Society is changing so rapidly that even those who seemed adequately prepared for life a generation ago have now found that their education is out of date. If this is true at a general level, and I believe it is, the lag is bound to be felt even more forcefully in our inner-city areas. If, in the inner city as in the affluent suburb, we do not think of the entire community (its people and its facilities) as the school, then I can confidently predict an increase in deliquency, crime, and the numbers of our people on welfare rolls.

We must start thinking of our schools as centers for human resource programs of every conceivable nature. They should provide academic, vocational, cultural, recreational, health, and related services according to goals and objectives of a given area and personal needs. If we conceive the above as the role of the school, the school would become an invitation to all—to the very young, to the very needy, to citizens of all ages. Opportunities would be provided for self-improvement in basic skills and every other means of self-fulfillment.

I am convinced that a school that denies any of its people the opportunity to actively participate in meaningful activities that are career centered and in decision-making activities is obsolete and does not deserve our continued support. School experiences must be relevant to life experiences and employment opportunities. Schools must become accessible to every resident, young and old, on a seven-day week, year-round basis. The school is a public instrument and must be used for the training of all of the people. Since it is the principal institution for the training of all people, it is imperative that it be provided with the resources to operate on a full-time basis. I believe that our present schools could be operated more efficiently without new money, but we cannot make full use of our school facilities without providing additional tax revenue for their extended use and operation. I feel that this is a legal and moral responsibility of our government and anything less would be a serious failure to discharge our responsibility for the education of all of our people.

Let us start by taking a *community inventory of facilities* available for educational and recreational purposes. Once we know what is available, we can then make plans for using all of the space, all of the equipment, and all of the staff. We might discover when we do this that there is no need for a new wing on an existing building and that possibly the new school could be delayed indefinitely.

Now let us consider scheduling use of the facilities on a twelve-month basis. Teachers and administrators will be given an opportunity to work either a twelve-month year (with one month vacation), or a nine-month year, as they now do, and be paid accordingly. Students would be scheduled for three of four semesters and could select a vacation period consistent with the family wishes and interests.

Parochial and private school students would be given open access to courses that such schools do not offer as well as to the media (library, audio-visual) facilities, gymnasium and recreational facilities, science laboratories, and all occupational courses.

On a statewise basis, Massachusetts has become a pace-setter for the twelve-month school and community use of school property.

In 1970, the General Court of the Commonwealth enacted into law the following section under Chapter Seventy-one of the General Laws. It reads as follows:

(a) *The purpose of this section is to provide for the maximum use of school facilities as a focus for community life. School facilities under this section shall be available for use at all feasible times by persons of all ages for educational purposes, cultural, recreational and leisure time activities, the dispensing of social services, neighborhood group meetings and joint involvement of educators and the community in all aspects of education.*

(b) *The school committee or any other public agency or department of any city or town may file with the Department of Education a plan for maximum use of school facilities. The plan shall contain a description of the programs which shall be established under this section, an estimate of the costs of such programs, an enumeration of the specific schools designated for maximum use, a provision for the maximum possible participation of community residents in the planning and implementation of all programs and such other information as the Commissioner of Education may require. Plans shall be considered in the order in which they are filed except that if a plan filed by the school committee of a city or town is one of two or more plans being considered at the same time for such city or town, the plan proposed by the school committee shall be considered prior to other plans. The Commissioner may, within a reasonable time, approve, reject, or modify plans submitted to the Department. The Commissioner shall have the power to withhold funds authorized under this section from agencies which fail to comply with the provisions of or any regulation promulgated pursuant to this section. There shall be employed in the Department of Education two persons whose duties shall be to assist local agencies in the development, implementation, supervision and coordination of plans proposed under the provisions of this section.*

(c) *An approved plan shall be administered by the proposing agency. Such agency shall appoint a director who shall be a salaried, full-time employee, not subject to the provisions of chapter thirty-one of the General Laws, to implement and carry out the plan.*

(d) *The Commonwealth shall reimburse actual expenditures made pursuant to this section in the amount of fifty percent. Grants for the development of plans pursuant to paragraph (b) of this section shall be available, upon application to and approval by the Department of Education, in an amount not exceeding fifteen thousand dollars. In no event shall the appropriation under this section exceed one million dollars in any one year.*

(e) *The Commissioner of Education may, by regulation, further define the requirements for the content and operation of a plan proposed under this section.*

Figures 9.1 and 9.2 graphically display how Michigan communities organize for the complete use of school facilities on a twelve-month basis.

From Theory to Reality

As we move from theory to reality we must set goals and establish standards. The goal in the area of the community school is a simple one: make the school the nerve center for community development.

The subgoals to support this goal are as follows:

1. Fully utilize all public school facilities, staff, and equipment on a round-the-clock basis, seven days a week, three hundred and sixty-five days a year.
2. Make all public facilities and private facilities an extension of the school and use accordingly.

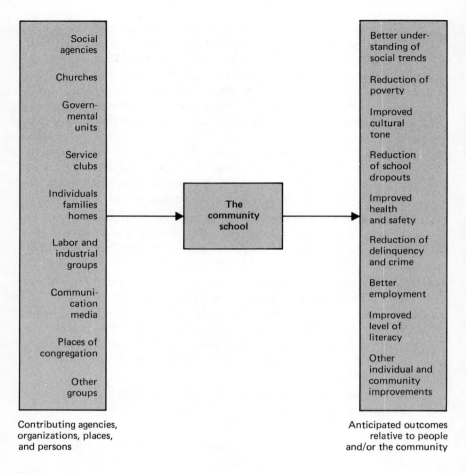

Fig. 9.1   Community education

3. Make business, labor, industry, social and governmental agencies, church, and social groups all part of the contributing team for community education.

4. Make the school a real-life microcosm of our society with people *of all ages* intermingling with one another in various action-oriented situations.

5. Make the school take the initiative by extending its walls and including within them challenging programs for all of the people.

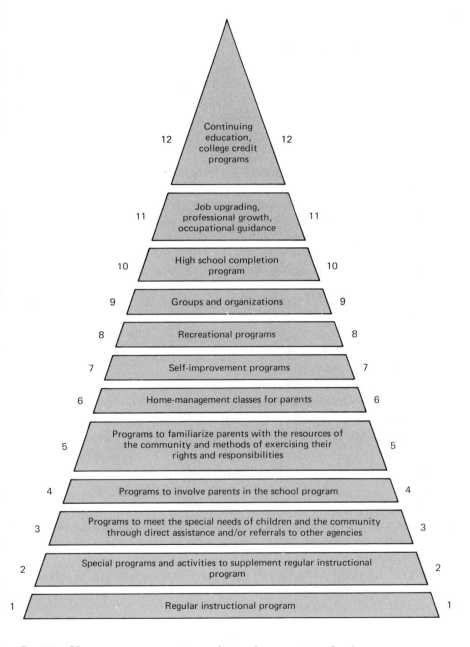

Fig. 9.2   Human resources center emphasis of community school program

6. Make the school take *responsibility* for programs that will provide equal opportunity for people of all ages.
7. Extend the use of all school facilities and services to people of all ages and to those attending *private, free,* and *parochial* schools.

The standards that must be set to accomplish the goals and subgoals are as follows:

1. Most communities will be fully utilizing all of the school's facilities and equipment on a round-the-clock basis within three years, with full supervision provided by trained staff, and monetary support for maintenance of buildings.
2. All communities will fully utilize all of the school's facilities and equipment within seven years.
3. Most of the professional staff will work a twelve-month year by within three years.
4. The entire professional staff will be on a twelve month year within seven years.
5. One-half of the enrollees will be attending school on a twelve-month arrangement within two years, with parents involved in programming around family needs and desires.
6. All enrollees will be on a twelve-month program within six years, with appropriate vacations arranged around family needs.
7. Central Boards of Education will all include *representation* of contributing agencies and organizations as well as individuals by 1975.
8. All employees of the district will spend part of their day serving in a contributing capacity with one of the social agencies or contributing groups.
9. All enrollees, within two years, will be required to have an ongoing learning experience with one of the social agencies.
10. Within three years, one-third of the operational budget will be earmarked for activities that are carried on outside of the straight subject matter (cognition areas) fields.
11. Within five years, one-half of the operational budget will be earmarked for community based programs and for those under five and over eighteen years of age.
12. Within three years, most school-district political boundaries will have been eliminated and mandated collaboration between urban and suburban communities will be in operation.

13. Within six years, all political boundaries (for educational purposes) will be eliminated and urban-suburban collaboration in every area will be in effect.

14. Within two years, 50 percent of the secondary school population will be earning credit toward graduation by providing help in local institutions (hospitals, libraries, homes for the elderly, houses of correction).

15. Within four years, all students twelve years and over will be required to contribute one-third of their scheduled time helping in local institutions.

16. Within three years, the school staff will spend one-third of its collective time planning and supervising programs that will take the student into the community and bring adults into the school.

17. Within five years, the school staff will spend one-half of its collective time planning and supervising programs that will take the student out and the community *into* the school.

18. Within one year, the tight regulations governing access to and use of school facilities will be eliminated.

19. Within two years, every citizen will have unlimited access to schools and their facilities.

20. Within three years, all laboratories, libraries, gymnasiums, and recreational space will be available to parochial and private school student population.

21. Within two years, all such health services will be available to all parochial and private schools.

22. Within two years, all transportation vehicles will be available to all parochial and private schools, free schools, and to the community.

In summary, the state must take the leadership and mandate community involvement. Only a bottoms-up approach involving thousands of our citizens will change the system. We cannot put the onus on one or two minority people who serve on city and state committees.

Parents, whatever their socioeconomic level or ethnic or racial group, young and old have a strong interest in their children's success in school and their own self-improvement. They should be brought in as full, participating partners, as decisions about the community school are being made.

The entire community—business, labor, church, social groups (with students, staff, and parents)—must have representation on community councils and, at this level, decisions should be made.

The community school then will become the people's school and will reflect in its program and operation the needs of every individual and every group.

Suggested Readings

Altshuler, Alan A. *Community Control: The Black Demand for Participation in Large American Cities.* Indianapolis, Ind.: Pegasus, 1970.

Batten, Thomas. *The Non-Directive Approach in Group and Community Work.* New York: Oxford University Press, 1967.

Brager, George. *Community Organization.* New York: Columbia University Press, 1957.

Clinard, Marshall. *Slums and Community Development.* New York: Free Press, 1966.

Conway, James A. *Understanding Communities.* Englewood Cliffs, N.J.: Prentice-Hall, 1974.

Grosser, Charles. *New Directions in Community Organization.* New York: Praeger, 1973.

Hill, Michael J. *Community Action and Race Relations.* New York: Oxford University Press, 1971.

Jacob, Philip E. *The Integration of Political Communities.* Philadelphia: Lippincott, 1964.

Lewis, Eugene. *The Urban Political System.* Hinsdale, Ill.: Dryden Press, 1973.

Mead, Margaret. *The Wagon and the Store.* Chicago: Rand-McNally, 1967.

Miller, Paul A. *Community Health Action.* East Lansing, Mich.: Michigan State Press, 1973.

Murphy, Campbell G. *Community Organization Practice.* Boston: Houghton Mifflin, 1954.

Pearlman, Robert. *Community Organization and Social Planning.* New York: Wiley, 1972.

Presthus, Robert V. *Men at the Top.* New York: Oxford University Press, 1964.

Zimmerman, J.E. *Community Control in Large Cities.* New York: St. Martin's Press, 1973.

Dorcey Davy
José Llanes

Bilingual/ crosscultural education

10

In their chapter, Drs. Davy and Llanes offer us an alternative to the "melt-ing-pot" model of schooling. This model they refer to as the "salad bowl." They point out that initially our schools reflected many languages and cul-tures and then were changed to reflect only the dominant language and cul-ture of the time. They outline the negative effects of such practices and indicate the potential benefits of incorporating bilingual/crosscultural education into today's public schools. They are in accord with Fantini and Sullivan in the belief that viable options must be offered within the public school system if that system is to survive (see Chapters 8 and 9).

Dorcey Davy   **José Llanes**

Dr. Dorcey Davy is Director of Teacher Education Programs at the University of San Francisco and Director of the Curriculum and Instruction Division of the Doctoral Program. His professional experience includes work in international development with the Ford Foundation and in teacher education with the University of Chicago and the University of California at Davis. His interests include multicultural education, teacher education, and international development.

Dr. Llanes is a sociologist with a background in bilingual education research. He is the director of the Multicultural Program of the University of San Francisco, which provides graduate degrees in bilingual education.

It has been said that the school represents the final synthesis of ideas, values, and attitudes prevailing in society at large. Thus, as the United States evolved from an agricultural and individualistic society to an industrialized and collective society, the schools began to synthesize this evolution through the use of uniform texts, the classification of children by grade level, the placement of desks and chairs in neat "production-style" rows, and—perhaps most important—the design of curricula that would transmit the ideas and ideals of the collective/industrialized society to the exclusion of those of the rural/agricultural, Native American, immigrant, black, and other minorities.

The melting-pot concept of socialization and acculturation was born of this synthesis.[1] Implied in this concept was the belief that melting down the values, languages, and customs of the minority cultures and amalgamating these melted ores (in carefully controlled amounts) with the basic ore of the northwestern European culture would produce a stronger and more useful metal as it came out of the melting pot. The character of the new metal would reflect the basic values and attitudes of the northwestern European culture, the language of that culture, its symbols, its spiritual beliefs, and its system of socialization—in short, its entire intellectual and social heritage—to the exclusion of others.

The melting-pot concept became a patriotic American slogan,[2] and while it was used to extend a liberal "welcome mat" to those of other languages and cultures who wished to partake of the American dream, it stemmed from assumptions about America and its development that were essentially inaccurate and incomplete.

When the northwestern European culture arrived on the shores of what is today the United States, there were other cultures already represented here. Unlike the northwestern European, the Native American had not thought of devising such a grandiose scheme of social acceptance for the Pilgrims. Instead, the Native Americans allowed the new arrivals to settle and propagate without attempting to impose their language and customs on them. Indeed, in early recognition of the right of cultures to maintain and transmit their values, knowledge, and attitudes to their children, the new European arrivals to North America quickly established an independent form of schooling for their youngsters, using the language of the home. There is no record of Native American interference with this practice.

The same is true of the French immigrants to the southern United States, the Spanish to California, and later, the northern Europeans to the Midwest and the West. It is fair to say that before industrialization began to change the face of society, the United States was a "salad bowl" where each component part remained just what it was, readily identifiable and contributing to the whole with no loss of identity.

But as we melted ores to build locomotives and automobiles, we decided to carry this practice to people, and today we have begun to realize that the practice carries with it dangerous side effects that weaken the social fiber of society by causing learning dysfunctions, the collapse of the family structure, and the alienation of students—resulting in intolerably high dropout rates among the culturally and linquistically different.[3]

The Melting Pot Today

For the grandsons and granddaughters of those who devised the melting-pot concept of education, school tends to be a very agreeable place. The language of the home is spoken so there is no need to learn another. The storybook characters of early childhood now bring new and interesting knowledge. Jack and Jill go up the hill and inside the pail of water is the letter A or the number 4; and as William James said in 1906, "interest is shed from point to point until it suffuses the entire system of objects of thought."[4] The school becomes an extension of the home and the child's development continues uninterrupted.

But we know that for many children who come from a culturally and linguistically different home environment the school does not provide the same opportunity to continue their development uninterrupted.[5] For many, the school represents a totally alien environment where a different language is spoken and where they are supposed to acquire a different view of "correctness"—a different set of behaviors—if they expect to win the approval of their teachers and the acceptance of their peers. This sudden change in language, values, and attitudes is not easy to assimilate, and even for those who manage to learn the new language, values, and attitudes in a short period of time, there will remain a nagging doubt about themselves, the appropriateness of the language they were taught at home, and the desirability of being who they are and belonging to a family group whose every characteristic is so different from those found in school.

The Salad Bowl Today

"If you're not all right the way you are it takes a lot of effort to get better. Realize you're all right the way you are, and you'll get better naturally."[6] This aphorism may be taken as a central theme of the modern salad-bowl concept. The concept embodies the idea that the quality of the salad is a function of each component being just what it is. It is not necessary to melt down one's cultural heritage and attempt to become an amalgam. From this point of view the national cultural flavor shall be unique and distinctive; each component of the salad may be readily identified and each shall contribute to the flavor of the whole without losing its identity.

If we adopt this concept, we can build learning environments where the language, values, and attitudes of the home are maintained, and grant the culturally and linguistically different the same opportunity to succeed as those in the majority enjoy. Clearly the child must learn the English language eventually; the child must also learn the symbols of the majority culture eventually; yet we must first accept the child as he or she is. We must strive to build a secure and stable emotional base, involving positive views of self and respect for self and others, before we attempt to teach what we want the child to know. This is an ancient and respected notion of education, substantiated by research and originating in the thought of Plato.[7] Plato said that in order for education to accomplish its purposes, reason must have an adequate emotional base. Teachers have no alternative but to help build this emotional base first, before they attempt to deal with the reasoning processes.

The salad-bowl concept is central and vital to education of the nation's children. The school classroom needs to provide a safe space for each child to experience that it is all right for him or her to be just the person he or she is. Once this can be realized, a great portion of the child's conscious and unconscious mental facilities are freed for the great adventure of learning.

Bilingual/Crosscultural Schooling

The central theme of the melting-pot philosophy is efficiency. One language means one set of materials, one culture means one teacher, one criteria for emotional development translates into standardized tests, and so on. By that measure of efficiency, the salad-bowl concept cannot be said to be more efficient. The addition of a language other than English as the medium of instruction for some means that a second system of instruction must be developed and operated alongside the already established system of instruction. Because of that additional expense, few school systems attempted to establish bilingual programs until 1967, when the Bilingual Education Act began to provide school systems with the federal funds needed to encourage new bilingual programs.

While it had been known for some time that the melting-pot concept was not working, school systems chose to ignore the 80-percent dropout rates of Mexican American high school students, for example, rather than make available the money and resources needed to try something different.

It took a geopolitical accident to begin the practice of bilingual education on a large scale. Beginning in 1959, political refugees from Cuba arrived in Miami and for the most part remained there. Handling such a massive immigration of culturally and linguistically different people was a major problem for the Dade County School System. Since many of the new immigrants were Cuban credentialed teachers, the school system began to hire them as teacher's aides and classroom paraprofessionals in an effort to offer some attention and instruction to the newly arrived Spanish-speaking students. These aides and paraprofessionals, left largely to their own resources, began to parallel the English-speaking system; by 1965, Dade County Schools were capable of providing instruction in two languages with a nearly equal level of quality. This startling development gave some impetus to the long struggle the Mexican Americans of the West and Southwest and the Puerto Ricans of New York had been engaged in for many years—to bring recognition of their language and heritage to their school environment.[8]

Federal funds provided incentives to school districts to begin new bilingual programs, yet they could only provide the *means* for those who *wanted* to alter their school system to allow for equal opportunity. There remain many school systems that adhere firmly to the melting-pot philosophy, and it was not until 1974 that this philosophy was challenged in the Supreme Court. In its famous *Lau* v. *Nichols* decision, the Supreme Court ruled that failure of the San Francisco School District to provide comprehensible instruction for its non-English-speaking Chinese students was a violation of their civil rights.

While the Supreme Court decision is welcomed by many as a recognition of the basic principles that were abandoned in the wake of the melting-pot's ideological birth, it will not bring about the desired change in the attitude of the dominant majority. For that change to take place, educators must learn to accept different styles of learning, communicating, and interacting on the part of the students. Educators must learn to use these different styles to promote the educational and emotional development of the students. They must learn to involve the parents of the student in the student's educational process. If the salad is to be left in the bowl and not put in the blender, a great deal of responsibility for the child's development must be put back in the hands of the parents.

Bilingual/Crosscultural Learning

We said earlier that the school represents the final synthesis of ideas, values, and attitudes prevailing in society at large. Bilingual/crosscultural schooling avoids the process of synthesization (often called acculturation) and seeks to maintain the ideas, values, and attitudes of each segment of society. The principles are simple, but their execution in the environment of the present-day school is not easy. The execution of these principles involves the granting of choices to parents and students. There is not one form of child rearing among a given subculture. The northwestern Europeans, for example, are mostly Protestant, but there are some Catholics, Jews, and even agnostics among them. The Germanic influence is strong in some homes, yet others are more influenced by the Anglican customs. These differences may be too insignificant for a synthesis, but they remain powerful determinants of perception-behavior phenomena; that is, they remain the prime indicators of how we perceive a certain development and how that development causes us to act. Language, as a system of symbols, is inextricably tied to culture in a way we cannot fully understand. Wallwork suggested that for most people language and thought are mutually interdependent: "To some extent, we are controlled in our thoughts and actions by the language we know."[9] What significance does this interdependence hold for teachers working with linguistically and culturally different children? We do not know the complete answer to that question, but we do have some indications. In several instances where the language of the home has been developed and maintained alongside the language of the school, we find that children do no worse than in monolingual environments and sometimes better. Wallace Lambert compared the abilities of ten-year-old French-Canadian monolinguals with bilinguals of comparable socioeconomic and home background. The 1962 and 1969 analysis of this study "showed the bilinguals to be much superior on measure of intelligence, reliably further ahead in school grade, significantly better than the monolinguals in school work in general, and more sympathetic in their attitudes toward English-speaking Canadians."[10] These findings were in sharp contrast with the earlier findings of Ladd (1933), where children in the third, fourth, and fifth grades from other than English-language backgrounds who were taught only in English were compared to those from an English-language home background in tests of reading achievement. The analysis revealed that the monolinguals scored much higher.[11] These findings were interpreted by the teaching community to mean that it was desirable to "discourage the use of other than English in the home, so that children would not grow up as bilinguals."[12] But how, may we ask, can any institution or profession in a free country undertake the task of "discouraging the use of a language other than English in the home"? Children from linguistically different homes will come to school with knowledge of another language. What can the schools do to help them develop as bilinguals?

The Lambert studies cited earlier tell us that it is productive to use the home language as one of the mediums of instruction. It is not only productive from the point of view of better school performance, but it also contributes toward the acceptance and understanding of other cultures. This latter benefit of bilingual education is what we mean by the crosscultural benefit. Once the language, values, and attitudes of the home are recognized, utilized, and fully enfranchised into the school environment, the language, values, and attitudes of other cultures are easily and willingly assimilated. The child does not become "acculturated"—a process by which one person adapts to another culture to the partial displacement of his or her own—but becomes "encul-turated"—a process by which one person adopts some of the values of another culture, willingly assimilating its symbols alongside his or her own.

In this chapter, we have attempted to point out that the child arrives on his or her first day of school with certain emotional and intellectual character-istics that are acquired in the home environment. These characteristics correspond to the culture of the child's environment and for the most part rep-resent the values and attitudes of the parents. The school must recognize these "internalized values and attitudes," as well as the language that embodies them, and continue to develop them. John Dewey, in his work *My Pedological Creed*, stated the principle this way: "The process of education," Dewey said, "must be conducted within the reality of the existing world and not simply be a preparation for the future."[13] The "reality of the existing world" is pluralistic and diverse and so must be the process of education. Bilingual/crosscultural education is a tool that can be used to bring the schools closer to the reality of the world as it is presently constituted.

Summary

The melting-pot philosophy was born as a short-term and shortsighted response to the demands of the new industrialized America. It created school environments where only certain kinds of people—that is, members of the northwestern European culture—could find emotional and intellectual fulfill-ment.

The pluralistic or salad-bowl concept is older, and is more closely attuned to the needs of the school populations.

In educational terms, practices that demand acculturation have not suc-ceeded. Bilingual/crosscultural schooling, however, has proven to be an effec-tive process for those who come from linguistically and culturally different en-vironments.

The Supreme Court has reaffirmed the illegality of the melting-pot con-cept of schooling and Congress has voted funds to promote the practice of bi-lingual education.

Notes and References

1. Ellwood P. Cubberly, *Changing Conception of Education* (Boston: Houghton Mifflin, 1909), pp. 15–16. "The primary task of the education process is to assimi-late and amalgamate these people as part of our American race, and to implant in their children, so far as can be done, the Anglo Saxon conception of righteous-ness, law and order, and popular government."
2. Isreal Zangwill, *The Melting Pot* (New York: Macmillan, 1909), p. 37.

3. U.S. Congress, Senate Committee on Labor and Public Welfare, *Bilingual Education, Hearings,* before a Special Subcommittee on Bilingual Education of the Committee on Labor and Public Welfare, U.S. Senate, on S. 428, to amend the ESEA of 1965, 90th Cong., 1st Sess., 1967, Vol. 1, p. 52.

4. William James, *Talks to Teachers on Psychology: and to Students on Some of Life's Ideals* (New York: H. Holt, 1914), pp. 95–96.

5. Blandina Cardenas and Jose A. Cardenas, "The Theory of Incompatibilities," invited address presented at the Issues of Leadership for Mexican American School Board Members Conference, San Antonio, 1973; Thomas Carter, *Mexican Americans in School: A History of Educational Neglect* (College Entrance Examination, 1970); Tomas Arciniega, "Public Education's Response to the Mexican American" (El Paso, Texas: Innovative Resources, 1971); Manuel Ramirez III and A. Castaneda, *Cultural Democracy in Education and Mexican American Children* (New York: Seminar Press, 1973).

6. Werner Erherd, *EST Book of Aphorisms* (San Francisco: Erherd Seminar Training, 1973).

7. Plato, *The Republic,* Book II.

8. No account of the Mexican American equal education movement is complete without recognition of the leadership of Dr. George I. Sanchez, who since the early 1930s called for reform of testing practices and a form of bilingual education. With attorneys like Gus Garcia, Carlos Cadena, and Cristobal P. Aldrete, Dr. Sanchez pursued through litigation and administrative challenge the reforms needed by the Chicano.

9. Jean Wallwork, *Language and Linguistics* (London: Heinemann Educational, 1969), p. 10.

10. Elizabeth Peal and W.E. Lambert, "The Relation of Bilingualism to Intelligence," *Psychol. Monogr.* 76, No. 27 (1962), 1–23.

11. M.R. Ladd, *The Relation of Social, Economic and Personality Characteristics to Reading Ability* (New York: Columbia University Press, 1933), p. 100.

12. Moses Hoffman, *The Measurement of Bilingual Background* (New York: Columbia University Teacher's College, 1934), p. 38.

13. John Dewey, *My Pedological Creed* (report of the Progressive Education Association, 1929).

Suggested Readings

Anderson, Theodore. *Bilingual Schooling in the U.S.* Washington, D.C.: Superintendent of Documents, 1970.

Castaneda, Alfredo. *Educational Needs of Minority Groups.* Lincoln, Neb: Professional Educator's Publicaions, 1972.

James, William. *Talks to Teachers on Psychology: And to Students on Some of Life's Ideals.* New York: Henry Holt, 1914.

Philip J. Burke

The handicapped – a "special" population requiring a "special" education?

11

Dr. Burke's chapter on the handicapped vividly illustrates how another group is denied a viable education because of the melting-pot model. Problems of handicapped children parallel in many ways the problems of those who come from homes where the family language is not English or those who have been discriminated against because of race. Thus, the story told in this chapter has marked similarities to the ideas expressed in Chapters 10 and 12. The suggestions of Fantini and Sullivan in Chapters 8 and 9 take on new importance when viewed in light of the material that is presented in this chapter.

Philip J. Burke

Dr. Burke is Chief, Special Projects and Comprehensive Programs Branch in the Bureau of Education for the Handicapped, U.S. Office of Education. He also serves as professional advocate and consultant for personnel preparation programs in special education administration, mental retardation, and the severely and profoundly handicapped. In this capacity he has traveled widely in an effort to improve educational and training programs for handicapped children. Prior to his appointment with the U.S. Office of Education, he served as a teacher of the mentally retarded and severely handicapped, and taught at several universities.

A free society will be judged by its concern and provision for the well-being of its members most in need. Words to this effect have been written and spoken through the ages. In his inaugural address, John F. Kennedy paraphrased Luke 12:48: "If a free society cannot help the many who are poor, it cannot save the few who are rich." These words are now carved into a stone monument at a hillside grave in Arlington. To stand and read them is a stirring experience, calling to mind the visions of a promise. If these words were true two thousand years ago or even a decade ago, one can legitimately ask what our society currently does to guarantee the rights of its members, especially those in need of special help. What does the record show? One can choose to review the history on civil rights, or the treatment of minorities. Or the record can be reviewed in both areas as it relates to our nation's handicapped citizens.

Exclusion of the Handicapped by Schools

Edwin W. Martin, Deputy Commissioner of the Bureau of Education for the Handicapped, U. S. Office of Education, once characterized the efforts to obtain a free and appropriate education for handicapped children as "the next civil rights movement." To realize the dream of an appropriate education for their children, parents of the handicapped have united and taken the public schools to court. And they are succeeding in their efforts to compel the schools to provide an education appropriate to the needs of their children.

In a suit brought by the Pennsylvania Association of Retarded Children (1971) in Federal Court, a decision was rendered that clearly stated that free public school education should be provided for mentally retarded persons. In a later suit (*Mills* v. *Board of Education of the District of Columbia*, 1972) it was decided that all handicapped children, not just those labeled as mentally retarded, have a right to a public education. In addition, the Mills case is considered "a final and irrevocable determination of plaintiffs' constitutional rights.[1] In his summary statement, U. S. District Court Judge Joseph C. Waddy stated:

> *That no child eligible for a publicly supported education in the District of Columbia public schools shall be excluded from a regular public school assignment by a Rule, Policy or Practice of the Board of Education of the District of Columbia or its agents unless such child is provided: (a) adequate alternative educational services suited to the child's needs, which may include special education or tuition grants, and (b) a constitutionally adequate prior hearing and periodic review of the child's status, progress, and the adequacy of any educational alternative.[2]*

The record shows that handicapped children have frequently been denied educational programs appropriate to their special needs. In fact, as of this writing over twenty-eight states are involved in some stage of adjudication regarding the provision of appropriate educational services for the handicapped.

This new civil rights movement comes after a long history of isolation and denial for the handicapped. Historically, the handicapped have been considered different and unacceptable by society. Large institutions have been built in isolated locales and many decisions have been made that have perpetuated the isolation of the handicapped. In recent history, it has been a quiet and almost imperceptible force that has caused such exclusion. Few politicians have ever spoken against the handicapped directly and the exclusionary process has never involved riots or civil strife. The arguments are typically based on economics. For example, in the Mills case the District of Columbia argued that insufficient funds were available to "afford plaintiffs the relief sought unless Congress appropriated the needed funds or funds were diverted from other educational services." This argument has had many variations and has been used to justify the lack of planning to install elevators in new subway construction projects, the shortage of public transportation and public buildings easily accessible to physically handicapped persons, and numerous other instances where the handicapped were last in the thoughts of society.

The Handicapped—A Historical Perspective

To gain a perspective on this most pervasive exclusionary force in society it can be seen that throughout the centuries people have had numerous difficulties dealing with those among them who through accident, birth, or disease were unable to function in the same manner as their peer group. There have been many episodes of persecution, neglect, and mistreatment. And where such episodes did not occur, little was done to assist the handicapped in any meaningful way. The reasons for this phenomenon are not thoroughly understood. It appears that the key to the exclusion or rejection of the handicapped is the perception of difference.[3] It is known that being different involves a process of being "set apart" that may result in rejection. This becomes very acute during adolescence, when high value is placed on conformity and even small deviations in behavior or appearance, perceived negatively, can result in extreme forms of rejection. This little understood phenomenon has existed throughout man's history. It is significant that the term *idiot* is a derivative of the Greek *idiotas*, or *idios*, a term that communicated the meaning "peculiar person" and one to be excluded.

During the seventeenth century several efforts were made to organize services for the severely handicapped. The result usually involved the creation of an institution. From the earliest times, institutions were designed primarily to provide a form of custodial care. Little provision was made for educational programs.

During the nineteenth century physicians such as Itard, Sequin, Montessori, and Decroly made major contributions to the understanding of the education of the mentally defective child. The work of Itard, described in his book *The Wild Boy of Aveyron*, is extremely informative concerning the educational training and concerns at the beginning of the nineteenth century.[4] The earliest and most significant work of Maria Montessori was with the mentally deficient children she found housed in insane asylums. She organized the Orthophrenic School for the Cure of the Feebleminded. In addition to working with children classified as feebleminded, she developed training programs for teachers of mentally defective children. Possibly her major contributions involved the understanding of mental deficiency as a pedagogical rather than a medical problem and her development of procedures and materials to teach retarded children to read and write. Those procedures and materials were later expanded and refined in her school, Case Dei Bambina, and are now world famous.[5]

Throughout history the handicapped child was educated either at home or in a residential institution. With the advent of compulsory education laws enacted in the latter half of the nineteenth century, a few handicapped children enrolled in public schools. Throughout the past hundred years, however, though many advancements have been made, the handicapped have been excluded from school programs by either legal or administrative fiat. This is particularly true for the more severely handicapped. The public schools frequently defined certain standards for admission that excluded the handicapped. By requiring that a child be fully toilet trained or have a mental age of six years, the public schools could remand severely handicapped children to their homes for years. The constant care and attention required of the parents in such cases makes institutionalization for the child a more acceptable alternative. And thus a cycle of exclusion is perpetuated. Only recently, as cited in Judge Waddy's decision, has the constitutional right to a free and appropriate education been established by the courts. And there is no longer any question that such education is the responsibility of the state and its system of public education.

Throughout the nineteenth and early twentieth centuries, the blind and deaf children who had no secondary handicaps (such as retardation) beyond their sensory deficit fared much better than the retarded, seriously disturbed, and other severely handicapped. Though the pattern of service for children with sensory disorders predominantly involved the large state institution or state school, the emphasis on the educational program for such children far surpassed the purely custodial service provided for other handicapped children. Unfortunately many of the early services for the deaf or blind were not readily available to children having additional handicaps, such as the deaf-retarded or blind-retarded.

There is a long and distinguished history of advocacy for both the deaf and blind that resulted in some of the earliest support for programs from state governments as well as from the federal government.

One of the earliest pioneers in the education of the deaf was Thomas Hopkins Gallaudet. He was a teacher as well as a trainer of teachers. In 1817 he founded the American Asylum for the Deaf in West Hartford, Connecticut. This was our nation's first formal educational institution for the handicapped. Gallaudet was memorialized for his work when the only liberal arts college for the deaf in the world, located in Washington, D. C., was named Gallaudet College.

In 1829 the Massachusetts state legislature voted funds for the establishment of the New England Asylum for the Blind. It was soon renamed the Perkins School for the Blind. An early graduate of the Perkins Institute named Anne Sullivan became a famous teacher with an even more famous student who was both deaf and blind—Helen Keller.

Efforts to integrate the deaf and blind into the basic public school have frequently been resisted despite the fact that for many of these children the basic program need not be substantially altered. With the use of special support services and mechanical aids to convert the printed and spoken word into a form that can be utilized despite sensory deficits, these children have functioned quite well.

Historically the terms mentally deficient and feebleminded have been used to describe a portion of the handicapped population. However, the population of children considered handicapped varies widely, depending on the nature of the handicap, the relative degree of severity, and the environment in which the judgment is made. It should also be understood that many of the children considered handicapped today probably would not have been so identified during earlier historical periods. With the advent of compulsory school attendance and the shift from an agrarian to an industrial society, with concomitant shifts in the complexity of life, a greater proportion of the population has come to be considered handicapped. Also, the increased development and use of assessment and diagnostic instruments by psychologists and educators has facilitated the identification of learning problems that children manifest in school, and frequently such problems are defined as, or are associated with, a handicap. For example, Alfred Binet developed his age scale for testing intelligence "to furnish to the teacher a first means by which he may single out mentally backward children...."[6] This increased capacity to identify learning problems has frequently compounded the difficulties experienced by the handicapped in schools. All too often the problems have been documented, while efforts devoted to their remediation have been meager. At the same time, many children labeled handicapped by test devices have been assumed to have difficulties in school when they do not. But because they carried the label, and the stereotypic picture of persons with that label called for a given set of school difficulties, they often have been treated as if they fit the stereotype. Additionally, the differences between the handicapped and other children have too frequently been exaggerated so as to render a distorted picture of the total child. In this sense the diagnostic and assessment instruments have been inappropriately applied.

Terminology—Severity of Handicap and the Effects of Labels

Children may have cognitive, affective, physical, or essentially undefined problems that require special programming for them to achieve educationally. Sometimes the cause of the handicap is understood. In many instances it is not, and in an educational sense the cause of the handicap is frequently not important. Rather, emphasis should be placed on the positive aspect of what a child *can* do. Although terminology is important and must be dealt with in any detailed discussion of handicapped children, it is important that a term not be used as a negative label for a child and his or her ability to function. The most frequently encountered terminology or classifications used to describe the handicapped are as follows: mentally retarded, emotionally disturbed, learning disability, visually handicapped, crippled and other health impaired, multihandicapped, deaf, hard of hearing, speech impaired, and deaf-blind. Again, it should be understood that the distinction between the handicapped and nonhandicapped is far from clear when one considers the basic indices or manifestations of learning problems in the schools.

In an analysis of one school population the incidence of variables such as spending an extra year in kindergarten, being held back a year in grade, and being referred for speech or counseling services, placement in special classes, or intensive reading assistance, were examined.[7] Depending upon the list of variables used, it was found that up to 41.6 percent of the total population of children from kindergarten through the third grade, in over 200 districts, were involved. Surely all of these children are not "handicapped." Such findings indicate that school systems and teachers should develop a concept of educational programming wherein all children and their learning needs are viewed as falling in a range that has few, if any, discrete disjunctions. At the very least, a flexible system of services should be designed to enable all children to receive full opportunity to be educated. All too frequently any special assistance for the child who is different, if offered, is in a dichotomous system and, to get that specialized help, children must be labeled as handicapped. This labeling process often results in labeling as handicapped a disproportionate number of black and bilingual children.

The severity of the handicap is a crucial factor that has serious implications for educational programming. For example, retardation can be quite severe or very mild. A great deal of thought and research has gone into the definition of each area of handicap by degree of severity. In mental retardation the terminology used at the turn of the century was as follows: idiot (to describe the most severely retarded); imbecile (to describe the more moderately retarded); and moron (to describe the moderately to mildly retarded). These terms quickly became labels of derogation, with the main connotation focused on disability. Even dictionaries have added secondary meanings to the terms reflecting their slang usage. Revised terminology in popular usage today would classify retardation as profound, severe, and moderate to mild, with the classification focused on adaptive behavior. That is, a total assessment of the child is called for, including consideration of all relevant performance variables with emphasis on what the child is capable of doing. Unfortunately, the terms "profound retardation" and "severe retardation" will eventually be interpreted as labels, and they too will create a stereotyped image of the child who carries the label. Even a brief encounter with several handicapped children "labeled uniformly" will reveal to the most inexpert eyes and ears that they are truly distinct and individual. Many severely handicapped children can read, some "blind" children can read print, and the understanding of their true heterogeneity increases as observation and interaction increase. In fact, one eventually comes to the realization that even the most severely handicapped child is more like a "normal" peer than different. It would be so much better if children could be referred to as John or Mary and not have to be labeled to describe some aspect of their behavior. Perhaps someday, instead of saying that Mary is "gifted" or "delinquent" or "retarded" or "deaf," we can say that Mary is a child of certain height and weight with brown hair, and continue to outline her attributes in descriptive terminology that emphasizes her abilities, while concentrating on specific measures designed to remediate shortcomings where and when they are identified.

The Handicapped Population and Services

In the United States today it is estimated that there are 7,886,000 handicapped children from birth to nineteen years of age (see Table 11.1). It is estimated that less than 50 percent of school-aged handicapped children are properly served in educational programs today. Thus, a great deal remains to be done if handicapped children are to receive appropriate educational programs. There is currently a great deal of interest in preschool and early childhood programs for the handicapped. It is widely believed that early intervention programs are particularly important and effective with the handicapped child. Recent federal legislation[8] has strongly emphasized this need, but as evidenced in Table 11.1, less than 22 percent of the preschool handicapped population are currently receiving an appropriate educational program. One certain analysis of these data is that a great number of additional teachers and specialists need to be prepared if adequate educational programming is to be provided for the handicapped.

Table 11.1
Estimated number of handicapped children served and unserved by type of handicap

	1974–1975 Served (projected)*	1974–1975 unserved	Total handicapped children served and unserved†	% Served	% Unserved
Total age 0–19	3,947,000	3,939,000	7,886,000	50%	50%
Total age 6–19	3,687,000	3,062,000	6,699,000	55	45
Total age 0–5	260,000	927,000	1,187,000	22	78
Speech impaired	1,850,000	443,000	2,293,000	81	19
Mentally retarded	1,250,000	257,000	1,507,000	83	17
Learning disabilities	235,000	1,731,000	1,966,000	12	88
Emotionally disturbed	230,000	1,080,000	1,310,000	18	82
Crippled and other health impaired	235,000	93,000	328,000	72	28
Deaf	35,000	14,000	49,000	71	29
Hard of hearing	60,000	268,000	328,000	18	82
Visually handicapped	39,000	27,000	66,000	59	41
Deaf-blind and other multihandicapped	13,000	27,000	40,000	33	67

* Estimated total numbers of handicapped children served, obtained from SEA's fall and winter 1975. Information by type of handicap was not available and is projected from data provided by SEA's for school year 1972–1973.

† Total number of handicapped children ages 0–19 provided on basis of estimates obtained from various sources, including national agencies and organizations, plus state and local directors of special education. According to these sources the incidence levels by types of handicap are as follows: speech impaired 3.5%, mentally retarded 2.3%, learning disabled 3.0%, emotionally disturbed 2.0%, crippled and other health impaired 0.5%, deaf 0.075%, hard of hearing 0.5%, visually handicapped 0.1%, deaf-blind and other multihandicapped 0.06%. The total number of handicapped children in the above categories represents 12.035% of all school-age children from 6–19 and 6.018% of all children age 0–5. The population figures to which the incidence rates were applied were obtained from the Bureau of Census and reflect the population as of July 1, 1974.

USOB/BEH/ASB
March 4, 1975

There are many varieties of direct educational and support services required for the handicapped. Some are distinct and appropriate for a single category alone, such as interpreters for the deaf. However, many services have common elements in terms of assessment and remediation. For example, though children may be considered "emotionally disturbed" or "learning disabled" or "educationally handicapped," the basic process of defining their problems in learning can usually be viewed from a common base. If the problem is in reading or arithmetic concepts, a single consulting, itinerant, or resource teacher may serve to assist the learning of a diverse group of handicapped children in these areas.

The expanding effort to provide a more normalized environment for the handicapped has caused a pervasive emphasis on programs to bring the handicapped in closer contact with society and their "normal" peers. Philosophically there is a strong movement underway to de-institutionalize the handicapped, where possible, with a de-emphasis on large institutions and a concurrent popularization of community-based efforts such as halfway houses, group homes, and foster homes. In the public schools a parallel effort is frequently characterized as *mainstreaming*. In this effort, handicapped children are placed in regular elementary and secondary classrooms and specialized support services are provided for a child and the classroom teacher. These movements represent a counter-response to the exclusionary trends cited earlier. But however, zealously pursued, without appropriate preparation for the child and parent and without adequate training and support for the classroom teacher, some of these efforts can easily end in failure. In fact, some of the efforts to place the previously institutionalized handicapped children into the community have met with strong resistance. Also, some of the handicapped children who have been mainstreamed no longer enjoy going to school, and it has been reported that a high dropout rate is developing, particularly among the secondary-level moderate to mildly handicapped. Frequently in such cases, the necessary special support services for the regular classroom teacher have never materialized and the teacher has been left to struggle with an overwhelmingly difficult situation.

The term generally used today to describe educational programs for handicapped children is *special education*. The exact first usage of the term is not known, but it has come to have the same meaning as exceptional child education or education that is provided outside or beyond that normally contemplated to educate the "normal" child. The form and substance of special education vary greatly. In some school districts there are separate school buildings for the handicapped. In others there are special classes, where the children may be housed in a regular school but receive all of their educational program from a special teacher in a segregated, self-contained room. In some schools children may receive their basic instruction in the regular program, but may go to a resource teacher for special help for part of the school day. Some programs provide itinerant services that may involve a weekly instructional session for a child with a vision or speech problem requiring only brief, but sustained, intervention. Some school service delivery systems may emphasize one of these programs or have a combination of all of them. Serving the handicapped children of the St. Louis area, there is a special school district with its own tax base. Currently, however, the trend is toward a more integrated model of services that allows the child to interact with the general school population as much as possible.

Special Education as a Career

The challenges to the person choosing a career in special education are enormous. On a cold January morning in 1961, John F. Kennedy issued a challenge to those embarking on new careers. It was his belief that "of those to whom much is given, much is required," and that success could be measured by a person's courage, judgment, integrity, and dedication. Competence was assumed in his assessment. An earnest commitment to a career in special education requires not only a dedication to competence, for in few other professions is skill so surely tested, but a dedication to the rights of handicapped children and the frequently desperate and anguished expectations of parents who must have a constant and helpful role in their child's education if it is to be a success. There must be a special expectation for patience, a tolerance for deviance, and a willingness to spend the extra time and effort needed to generate optimism in the children and true progress in their learning. A humanistic point of view is required, but not in the sense that a teacher should have extra reserves of compassion or love for the children or the belief that all will be fine if the children know that someone cares. It has been found that teachers of the handicapped have too easily developed low expectations for these children and, as a result, the children have learned little, thereby fulfilling the teacher's negative prophecy. Because of such limited expectations, many programs for the handicapped in the past have concentrated their efforts on practical skills, arts, and crafts, or on a limited vocational outlook, unnecessarily restricting the handicapped in their career and academic choices. Rather, the teacher should understand that he or she will get along with the handicapped as with any group of children. Some children will be strongly liked and even loved, others will be distant, and some may tax the personal tolerance of the most stable teacher. However, no matter how severely handicapped a child may be, he or she has a great capacity to learn and a basic right that that capacity be challenged in a appropriate manner. Perhaps the strongest recommendation to someone considering a career in education for the handicapped is to go out and experience what it is like to work with them. Most professional preparation programs at the undergraduate level now require experience with the handicapped as a pre-requisite for majoring in special education. This is an excellent idea, but the experience should come in several settings and with a range of severity of handicaps. At the least, that experience should continue over a six-month period, with a good portion of the time invested in educational programs for children. Such an experience will allow a general understanding of what it is like to work with the children and, most important, how one feels about the experience.

The opinion has been offered that the more severely handicapped the child, the more skillful a teacher must be to render an appropriate educational service.[9] This is contrary to many current educational practices, particularly those in institutional settings where a great deal of on-the-job training of aides has been practiced where the aide may be the primary source of program experience for the severely handicapped.

The educational roles and possible careers in special education are quite varied. They range from aide or paraprofessional to master teacher, super-visor, or administrator. Teaching is primarily of two varieties, either directly with the children throughout the day (such as in a special class) or partially direct or intermittent (such as in a resource room program), where the primaiy relationship may be with the general classroom teacher while services for the child are rendered in an indirect fashion. The latter would require a teacher with excellent experience or training or, preferably, both. Clinical programs are also available for those considering a career as a speech pathologist or audiologist. Graduate programs are widely available for training at the mas-ters and doctoral level. Though it is still possible in many states to receive a teaching license with a bachelor's degree, the tendency to require additional graduate work prior to final certification is widespread and growing in popularity. Current preparation programs tend to be general in nature (with regard to area of handicap) at the undergraduate level, with specialization coming through graduate work. The most productive and effective programs appear to have a solid core of work in the areas of assessment, diagnosis, and specific understanding of teaching approaches and methodology. Also, the programs with heavy and early emphasis on experience with children and skill utilization, and with close supervision and systematic student followup by the key faculty members, would appear to hold the most promise for a successful training experience. In choosing a program of preparation, these issues should be thoroughly discussed with the faculty or program chairperson. (For information concerning programs and student support, write Closer Look, P. O. Box 1492, Washington, D. C. 20013, and request the career preparation brochure.)

There is a surplus of general classroom teachers, but special education is still in need of qualified teachers and other personnel. It may be necessary to go outside of attractive metropolitan areas to find these positions, but they are available in every state. It now appears that, with the passage of the most recent federal legislation, a substantial federal investment will be made in local education agency programs for the handicapped and this should bring about an even greater demand for the services of well-qualified personnel.

A Special Challenge

It has often been stated that special education has led the way in educational innovations, providing a preview of educational practices to come. This can be debated, but there can be no disagreement that special education has been faced with the challenge of providing educational programs for those children presenting the most severe educational challenges. Many of the most encouraging developments in instructional technology, computer-assisted instruction, behavior modification, affective education, and educational ecology have been developed and refined in special education. In most cases the developments have come in response to the challenges presented by the children. Also, there is a certain freedom that operates when one is faced with the knowledge that all conventional procedures are unsuccessful. In large part these were the challenges presented to Montessori in the last century. The challenge in special education is exciting and the potential benefit for all children is great. The recent legal decisions regarding the constitutional rights of the handicapped, which will surely have eventual implications for all children, are encouraging developments in our society.

In keeping with the innovative role special education has served, it should be noted that the most recent federal legislation affecting educational services for the handicapped[10] requires each local public agency to develop an individualized educational program for each child. This must involve the teacher working in consultation with the child's parent or guardian. In appropriate instances the child should also be involved. This task involves three fundamental elements: (1) each child must have an educational plan that is tailored to achieve his or her maximum potential; (2) all principals in the child's educational environment, including the child, must have the opportunity for input in the development of an individualized program of instruction; and (3) individualization is defined as meaning specific elements of a program and appropriate timelines and projected accomplishments. The need for periodic review of those specifics is outlined. Every effort is made in the language of the law to enhance educational and fiscal accountability.[11] The magnitude of this requirement and its effect on school programs is impossible to estimate. However, its significance can hardly be overstated.

This law also requires that "due process" procedures be established in each local education agency so that children and their parents may present complaints relating to the maintenance of their educational rights. Thus, educational and placement decisions regarding handicapped children will undergo additional and stringent scrutiny. This development can only intensify the need for highly skilled and competent personnel to be involved in the education of these children.

Special Education and the Future

It can be seen that special education as a career presents a unique and challenging opportunity to provide a valuable service both to individual children and to society. The historical trend has been to move from a position of exclusion to a more reasonable address of the problems, but without complete acceptance of the handicapped. Some of the most significant developments in this nation have come as a result of court decisions wherein the constitutionality of appropriate educational services for the handicapped has been established. The effort must now be made in the schools and in other educational settings to insure that the services the handicapped need so badly, and have a right to, are provided. An adequate or acceptable program for the handicapped can be provided only by well-qualified personnel working with acceptable facilities, materials, and support services. If these services are to be provided as both the law and courts have required, there will be a need for many new personnel as well as stringent requirements for the retraining of existing staff in most systems.

The handicapped are a "special population" requiring a "special education." Unfortunately, a "special education" has all too frequently been required because the basic educational system has not perceived the education of the handicapped as a central responsibility. The special needs of the handicapped are not so great as to require a separate system. The handicapped are more like than unlike their "normal" peers. The responsibility for the educational needs of the handicapped has only recently been placed squarely on the shoulders of the public education system. The challenge is now there for all educators, "special" and "regular" alike, to see that these children are properly educated. And perhaps in the future the basic educational programming available to children will be adequate and flexible enough to account for the needs of all children, even those who are now considered "special." Several state legislatures have now mandated that all teachers have some specialized training in the education of handicapped children and this idea appears to be growing in popularity.

If our society can provide a high standard of service to its members most in need and least able to advocate their rights, then perhaps the total outlook for our society can and should be optimistic. Perhaps some day it will not be necessary to write separate chapters about the handicapped in educational texts.

References

1. P. Friedman, *Mental Retardation and the Law: A Report on Status of Current Court Cases* (Washington, D. C.: Office of Mental Retardation Coordination, Department of Health Education, and Welfare, 1972).

2. Alan Abeson, (Ed.), *A Continuing Summary of Pending and Completed Litigation Regarding the Education of Handicapped Children* (Arlington, Va: The Council for Exceptional Children's State—Federal Information Clearinghouse for Exceptional Children, 1973), pp. 1–5.

3. Beatrice A. Wright, *Physical Disability—A Psychological Approach* (New York and Evanston: Harper & Row, 1960).

4. Jean Marc Gaspard Itard, *The Wild Boy of Aveyron* (translated by George and Muriel Humphrey) (New York: Appleton-Century-Crofts, 1932).

5. Maria Montessori, *Montessori Method* (translated by Anne E. George) (New York: Frederich A. Stokes, 1912).

6. Alfred Binet and T. Simon, *Mentally Defective Children* (translated by W. B. Drummond) (New York: Longmans, Green and Company, 1914).

7. Rosalyn Rubin and Bruce Balow, "Learning and Behavior Disorders: Longitudinal Study," *Exceptional Children* 38 (1971), 293–299.

8. PL 94-142, *Education for All Handicapped Children Act of 1975.* 20 United States Code 1401.

9. Edward Sontag, Philip J. Burke, and Robert York, "Considerations for Serving the Severely Handicapped in the Public Schools," *Education and Training of the Mentally Retarded* 8 No. 2 (April 1973), 20–26.

10. PL 94-142, *Education for All Handicapped Children Act of 1975.*

11. PL 94-142, *Education for All Handicapped Children Act of 1975.*

Suggested Readings

Blatt, Burton. *Christmas in Purgatory: A Photographic Essay on Mental Retardation.* Boston: Allyn and Bacon, 1966.

Cruickshank, William, *et. al. Misfits in the Public Schools.* Syracuse, N.Y.: Syracuse University Press, 1969.

Dunn, Lloyd (Ed.). *Exceptional Children in the Schools: Special Education in Transition.* New York: Holt, Rhinehart & Winston, 1973.

Haring, Norris. *Behavior of Exceptional Children—An Introduction to Special Education.* Columbus, Ohio: Merrill, 1974.

Itard, Jean Marc Gaspard. *The Wild Boy of Aveyron,* trans. by George and Muriel Humphrey. New York: Appleton-Century-Crofts, 1932.

Kirk, Samuel. *Exceptional Children: Educational Resources and Perspectives.* Boston: Houghton Mifflin, 1974.

Robinson, Halbert T., and Nancy Robinson. *The Mentally Retarded Children.* New York: McGraw-Hill, 1975.

Szasz, Thomas S. *The Manufacture of Madness; a Comparative Study of the Inquisition and the Mental Health Movement.* New York: Harper & Row, 1970.

Wright, Beatrice, A. *Physical Disability—A Psychological Approach.* New York: Harper & Row, 1960.

Robert L. Green
Janet Brydon
Wanda Herndon

Beyond race, sex, and social class: toward democracy in education

12

This chapter by Dr. Green, Ms. Brydon, and Ms. Herndon marshals a great deal of experimental evidence that supports the hypothesis that the schools are far from equitable in their treatment of children. Children from minority groups, from the lower socioeconomic class, and of the female sex all suffer discrimination, overt and covert. When you add such special groups as the handicapped (see Chapter 11) the bilingual (see Chapter 10) and so forth it becomes evident that dramatic alterations in the structures of the schools (such as suggested by Fantini and Sullivan in Chapters 8 and 9) must be made if our educational institutions are really to help us achieve a democratic society here in the United States.

Robert L. Green   **Janet Brydon**   **Wanda Herndon**

Robert L. Green is Professor of Educational Psychology and Dean of the College of Urban Development at Michigan State University. He is a lecturer and consultant, particularly in matters of educational testing and school desegregation. He has published many articles in professional journals and is the author of several books.

Janet Brydon, with a bachelor's degree in English Literature from Michigan State University, has served as editorial assistant at MSU Information Services, research associate at MSU's College of Urban Development, and freelance editorial consultant.

Wanda Herndon earned her BA in Journalism at MSU in 1974. For the past two years she has been employed as a staff committee aide in the Michigan House of Representatives, working with the Committee on Military and Veterans Affairs. She worked during 1975 as a research assistant in the College of Urban Development at MSU.

Lip service is often given to the ideal of democracy in United States education, yet democracy is not a reality. First-grade children learn to salute the flag and recite, "One nation under God, with liberty and justice for all," yet they do not see liberty and justice being practiced in their schools. From Little Rock to Boston, teachers and children are facing abuse and limited opportunities due to racism, sexism, and social class discrimination. Only if educators become aware of this discrimination and work to eliminate it will the goal of educational democracy become a reality.

An educational ideal was expressed by John Dewey as early as 1900 when the American public education system was relatively young. Dewey describes the school as a place where the individual and society are one: "Only by being true to the full growth of all individuals who make it up, can society by chance be true to itself."[1] Seventy-five years have passed and public education still does not contribute to the "full growth of all individuals." Some children are educated to be useful, responsible adults, while many others become school and societal dropouts. American education opens up vast opportunities for some and limits opportunity for others.

Racism in Education

Racism is perhaps the strongest force working against educational democracy. Segregation still isolates many minority children from modern education facilities. The Coleman Report stated that "Negro pupils have fewer of some of the facilities that seem most related to achievement."[2] In 1967, thirty of the school buildings that housed black students in Detroit had been dedicated during President Grant's administration.[3]

Even in newly desegregated schools, racism takes its toll among teachers and students. The National Education Association estimated the number of black teachers displaced from jobs in seventeen southern and border states to be 39,386 in 1972, an increase of 6,490 over 1970.[4] The Race Relations Information Center reported that a black principal with twenty-five years' experience was assigned to teach seventh-grade social studies and history. It also tells that a home economics teacher with twenty-three years' experience was fired for "incompetence" five days after signing her new contract to teach second grade.[5]

The most serious racial oppression, however, occurs not in overt practices against students and teachers—pupil assignment, teacher displacement, and so on—but in more subtle practices in the classroom. Prejudicial teacher attitudes toward black children are perhaps the most harmful of practices because they are difficult to document and to eliminate.

The 1967 Public School Racial Census by the Michigan State Department of Education showed that teacher attitudes toward students were more negative in classes with large numbers of black students.[6] Studies by Eleanor Leacock support this finding.[7] Leacock surveyed four schools, two poor and two middle-income. One school in each income level was predominantly black, one predominantly white. Leacock found that teachers were more likely to have negative attitudes toward black children than white, 43 to 17 percent.

Robert Rosenthal has shown that teachers having negative attitudes and perceptions of their students do not teach them as well as teachers who believe in their children's ability.[8] In a related study, J. Michael Palardy tested the folk belief that girls have an easier time learning to read than boys.[9] Palardy matched five teachers who had high expectations for girl readers with five who believed boys could learn to read as well as girls. He found that girls were better readers when their teachers expected them to be, while boys' reading ability equaled girls' when teachers believed it would.

Subtle racism is also evidenced in the use of standardized IQ and achievement tests. For example, in one midwestern city, second graders were divided into twelve different ability groups or "tracks" on the basis of their scores on reading tests.[10] The majority of white children were placed in upper-level tracks, while the majority of poor black children were assigned to low-level groups. During twelve years of schooling, the children remained in these same groups. Thus the majority of black children were given simplified curriculum that would prepare them perhaps for trade school, but not professional school or college. This tracking limited their educational opportunities and their future career or employment choices.

Consequences of Racism

Racial isolation, whether within school systems or within individual schools, tends to perpetuate racial prejudice. J. Kenneth Morland has shown that by the end of high school in a segregated school system, black children develop favorable attitudes about their own racial group, but highly unfavorable attitudes about whites.[11] White children consistently show, from elementary through high school, a favorable ranking of their own race and an unfavorable ranking of blacks.

On the other hand, whites who have attended multiracial schools tend to seek racially mixed situations, have a greater probability of having black friends, appear more interested in having their children attend multiracial schools, and more frequently indicate that they would go out of their way to obtain housing in multiracial neighborhoods than whites who attended racially isolated schools.[12] Blacks and whites who have attended multiracial schools live in multiracial neighborhoods and have close friends of another race more often than those who have attended segregated schools.[13]

Social Class Discrimination

Income level, a second factor underlying discrimination in our schools, is closely related to race. For example, teachers are often guilty of assuming that children who live in public housing or who are on welfare cannot learn.[14] Eleanor Leacock, whose studies pointed out teachers' racial prejudice, also learned that teachers favored middle-income over lower-income children, 40 to 20 percent.[15]

Like racial prejudice, income class discrimination shows up in standardized tests. Chuck Stone, former director of minority affairs for the Educational Testing Service, reports that there is a positive correlation between income status and test score.[16] Children who come from middle- or upper-income families tend to make higher scores than children from low-income families. This shows that standardized test questions are geared to children from more well-to-do backgrounds. The majority of these children are white.

Social Class and Achievement

According to the Coleman Report, *Equality of Educational Opportunity*, socioeconomic background bears a strong relationship to achievement.[17] The report showed that when children from well-educated, more affluent families are placed in schools where most pupils do not come from such a background, their achievement does not suffer. Yet when a low-income child is placed in a school with those whose parents could afford to give them greater learning opportunities at home, the low-income child's achievement is likely to increase.

The "Racial Isolation" report of the U.S. Commission on Civil Rights supports these findings. These data show that low-income black children who attend school with a majority of other low-income black children do not perform as well as black children who attend school with a substantial majority of white, middle-income pupils.[18]

Sexism in Education

Sexism is a third factor that limits the educational opportunities available to American children. Schools tend to provide a shrinkage rather than an expansion of alternatives by directing girls to the dolls and toy dishes and boys to the trucks.[19] A rationale for this separation of the sexes was offered in an article in the Santa Ana (Calif.) *Register*:

> . . .the "all girl" class teacher has a chance to plan female-type activities, now that the boys are taught separately.

> Mrs. Markum says, "We can orient instruction to the needs and interests of girls.
>
> "The other day they counted by tens up to a hundred by shaking up an instant pudding mix. This is a girl-attitude approach to mathematics," she says...[20]

Such "girl-attitude" approaches trap women into the same occupations and societal roles they have assumed for years. Women teachers in elementary and secondary schools, themselves limited to a career choice of housewife, nurse, or teacher, help perpetuate the women-trap. Opportunities are further limited by career counseling that discourages girls and boys from pursuing jobs currently dominated by the opposite sex. Girls are also limited by the scarcity of role models provided by adults in the school.

Psychological studies have shown that children can best develop satisfactory sex roles by having many models to choose from. Yet schools hardly provide a diversity of models: 80 percent of elementary school teachers are women, while 80 percent of principals are men.[21]

Both boys and girls suffer from the rigid divisions of tasks they are assigned and the sexist examples to which they are exposed. Some schools have recently initiated equalization programs, yet the majority still designate activities along traditional lines.[22]

Revising Traditional Curricula

Racism, social class discrimination, and sexism are evident in most elementary and high school curricula. Traditional curricula, relating only to the white, middle-income experience, transmit negative perceptions to minority and poor children, fostering doubts and anxieties about their cultures and backgrounds.[23] Available textbooks often perpetuate false representations of women and racial and ethnic minority groups.[24] Such books, depicting certain racial, religious, or ethnic segments of our population as less worthy, do not assist students in recognizing the basic similarities among all people. They do not make clear that all minority groups have played an important part in United States history.[25]

Evaluation of textbooks has begun in some states, but it has been slow. A Michigan task force to identify and eliminate sexism in Michigan education spent ten months just trying to break through bureaucratic obstacles and bolster attendance at meetings.[26] At this rate, as a reporter aptly observed, "it may be some time before school children in Michigan win freedom from textbooks showing Dick and Jane waving good-bye to father as he heads for the office leaving mother at home with the dirty dishes."[27]

To help teachers and future teachers avoid discriminatory reading materials, the Michigan State University Urban Affairs Library has developed a multi-ethnic children's book collection. Each volume is accompanied by a critical review to aid teachers in choosing between high- and low-quality literature. Such projects combined with a conscientious effort by educators to eliminate discriminatory attitudes and practices among their ranks can do a great deal to foster positive attitudes among school children.

Politics and Educational Policy

Action within the educational system, however, is not enough to eradicate racism, sexism, and social class discrimination in our public schools. Educators must look outside the immediate confines of the school yard to the political sector of society, for education is largely influenced by outside forces with political interests. For example, racist viewpoints have not been eliminated from textbooks because publishers print what sells. Those who purchase texts—ultimately the school board—are giving the publisher a stamp of approval.

A careful look at school boards, however, reveals that they are not omnipotent. Board members are usually elected by district residents and are responsible to a very sensitive constituency. A board that acts counter to the expressed wishes of its constituents finds itself in trouble. For instance, in November 1972, school-board members in Lansing, Michigan, were recalled because they took a liberal stand in favor of busing and desegregation.

A year later, angry parents in Kanawha County, West Virginia, demanded and got the resignation of the school-board president and school superintendent in a heated dispute over textbooks that the parents labeled "anti-American, un-Christian and obscene."[28] One of the organizers of this protest was Alice Moore, a self-described "politician" who was elected several years ago on a stop-sex-education platform.[29]

Of course, most school-board members never face such controversy. In the past, many have been unrestrained in determining educational policies and practices. In Federal District Court, for example, Judge Stephen Roth found the Detroit school board guilty of the following practices:

> *The Board has created and altered attendance zones, maintained and altered grade structures and created and altered feeder school patterns in a manner which has had the natural, probable and actual effect of continuing black and white pupils in racially segregated schools. . . . Throughout the last decade (and presently) school attendance zones of opposite racial composition have been separated by north-south boundary lines, despite the Board's awareness (since at least 1962) that drawing boundaries in an east-west direction would result in significant integration. . . . There has never been a feeder pattern or zoning change which placed a predominantly white residential area into a predominantly black school zone or feeder pattern.*[30]

A statement by Judge Damon Keith in the Pontiac school case applies equally to the Detroit situation:

> *When the power to act is available, failure to take necessary steps so as to negate or alleviate a situation which is harmful is as wrong as the taking of affirmative steps to advance the situation. Sins of omission can be as serious as sins of commission: Where a board of education has contributed and played a major role in the development and growth of a segregated situation, the Board is guilty of de jure segregation.*[31]

Allocation of Resources

Like the assignment of pupils, the allocation of resources is also political. Property taxes have traditionally been the means of educational financing. This has meant that white flight, gerrymandering of districts, and assignment of blacks to all-black schools have enabled middle-income and wealthy whites to keep their children in well-equipped schools while the poor and minority children attend schools with little monetary support. The consequence for education is that the very students who may most need the added dollars are the ones whose chances of receiving them are the least. For example, former Detroit school superintendent Norman Drachler reported to the Kerner Commission that "25 school boards in communities surrounding Detroit spend up to $500 more per year per pupil than the city of Detroit."[32]

Women, like racial minorities, also have found little financial support for their programs. A National Education Association survey turned up the following startling summary:

> *One Michigan school district spent ten times more on boys' athletics than on girls'. A similar ratio was found in a Pennsylvania district. A study in Texas indicated that approximately ten million dollars worth of public facilities were, for practical purposes, unavailable to girls. A second Texas school district exhibited the same pattern. In a study of 60 junior and senior high schools in the state of Washington, not one of the schools reported a girls' physical education budget that was even 50 percent of the budget for boys. The 10:1 ratio of expenditures seemed to prevail as a general benchmark.*[33]

Not until 1974, when the Department of Health, Education, and Welfare proposed regulations to implement Title IX of the Education Amendments of 1972, were there any concrete guidelines for eliminating such inequities. Title IX, which prohibits sex discrimination, can make a difference. However, this legislative go-ahead for change will be minimal unless teachers actively support it.

Federal Government and Educational Democracy

Democracy in education has received the approval of the federal government. Title IX has given legitimacy to women's rights in education. The Civil Rights Acts of the 1960s boosted the antiracism cause. An antibusing amendment, which would have prevented the federal government from cutting off financial aid to school systems that disobeyed desegregation orders, was defeated in the U.S. Senate on October 9, 1974.

The federal courts also have supported the quest for equality. U.S. District Court Judge William E. Doyle issued a restraining order on September 27, 1974, prohibiting Denver, Colorado, residents from boycotting school busing.[34] U.S. District Court Judge W. Arthur Garrity has continually supported the desegregation of Boston public schools, first with a busing order, then with fines to school-board members who refused to go along with the order.

But even with congressional and judicial support for equal opportunity, there is still federal footdragging. A 117-page report by the Center for National Policy Review stated, "Northern schools today are far more segregated than those in the South."[35] Of eighty-four civil rights compliance reviews conducted in the North, the study found that fifty-two are still open and unresolved. The average age of the unresolved cases exceeds thirty-seven months. "While a few staff investigations have been shaky," the report said, "HEW's files literally bulge with documented evidence of violations of law."

Recommendations

The Government has legally adopted the banner of educational democracy, but educators must make sure there is more involved than just a show of colors. Teachers and administrators must become public watchdogs, finding and speaking out against inconsistencies and oversights in agency enforcement practices.

Educators must also support "positive action" programs in the public sector, such as state-sponsored training of school-board members. Alerting board members to the needs and concerns of racial and ethnic minorities and women would greatly assist the members in formulating equitable policies. When school boards become more concerned with educational quality than political questions, educational policies will be more effective.

At the same time, educators must watch their own practices. Educational programs still need reform. For instance, more women and minorities are needed on educational faculties at all levels. While white, middle-income teachers can teach an understanding of black, Native American, or Chicano concerns and male teachers are capable of giving women equal treatment in the classroom, minority faculty members are important because they can give

194 *Perspectives on Education*

special support to minorities, provide a check against discrimination, and serve as role models.

Colleges of education must develop courses and field experience programs to help foster an understanding of minority concerns among teachers. Such a program has been set up through the joint effort of Michigan State University Colleges of Urban Development and Education. A double major is offered to students who are interested in urban education. Combining urban and ethnic studies courses, traditional education courses, and practice teaching in the city, it prepares future teachers for democratic behavior in the inner city class-room.

Conclusion

Quality education and equal educational opportunity go hand in hand with equality and justice in other institutions such as employment and housing. Children who are treated fairly in classrooms and who learn that people of other races, sex, or social strata are not very different from themselves will tend to carry their experience and attitudes with them into adult life. As residents, many will seek housing in racially and economically mixed neighborhoods. As business people, they will seek to be equal opportunity employers, in the true sense of the phrase. As parents, they will seek to give their children an unbiased view of the world. On the other hand, those children—white, black, rich, poor, male, and female—who are steeped in prejudice throughout their educational careers will probably perpetuate those prejudices throughout their lives.

Thus educators must choose which legacy they will help to preserve in the United States. Schooling can be the key to creating real democracy in American society. By espousing nonracist, nonsexist, and nonclassist beliefs and acting according to those beliefs, educators can do much to help make democracy a reality.

References

1. John Dewey, "The School and Social Progress," *School and Society* (Chicago: University of Chicago Press, 1900).

2. James S. Coleman, *et al., Equality of Educational Opportunity* (Washington, D.C.: U.S. Government Printing Office, 1966).

3. Robert L. Green, "Racism in American Education," *Phi Delta Kappan* 53 (January 1972), 274–276.

4. "Discrimination has Cost Minority Educators over 200,000 Jobs, NEA Official Asserts," National Education Association Press Release, October 19, 1973.

5. Robert W. Hooker, *Displacement of Black Teachers in the Eleven Southern States* (Nashville, Tenn.: Race Relations Information Center, December, 1970).

6. Robert L. Green, "Northern School Desegregation: Educational, Legal, and Political Issues," *Uses of the Sociology of Education*, Seventy-third Yearbook of the National Society for the Study of Education, Part I (Chicago: Distributed by the University of Chicago Press, 1974).

7. Robert Rosenthal, "The Pygmalion Effect Lives," *Psychology Today* 7 (September 1973), 56–63.

8. Rosenthal, "The Pygmalion Effect Lives."

9. Rosenthal, "The Pygmalion Effect Lives."

10. Robert L. Green, "The Awesome Danger of Intelligence Tests," *Ebony* 29 (August 1974), 68–72.

11. J. Kenneth Morland, "Racial Attitudes in School Children: From Kindergarten Through High School," U.S. Department of Health, Education and Welfare, Office of Education, National Center for Educational Research and Development, Project No. 2-c-009, Grant No. OEG-3-72-0014, November, 1972.

12. Robert L. Green, "The Sociology of Multiracial Schools," *Inequality in Education* 9 (August 3, 1971), 25–27.

13. Meyer Weinberg, *Desegregation Research: An Appraisal* (Bloomington, Ind.: Phi Delta Kappa, 1970).

14. Green, "Northern School Desegregation."

15. Rosenthal, "The Pygmalion Effect Lives."

16. Green, "The Awesome Danger of Intelligence Tests."

17. Coleman, *Equality of Educational Opportunity.*

18. U.S. Commission on Civil Rights, *Racial Isolation in the Public Schools*, 2 vols. (Washington, D.C.: U.S. Government Printing Office, 1967).

19. Jean Bernstein, "The Elementary School: Training Ground for Sex Role Stereotypes," *Personnel and Guidance Journal* 51 (October 1972), 97–103.

20. "No Comment," *MS.* 3 (December 1974), 110. Reprinted with permission.

21. Bernstein, "The Elementary School."

22. "Starting Off Equal," *Parents Magazine* 49 (September 1974), 37–39.

23. John Aragon, "Alienation in the Schools: The Unwanted, Excluded and Uninvolved," *Student Displacement/Exclusion: Violations of Civil and Human Rights*, Report of the 11th National NEA Conference on Civil and Human Rights in Education (Washington, D.C.: National Education Association, 1973).

24. Max Rosenberg, "Evaluate Your Textbooks for Racism and Sexism," *Educational Leadership* 37 (November 1973), 107–109.

25. Rosenberg, "Evaluate Your Textbooks."

26. Willah Weddon, "Task Force on Sexism in Schools Flounders," Lansing, Mich. *State Journal*, August 20, 1974.

27. Weddon, "Task Force on Sexism in Schools Flounders."

28. "Schoolbooks That Stirred Up a Storm," *U.S. News & World Report* 77 (November 4, 1974), 61–72.

29. Curtis Seltzer, "A Confusion of Goals," *Nation* 219 (November 2, 1974), 430–435.

30. *Bradley et al.* v. *Milliken et al.*, U.S. District Court (E.D. Michigan) Civil Action 35257, September 27, 1971, "Ruling on Issue of Segregation."

31. Green, "Northern School Desegregation."

32. *Report of the National Advisory Commission on Civil Disorders* (New York: New York Times Co., 1968).

33. *Education for Survival*, Final Report Sex Role Stereotypes Project, USOE-0-72-2507, July 1973 (Washington, D.C.: National Education Association, 1973).

34. "U.S. Judge Bars Boycott of Denver School Busing," *New York Times*, October 11, 1974.

35. "Critics Say HEW Has Ignored Northern School Segregation," *Christian Science Monitor*, September 18, 1974.

Suggested Readings

Albert, Irene, and Pamela Sheldon. "Equality of Educational Opportunity." *Educational Leadership*, December 1966.

Allport, Gordon W. *The Nature of Prejudice*. Reading, Mass.: Addison-Wesley, 1954.

Andreas, Carol. *Sex and Caste in America*. Englewood Cliffs, N.J.: Prentice-Hall, 1971.

Banks, James A., and Jean D. Grambs (Eds.). *Black Self-Concept: Implications for Education and Social Science*. New York: McGraw-Hill, 1972.

Chisholm, S. "Sexism and Racism: One Battle to Fight." *Personnel and Guidance Journal*, 51 (1972), 123–125.

Dyer, Henry S. "Social Factors and Equal Educational Opportunity." Paper presented before the American Psychological Association, September 3, 1967.

Fox, David J. "Free Choice Open Enrollment-Elementary Schools." New York: Center for Urban Education, August 1966.

Gordon, Edmund W. "Equalizing Educational Opportunity in the Public School." *IRCD Bulletin*, November 1967.

Goslin, David A. "The School in A Changing Society." *American Journal of Orthopsychiatry*, October 1967.

Green, R.L. "After School Integration—What? Problems in Social Learning." *Personnel and Guidance Journal*, 44 (1966), 705.

Green, R.L. (Ed.). *Racial Crisis in American Education*. Chicago: Follett, 1969.

Green, R.L. "Northern School Desegregation: Educational, Legal and Political Issues." *73rd Yearbook of the National Society for the Study of Education*, 1974.

Hernton, Calvin. *Sex and Racism*. New York: Grove Press, 1965.

Jones, James M. *Prejudice and Racism*. Reading, Mass.: Addison-Wesley, 1972.

Knowles, L.L. and K. Prewitt. *Institutional Racism*. Englewood Cliffs, N.J.:Prentice-Hall, 1969.

Knox, Ellis O. *Democracy and the District of Columbia Schools. A Study of Recently Integrated Public Schools*. Washington, D.C.: Judd and Detweiler, 1957.

Ladner, Joyce. *Tomorrow's Tomorrow: The Black Woman*. New York: Doubleday, 1971.

McClure, G.; M. Friedman; K. Ries; T. Brunner; J. Hender; and B. Witwer. "Sex discrimination in the Schools." *Today's Education*, November, 1971.

Mosteller, Frederick, and Daniel Moynihan (Eds.). *On Equality of Educational Opportunity*. New York: Vintage Books, 1972.

National Commission on Professional Rights and Responsibilities, Detroit, Michigan. *A Study of Barriers to Equal Educational In A Large City*. Washington, D.C.: National Education Association, March 1967.

Pettigrew, Thomas F. "Race and Equal Educational Opportunity." *Harvard Educational Review*, Winter 1968.

Seward, Georgene H., and Robert C. Williamson. *Sex Roles in Changing Society*. New York: Random House, 1970.

Sowell, Thomas. *Black Education: Myths and Tragedies*. New York: David McKay, 1972.

Stacey, J.; S. Bereaud; and J. Daniel. *And Jill Came Tumbling After*. New York; Dell, 1974.

Sussman, Leila. "Democratization and Class Segregation in Puerto Rican Schooling: The U.S. Model Transplanted." *Sociology of Education*, **41** (1968).

Weinberg, Meyer. *The Education of the Minority Child*. Chicago: Integrated Education Associates, 1970.

Rhody McCoy

The teacher and the community

13

This chapter by Dr. McCoy gives us the views of one of the pioneers in the community control movement here in the United States. It is a view of schools that is far different from that presented in many conventional textbooks. It indicates in a very graphic manner how difficult it will be to initiate some of the changes suggested by Fantini and Sullivan in Chapters 8 and 9.

Rhody McCoy

Dr. McCoy is currently Dean of the School of Continuing Education at Federal City College in Washington, D.C. He has formerly taught at Mount Holyoke College, the University of Massachusetts, and Smith College. Dr. McCoy was the Unit Administrator (Assistant Superintendent) of Ocean Hill–Brownsville District 17a in Brooklyn, New York, from July 1967 to July 1970. He is on the Governor's Commission to Establish a Comprehensive Plan for School District Organization and Collaboration and is a member of the Massachusetts Advisory Council in Education.

Dr. McCoy has received numerous honors, awards, and citations, and has published many articles on education.

Two words that have invaded the minds of Americans in the last two decades are *teacher* and *community*. These two words have divided our society or, rather, they have been used to divide it. From another point of view, these two words are foundations of our society but they mean different things to different people.

To begin, let us take a look at your teacher or teachers. Whether or not this person is male or female, black or white, short or tall, plump or slim, he or she holds a significant position in your life. Remember if you can your first day of school. It was supposed to be an exciting and important day—at least that is what your parents told you. As it turned out, they took you to a new day-time home—new because most of your waking hours would be spent there, most of your activities would take place there, most of your new friends would be met there, and your future would start there. This new "home" had a smiling, friendly person there to receive you and introduce himself or herself to you as your teacher. The name was unimportant at the moment because all of this was frightening to you because you would now be separated from the persons who gave you love, warmth, and security. However, your parents felt in their hearts that this was a new and good experience for you. The smiling, friendly alien soon began to mold you, your personality, your behavior, your attitudes, and your life. You had embarked on the ship of change that poets call "the voyage of life."

Soon you met several other youngsters all dressed up and awed by this new experience. Their behavior varied from crying to sullenness, from attempts to escape to home to acceptance, from aggressiveness to withdrawal—all were unsuspecting that sooner or later they must conform or face an escalating degree of punishment. No one told you or your new companions anything about these persons called "teachers," other than perhaps their name, because either no one knew or no one felt it was important for you to know. Later you will discover how important it was and will be. This person began to "teach" you. If you can, recall that they taught you obedience, regulations, and compliance. They taught you where to hang your clothing, where to sit, how to be recognized, where the tools of learning were, the health process (toilets, and so on), fire regulations, and they taught you to "respect" each other and authority as represented by the teacher, the principal, and so forth. They did not teach you about or expose you to the intimacies of their personalities. You soon learned on your own the likes and dislikes of this person, and how to please him or her.

The formal learning process began with little regard for how and what you had learned but rather with what the teacher had been told you had to learn within an established time frame (either a semester or a year). Systematically you were taught the basic tool subjects in a sequence, regardless of whether you were ready to learn or receptive to learning at that time, and usually with no attention paid to your previous learning style and your mentor who prepared you for this new experience.

This process was modified with some degree of regularity as the teacher became aware that this objective process did not get the desired results. You were, then, identified or grouped. The groups usually consisted of the slow group, the average group, or the advanced group. Ironically, although you and your parents were unaware of the impact of this arrangement, it would be the beginning of your attitude and behavior toward school. As a result of this grouping process, the teacher spent less time with some pupils and more with others, and it would be many years later before you and your parents would begin to understand the full impact of this process. Gradually, if you were fortunate, you began to see other persons introduced into the learning set. They were guidance counselors, social workers, reading specialists, and maybe your parents or your classmates' parents, called paraprofessionals. All of these people were to assist you in the learning process. To varying degrees, your parents began to be more involved in school activities. They were involved out of concern—concern over your grades, concern over your behavior, concern about your progress, and concern about your future. Most of their concerns were generated because of some reference to your inability to learn at a pace or level set by the school system. You were told repeatedly during this period how important it was to acquire an education and how you would become a productive citizen.

What were you learning? Undoubtedly the teacher wanted you to be competent in the basic subjects—reading, writing, and arithmetic—but what were you learning? Undoubtedly you were learning or had learned submission, but what else? Had you learned about racism and what devastating effects it had and would continue to have on you? Had you learned about economic deprivation and its relationship to racism? Had you learned about unemployment and its effect on your family and your friends' families? Had you learned about poor housing and why certain classes of people still lived in poor housing? Had you learned about problems of health (eyes, teeth, bones) and how improper diet would effect your being? Had you been taught about institutions, their roles and functions, and how all of these aforementioned things would affect your future? Or had you been taught the "American dream"—that an education was essential to good housing, professionalism, economic security, good health, and a productive life. Is it not odd that while you were being taught about the American lifestyle you were in many instances being denied its opportunities and at the same time punished for not learning it?

As you read this passage, reflect on your experiences. Were you ever called a slow learner? Why did you receive low grades? Were you ever failed and, if so, why? Were you referred to reading specialists, social workers, and so on? Why? Did you notice your parents' increasing anger and frustration over your mediocre or failing performance?

You are capable right now of assessing these statements and concerns and you are capable of turning your education around. You can acquire an education and you must. As you read this chapter to its conclusion, you should have a more comprehensive picture of the "why" for education. Use this to reactivate your interest in school and in your future.

Let us go back now and look at the teacher—not the status symbol, but the teacher. This person, more often than not, was just like you and for a variety of reasons (economic, opportunity, career oriented, and circumstantial) proceeded through public schools, on to college, and then to teaching. He or she went through the same, if not worse, educational system. He or she graduated and was licensed to teach, and many are teaching you just as they learned and were taught. Thus, you are reflections of them and their times. After approximately nine months you are turned over to another teacher and, except for some configuration numbers like 60, 70, or 80, or grades A, B, and C, the process both repeats itself and is modified because of your age; it is not, however, modified by what you really have learned. The teachers and the teaching process are not totally at fault, for one would not expect to teach or be taught about the negative and painful things of life but rather about how to or why to avoid them. But there are other things missing. The teachers themselves are not measured by their background, their ability to teach, what they teach, how successful the pupils are, or even what the pupils have learned.

They are teachers and as such are rewarded for overcoming the same obstacles that confront you. They mean well, but once at the level of teacher they are not guided nor do they receive counsel by sincere, interested people to assist in the development of an effective learning environment. They are obedient to a system—a system whose major goals seem to be the rewards for attaining the gate-keeper status of teacher. Teaching should be one of our most important professions, for in our society it is through this process that our minds are developed, our attitudes formed, our personalities developed, and our futures projected.

There has been much talk over the last few years on the subject of equal educational opportunity or equity and quality education. This concern is for your benefit, you as the student, the pupil, the learner. Do you know what it means or how it affects you? Education means learning, and learning equips you to gather information, to make decisions, and to act. What, then, must you be looking at? Eventually, you must demand the type of education you or your children should receive.

Let us pursue this just a little more. Can you remember or visualize photographs or other pictures of your parents and their parents? Do you recall the background in those pictures? How do they compare with what you see around you today? If you can recall or visualize that background, then perhaps you can mentally address the point I am now making. Part of your education has taken place through your eyes; in fact, probably the most effective education process has been through your eyes. Television, magazines, newspapers, and actual real life unfolding daily in front of you have been instrumental in making you who and what you are. Oh yes, you hear too, but what you hear aside from such things as music and other sounds is people reacting to what they see. It is extremely important that you understand this. As you go from this printed text, begin to look at the images in front of your eyes through your brain. It will be exciting and above all it will educate you. Examine your books. See if they depict life as it really is and as you live it. If they do, then you are acculturated or assimilated; if they do not, then you are outside of the American mainstream.

Ask yourself why don't these images show life as it is—the crime, the poor housing, the jobless, the unhealthy, and other realities. The reason is that America is ashamed; but it will not remedy the situation. Not that it cannot; rather it will not. Therefore, it must urge you to accept the educational process for what it is. This process conditions you to accept your place in life, and to tolerate the dehumanizing practices, the menial tasks, and the obedience. You are rewarded in school (with As, Bs, or Cs) or punished (with failure) based on your reaction to this conditioning process. Unless I am totally in error, you have been exposed to crime on the streets, crime in government, and all phases and degrees of poverty either first hand or from your friends. You see poor housing conditions, infested buildings, the aged uncared for, and the jobless. (Yes, the young are jobless too.) You know of the loss of faith in a President; you know of the wars, legal and illegal. Yet you are taught about these things only superficially. I suggest that either your teachers are not substantially knowledgeable about them, or they reject them because of the pain, or they are ordered not to introduce them to you. You are relatively mature even at a young age, but the educational system, and even your teacher, ignores this basic fact. Thus, what is placed before you to learn is of no consequence.

You have a favorite subject. You learn about it, though its content is not one of the unpleasant subjects that I mentioned here. Why? Let's talk about James Brown, or Putney Swope. America created these characters for several reasons. One was to create an image, if you will, to stereotype modern black Americans so they will be seen as weird and ridiculous. A second was to provide recreation for blacks and to detour their thinking and actions away from the problems facing minorities. A third was for profit. You, all students, were a victim of this plot. You needed the recreation; it created employment for blacks and many blacks spent money attempting to emulate these characters.

Let me take just one illustration. The majority population is white. Do they dress like Shaft? Stores that sell these "stylish" clothes wait for blacks. Their prices are outrageous. Let me introduce a little humor in this example. This dude went into the neighborhood store and said, "I want to see your shirts." The storekeeper showed him some five-dollar shirts. "Man are you crazy I don't dig those." Next he was shown some ten-dollar shirts. "Listen man," he said, "if you don't know or have what I want I'll go down the street." The storekeeper then took him to the thirty-five-dollar shirts, knowing that they were what he wanted from the outset. Now doesn't that story tell you quite a few things? You hear similar stories, but not in school—not from your teacher. This story with variation takes place daily in poor and under-privileged areas.

Let us discuss, if you're still interested in what I say, a topic of current events. What recently happened in Boston and why? The media told us of the violence in the Boston schools and repeated with great frequency the fact that a black stabbed a white. The media also showed the brute force (numbers) of the police all decked out in battle dress. To protect whom? What was not played up in the media with the same intensity was the fact that the police claimed they could not cope with the white violence. Remember Watts, Kent State, and Washington, D.C.? They controlled the oppressed. But such situations are the overt manifestation, not the core.

When one examined urban schools, the "white schools" were in as bad shape as the "black schools." The blacks found little or nothing in the white schools that was relevant to them or that they figured was worth being injured for. The students were not told that in that area, housing and unemployment, as well as illiteracy, were just as acute as they were in other areas, particularly the black community. Why then such an uproar? The American educational system had struck a snag and it was backing up on them. Specifically, no one can define or has defined for students what quality or equity or educational opportunities are. Rather, the system is forcing minorities into accepting the standards of the white or dominant society. What minority students had been doing was rejecting the educational system, perhaps not knowing why, but thereby creating a challenge to the "American dream." This society had to get the students back into this oppressing process so they created a concept called desegregation, knowing full well that racist America would rebel. Even when the initial rebellion had died down (but not out), the educational needs of most students were not met. Yes, the reading skills and performance—as well as behavior—may improve, but in all honesty this really means that the minority students have regained their "senses" and are willing to accept their place in life. You probably remember Martin Luther King. He did not speak for all blacks when he was a national figure preaching nonviolence. This does not mean that blacks wanted or intended to be violent, but rather that they intended to challenge the oppressive system. Dr. King was more white America's hero. Do you find this hard to accept or understand? If you are black it means something deep.

Yes, Dr. King was to neutralize the interruptions of the economic system by blacks. He was to appeal to "whitey" to reconsider and remedy his atrocious acts toward black Americans. I cannot speak for Dr. King, but I knew and respected his honesty and sincerity and believed and hoped that his actions were strategies for change. History, however, has shown that he was used by the dominant society. As famous and important as he was and as needed was his theme of nonviolence, he could have been one of the first black national heroes. Yet today blacks cannot have a national holiday in recognition for what he did for white America.

History. Has your teacher explained to you about the judicial system and its relationship to you, starting with the Scotsboro Boys? Has your teacher explained to you the implications of the *Plessy* v. *Ferguson* decision? Have you read the Skelly Wright decision? Do you know about the Civil Rights decision in 1954? What does integration mean? Can you explain what decentralization means? Can you explain desegregation, de facto or de jure? Do you know or have you been taught how each of these has an impact on your education? Before I explain my meaning, let me make my most important statement. Learn the basic skills, particularly reading, but for one important reason—to learn. To learn means to think. To think means to know. To know means to act. To act based on knowledge is security. Security is survival. Survival is to be productive. Productivity breeds change. Change may mean dignity one day. Dignity *may* one day be the cohesive force that saves our nation. In short, you may be the savior of the nation and the architect for the future. I really should close, but I am compelled to discuss one or two more issues.

Recently I had to experience the two-barreled shock of both reading about and seeing blatant oppression. It is hard to believe that after almost twenty years blacks and whites still must fight to obtain a second-class education—an education denied to them by the very society who says they must have it. Hidden in the bowels of the article is the implication that white America is finding legitimate ways to opt out of their own commitment. Now they are in the process of redefining a word—integration (desegregation)—to help the Boston whites out of a predicament they created and incidentally did not define. Just for fun, to see if you really understand, look at the *New York Times*, January 26, 1975, in the "Week in Review" section. The second shock was *60 Minutes.* You know the TV show. Well, there was a section on Harlem and the media technicians really did a number on reawakening the stereotype in an effort to tell a story. More importantly, it told of the unemployment, poor housing, drugs, and so forth, and how the media helped to oppress blacks.

While the story was being told the technicians were in fact demonstrating the very oppressive act.

I just shared a look at your community with you and I hope you didn't like what you saw. You are a community; your family and friends. Experience, curiosity, quest for knowledge—these are the teachers despite the fact that there are people called teachers. Newspapers and TV people, ministers, politicians, and so forth are teachers. You have the very distinct privilage of selecting how and by whom you will be taught and more importantly examining what and how you have been taught until you are capable of deciding what you will be taught and why.

Peace.

Suggested Readings

Berube, Maurice R., and Marilyn Gittell (Eds.). *Confrontation at Ocean-Hill Brownsville*. New York: Praeger, 1969.

Mayer, Martin. *The Teachers' Strike—New York 1968*. New York: Harper & Row, 1969.

Urofsky, Melvin J. *Why Teachers Strike: Teachers' Rights and Community Control*. New York: Doubleday, 1970.

Ruth B. Love

Right to read: privilege or a right?

14

This chapter by Dr. Love indicates the scope of the reading problem here in the United States, and the efforts of one of the government programs specifically designed to help solve this problem. It is interesting to note that, like the preceding four chapters, this chapter again points out the difference between our rhetoric pertaining to education and the realities of the situation, and the discrepancy between what has been promised and what has been delivered.

Ruth B. Love

Dr. Love is currently Superintendent of the Oakland Unified School District in Oakland, California. From 1971 to 1975, Dr. Love was the Director of the Right to Read Effort at the U.S. Office of Education, Department of Health, Education, and Welfare.

Dr. Love is the recipient of numerous awards and citations, and is listed in *Who's Who in American Education*. She has some twenty-seven publications.

Recently we celebrated the bicentennial of the American nation. I think it is important that we understand what that means. Our bicentennial is and should be more than the observance of the anniversary of when we as a people began the successful struggle to wrest control of our own destiny from a colonial army.

The shot that has truly been heard around the world in the two centuries since our war for independence is not the sound of musketfire at Lexington and Concord, but rather the ringing declaration of these principles: "We hold these truths to be self-evident, that all men are created equal and endowed by their Creator with certain inalienable rights, and among these are life, liberty, and the pursuit of happiness." The significance of the bicentennial is not the historical fact that a ragged army of colonists defeated the greatest empire of its time, but rather that we instituted a system of government based on the consent of the governed. And even as our two centuries of history have been anguished at times by the struggle to perfect our system of government and to ensure that all men hold equal title in law to the meaning of the words of the Declaration of Independence, we became a beacon to the world of what free men can accomplish.

The rights that are celebrated in a general way in our Declaration of Independence have been spelled out over time very specifically. They were spelled out first in the Bill of Rights, which had to be drafted before the independent colonies would agree to form our United States of America, and then subsequently in the remaining amendments to our Constitution, and in our federal, state, and local laws. No nation on earth has so deliberately written specific legislation to protect individual rights as we have for the rights we assume as citizens.

Even so, there remain unwritten rights that, if not respected and equally granted to all, undermine all the others we have codified and made laws about. And the most important of these unwritten rights is the right to read.

Before the invention of moveable type in the fifteenth century, the ability to read was an elitist privilege. But Johann Gutenberg's accomplishment revolutionized all subsequent history, making possible not only light-year advances in the accumulation of knowledge but also the communication of that knowledge through systems of popular education. In a way, the evolution of the broad-based, representative system of government that we established in this country and whose anniversary we celebrate in our bicentennial can even be attributed to the invention of moveable type. The rights we have guaranteed under that system of government are clearly dependent on the right to read.

Throughout history, whenever one people have tried to subjugate another people, the trend has always been to imprison slaves in ignorance. The ancient Egyptians attempted to do it to the Israelites, and in our own history there are few more tragic episodes than the whites denying their slaves the right to read. Even our most expurgated history books now tell of the harsh beatings administered to slaves who attempted to learn to read the Bible, and of the repressive laws written to keep slaves illiterate and ignorant.

For there is no denying the adage that knowledge is power. When people learn to read and can assimilate knowledge, they can no longer be easily manipulated. And they cannot long remain chattels. Where at one time cynical attempts were made to subjugate people by denying them the wherewithal to achieve and accomplish, in the modern world we have recognized that the birthright of a free person is the right to read. More than a century ago in this country, we established the principle of free universal education. And when the Civil War was over, one of the first activities of reconstruction was to establish Freedmen's Schools to help repair the damage of centuries of servitude.

Yet now more than a century later, we are clearly failing to guarantee that birthright—the right to read—to all our citizens. At the beginning of this decade, there were more than 18½ million adult illiterates in this country. Simply stated, that means they cannot read well enough even to understand a newspaper.

Compounding that sad fact, there were at the same time seven million elementary and secondary school students with severe reading problems. In some large cities, an estimated 40 to 50 percent of school children are underachieving in reading.

In other words, approximately one-tenth of our people are functional illiterates or potential illiterates. No matter how you look at that fact, it represents a major social and economic problem for our society, and one that has gone unrecognized for far too long. In order to address this critical problem, the Right to Read Effort came into being. It is not a program, but rather a national campaign to eradicate illiteracy.

Right to Read As an Umbrella

Today, as in 1970, Right to Read is unique. It is not simply a legislated program, but rather an ambitious national thrust to focus on reading problems in the nation. It is a total effort, an umbrella under which all segments of the society, public and private, professional and nonprofessional, have united in a common goal—to ensure that by 1980, 99 percent of all school-age children under sixteen years of age living in the United States and 90 percent of all those over sixteen will possess and use literacy skills.

The National Right to Read Effort is designed to:

1. Stimulate national attention to reading needs
2. Determine what changes are required to alleviate reading problems

3. Identify existing resources, both public and private, that can be brought to bear on the problem

4. Initiate innovative and effective reading programs with all types of agencies and institutions that can contribute to the elimination of illiteracy in this country

5. Demonstrate, through the establishment of reading programs, effective techniques for the elimination of reading deficiencies, and thereby increase reading competencies

Right to Read has maintained its three-pronged strategy:

1. The establishment of demonstration programs

2. Designation of Right to Read states (administered through state education agencies)

3. Initiation and support of national impact programs or special emphasis projects

Although these components have not changed in five years, the activities and programs under each have increased, adding new directions and dimensions to the total Right to Read Effort.

Before detailing these activities, it is important to note another significant distinction of the Right to Read Effort. It is primarily a catalyst—using its budget, which has never been more than $12 million annually, solely as seed money. Because Right to Read philosophy and program guidelines stress the development of an effective reading program that will exist after the receipt of federal dollars, these Right to Read grants are essentially minimal funds provided to get things going. Right to Read encourages every grantee to enlist support from a wide variety of community resources and to work with local and state agencies so that they help continue the project when additional funds become necessary. Furthermore, program content emphasizes the training of existing staff, rather than the addition of new personnel, enabling the program to continue when federal money does not.

One measure of the success of this philosophy has been the ability of countless schools and communities to adopt the Right to Read name and principles—without using any Right to Read money. Following the Right to Read program guidelines, they have established their own "Right to Read" programs.

Demonstration Programs

A major part of the National Right to Read Effort is the demonstration of effective ways of eliminating functional illiteracy in the United States. To date, Right to Read has funded more than 200 school and community programs for preschoolers, school children, and adults. In fiscal year 1974 (July 1, 1973–June 30, 1974), the demonstration program component was expanded to include approximately $1.5 million for grants to 34 institutions of higher education for teacher preservice programs and in fiscal year 1975 over $1.2 million was included for more than 20 adult reading academies.

Each demonstration program plans the best possible program for its unique needs, using the materials, information, and assistance furnished by Right to Read. Every program follows certain guidelines. Each has a representative Unit Task Force responsible for the planning and successful implementation of the Right to Read program. Parental and community involvement as well as increased use of community resources are stressed. Emphasis is placed on the use of diagnostic-prescriptive and individualized instruction utilizing multiple reading methods. And, as mentioned earlier, a key focus is on the development of existing staff, rather than on the employment of new personnel.

School and Community-Based Programs

The school-based effort for fiscal year 1974 included the funding of over 100 small cities and 21 large cities, as well as 51 Emergency School Assistance Act schools. (Additional school-based projects were funded by the end of fiscal year 1975.) Grants varied from $20,000 to $100,000, depending on the type of program and the number of schools involved in each location.

In fiscal year 1974, more than 150 principals of school-based projects were trained in leadership seminars conducted by Bank Street College of Education, the National Association of Elementary School Principals, the National Association of Secondary School Principals, and George Washington University.

The community-based effort provided funds for 54 programs. These projects were aimed at increasing functional literacy for selected adult populations, utilizing functional, practical materials that relate to the interests and needs of the adult population. Highly diverse in terms of location, target population, program objectives, and content, they were conducted almost anywhere—fom prisons and warehouses to community colleges, storefronts, and libraries. Grants range from $30,000 to $60,000.

Teacher Preparation Programs

Thirty-four institutions of higher education were awarded funds in fiscal year 1974 to develop model programs for preparing elementary teachers to be effectively qualified to teach reading in all subject areas. First-year funds covered planning and developing a program. Second-year funds, for qualified applicants, were used for implementing the program.

As with all Right to Read demonstration programs, the first step in implementing these teacher preservice programs was to assess the needs of the existing program. For this reason, programs varied significantly from institution to institution, which makes it difficult to describe the programs more specifically. Every program did, however, emphasize practical development of skills in diagnosis and prescription and included plans for the evaluation and dissemination of the new program.

Adult Reading Academies

The newest component of the Right to Read demonstration projects, the adult reading academies, will be sponsored by teaching institutions, community organizations, libraries, civic clubs, and other nonprofit organizations. Relying heavily on the support of the private sector, these academies will train volunteers to teach reading to out-of-school youths and older adults not formally involved in any other educational program. These academies are largely an outgrowth of the community-based projects. Right to Read staff examined the activities and components of those programs in preparing regulations and guidelines for the new academies.

Right to Read States

Although the responsibility for the education of Americans traditionally has rested with the individual states, Right to Read invited the states to expand this role. Each state is presently involved in activities designed to carry out the four basic objectives of a Right to Read state. In addition to making a public commitment to place reading in the highest priority and to commit their systems fully to furthering the Right to Read Effort, all states agreed to establish and implement a systematic statewide approach toward the following:

1. Determining the scope of the reading problem through an assessment of need
2. Establishing developmental activities directed toward a coordinated statewide approach
3. Preparing local education agency (LEA) reading directors
4. Maintaining and supporting LEA efforts in reading program improvements

During fiscal year 1974, the Right to Read Office provided training seminars for state directors to teach them how to train local Right to Read directors, identify effective programs, and coordinate resources related to reading. A total of nine days was spent in seminars for state Right to Read directors. Similar seminars will be held for new state directors.

In turn, these state directors carried out programs resulting in the preparation of 1,227 local reading directors who each received 240 hours of training. Approximately 1,200 school districts were committed to and involved in building comprehensive K–12 grade reading programs. Almost 60,000 teachers received inservice training in the implementation of basic criteria for effective reading programs; and in the 1974–1975 school year, 3.7 million students were attending schools in Right to Read districts.

In addition to training local reading directors, the state education agencies are active in a variety of other activities designed to fulfill their individual state's assessed needs. For example, Ohio, concentrating on reading in the content areas, has developed The Teaching Teen Reading Series, a series of inservice training modules for junior and senior high school teachers. Emphasizing adult literacy, Maine and New Jersey have developed cooperative programs with universities and existing ABE efforts within the state. Indiana has prepared tutor training handbooks for local reading directors. Several other states are working on more effective procedures for identifying and validating demonstration programs, and still others are concentrating primarily on coordinating private sector resources.

Additional information on individual state projects may be obtained from the Right to Read director based in each state's Department of Education.

National Impact Programs

The programs funded under national impact efforts are those that have broad implications for education in general and embrace the concept of the multiplier effect. In other words, such specialized programs are designed either to reach massive numbers of people or for use with large sections of the population after their developmental stage has been completed.

The number of national impact projects has grown steadily, particularly in the areas of materials, dissemination, and informational/promotional activities. An important new component of the national impact program, however, is the involvement of the private sector. Responsibility for the private sector—business and industry, civic clubs and organizations, private citizens—did not come into Right to Read's jurisdiction until 1974. Major emphasis has been placed in the past few years on marshaling the vast resources of the private sector, and this will continue as an important thrust. The private sector activities are listed separately under the "What Can I Do?" section of this report, in an effort to illustrate how national projects can be replicated at local levels and to emphasize the role that every citizen can play in promoting the Right to Read Effort.

Materials/Dissemination

Validated and packaged programs. The American Institute of Research, Palo Alto, California, has been engaged in identifying, validating, and providing multimedia packaging of successful reading projects. Each package will contain a comprehensive case history of all the program components and procedures that made it effective. The product will be a systematically arranged projection of an exemplary (total school) reading program, which can be emulated either in part or in whole by other states or local education institutions. A catalog of more than two hundred promising programs that did not, however, meet the validation requirements will also be published.

Administrator's Handbook. A handbook based on the administrative seminars conducted for Right to Read principals. It was designed for use by state education agencies or others who are interested in leadership skills for principals in their roles as instructional leaders.

IRA reports. A series of six bimonthly reports, to be published by the International Reading Association, that focus on promising practices in Right to Read and non-Right to Read programs. Extra copies are available from the International Reading Association, 800 Barksdale Road, Newark, Delaware 19711.

Assessment Planning Handbook. A self-study guide that combines a revision of the Right to Read Needs Assessment Package and the Right to Read Program Planning Procedure. It presents a systematic process for planning a reading program, and is available from the Right to Read Office or the Government Printing Office.

Preschool Parent Kit. Prepared under a grant by the Urban Coalition, this is a prototype toy and book kit to be used by mothers of preschoolers to teach reading readiness skills. When completed, kits will be distributed to selected local Urban Coalitions, which will run three-day training sessions for parents.

Tutor training packages. Revisions and adaptations of original National Reading Center materials that deal with training volunteer tutors for elementary schools. Among them are the *Tutoring Resource Handbook for Teachers, Tutors' Resource Handbook,* and *Tutor-Trainers' Resource Handbook.* They are available from the Government Printing Office.

Tutor training filmstrips. A series of six filmstrips that can be used in conjunction with the tutor training handbooks or alone. Their titles are: "Organizing and Administering Your Tutor Program," "Talking to Tutors About Tutoring," "On Being a Reading Tutor," "Word Attack Skills," "Comprehension Skills," and "Work-Study Skills."

Adult literacy TV project. Two series of videotape reading instruction programs, each with twenty-five, thirty-minute lessons. One series in English and one in Spanish, they will be developed for use in multiple settings; that is, the home, adult basic education centers, community learning centers, and so forth. They are suitable for public, commercial, or closed-circuit TV.

Informational/Promotional Activities

Mini-assessment. A study of the reading competency of seventeen-year-olds still in school, conducted by the National Assessment of Educational Progress. Results will help determine types of reading programs that should be offered and will also indicate to high schools where they must improve their teaching skills. The results will also establish a baseline from which to measure reading progress for this age group and provide additional material to use in testing "the operational definition of functional literacy."

Gallup survey. A proposal submitted by the Gallup Organization to determine how the public views reading as a "basic living" requirement, how extensive the perceived reading problem is in America today, and how the public evaluates the national reading problem relative to other social problems.

Right to Read film. A twenty-eight minute, 16-millimeter, sound and color film highlighting and describing key strategies and tactics of the Right to Read Effort.

Radio and TV spots. Designed to elicit support of volunteers in the fight against illiteracy. These ads encourage both tutorial assistance and the donation of materials, space, equipment, and facilities.

Right to Read summer. An attempt not only to focus attention on the reading problem but to offer a variety of reading activities in numerous locations, such as parks and recreational centers, YMCAs, YWCAs, and colleges and universities. Depends greatly on private sector and general community support.

Organizing the Private Sector

What Can I Do?

Involving the private sector in the elimination of illiteracy is a critical thrust in the Right to Read's National Impact Program. Highlighted below are a few of the many ways in which the private sector can help. The first two—working with business and industry and with athletes—are projects of the national office, but can be replicated at the local level by interested community organizations. For additional ideas, send for the brochure entitled "You Can Help in the Right to Read Effort," available from the Right to Read Office, Room 2131, 400 Maryland Avenue S.W., Washington, D.C. 20202.

Working with business and industry

The first step in channeling the financial and human resources of business and industry is to bring key leaders together to discuss the reading problem and ways in which each company can help. At the national level, Right to Read is sponsoring seminars for representatives of a variety of businesses—from publishers and clothing retailers to food processors and bankers. Similar meetings can be held at state and community levels to identify ways in which local business and industry can aid the Right to Read Effort.

One area of involvement suggested by Right to Read is the establishment of on-the-job literacy classes. These could be designed not only to help staff improve reading and other communication skills, but also to expand "life skills" through such areas as consumer economics, health care, and nutrition. When possible, Right to Read would provide technical assistance for these "industrial academies."

Many of the companies attending the national seminars are also in the process of developing specific plans of action for other types of Right to Read activities. For example, cereal boxes produced by one major food manufacturer will carry short children's stories. Other suggestions include:

1. The establishment of "reading corners" in department stores—small areas for young children to select books or browse while mothers shop

2. The manufacture of T-shirts, sweatshirts, and other apparel that promote the reading habit

3. The establishment of special racks in supermarkets where books can be "purchased" with "book stamps" that have been distributed to disadvantaged children.

Working with athletes

Just as Right to Read is working with actor-athlete Roosevelt Grier to enlist the support of the National Football League and, hopefully, other athletic leagues, your community can also ask for help from its local heroes. Pete Rozelle, NFL Commissioner, has committed the support of the NFL. The Washington Redskins have received a contract to demonstrate the motivational value of athletes in helping to increase the child's reading ability. The program will be a model for reproduction in ten other NFL cities. Teacher training and curriculum models will be developed for use in the other cities.

How can these athletes help the Right to Read? As a motivational force in the community, they can encourage children and youths to learn to read, to improve their reading ability, and to become interested in books and other materials. Through talk-show appearances, speeches at school assemblies, and public service announcements that promote adult basic education programs and the importance of reading, these athletes may reach many children and youth who have lacked the motivation and interest in learning to read.

Reading Is Fundamental

Reading Is Fundamental, a program developed through private efforts to provide self-selected books for children, is an ideal activity for community organizations. The program's aim is a simple one: to motivate children to read by giving them inexpensive, attractive paperbacks about things they know. Each child is allowed to choose his or her own books and to keep them.

Each sponsoring organization must finance and administer its own program; however, once an agency, such as a PTA, women's club, fraternal organization, or business association, agrees to support the project, the national Reading Is Fundamental office helps with the organization, publicity, and book ordering.

Other programs

Other national impact efforts include support from a number of professional and educational associations. For example, the American Library Association has produced three brochures for Right to Read: "The Reading Management Team," "The Role of the Media Specialist," and "Essentials for a Literacy Campaign."

Right to Read has also been working with other Office of Education agencies on cooperative studies and projects to channel resources for the most effective approach to common problems.

Technical Assistance

No overview of the Right to Read Effort would be complete without a brief explanation of the critical role of the technical assistance arm of the Right to Read. This is essentially an ongoing service branch of the Right to Read Office and Right to Read field operations. In the past years, emphases have shifted somewhat in this department.

Although the four technical assistance teams initiated to work with the demonstration schools are still in existence, they are no longer funded through Right to Read. Some of the technical assistants, however, are still working through local school district budgets and are active in aiding states in their identification of demonstration programs and training of local Right to Read directors. These teams are based at Ball State University, City College of New York, University of Georgia, and the U. S. International University.

The major responsibility for technical assistance now falls on in-house technical assistants. Their chief duties are:

1. To provide technical assistance to the national office and to state education agencies

2. To serve as catalysts and liaisons between Right to Read and the private sector, providing technical assistance for the new adult academies and other Right to Read projects

The technical assistance branch includes scholars in residence who serve for one year and assume primary responsibility for professional expertise in reading and planning. Two important thrusts in coming months are the translation of research for the practitioner and the development of a total dissemination model for Right to Read.

Looking Ahead

Since 1970, when the Right to Read Effort was announced, the influence of this national thrust to eliminate illiteracy has been felt in hundreds of communities across the United States and in every state's Department of Education. Each year, as the three major components (demonstration programs, Right to Read states, and national impact projects) expand and refine, the Right to Read will have an even greater influence on the improvement of reading programs throughout the country.

However, even though the activities have increased and the significance has intensified, Right to Read is still only a catalyst, a process, an umbrella. The real success of the total effort depends on the involvement, or rather the commitment, of all segments of the society. Hopefully, the increased emphasis on private sector support will help unite the vast human and financial resources essential to the eradication of illiteracy in the United States.

Unlike most Health, Education, and Welfare programs, Right to Read began with no legislation. It was a concept, then a plan, later a program. The United States Congress utilized the staff's Right to Read strategy and enacted the National Reading Improvement Act. This represents another milestone in the long journey toward full literacy.

There is no denying that illiterate Americans are imprisoned in an ignorance more confining than iron bars and prison walls. For in the modern world the ability to read is a crucial and enriching asset in every aspect of human endeavor—political, economic, social, or religious. In fact, much of our success and fulfillment as human beings rests on our ability to read.

For example, to exercise effectively our rights as citizens or consumers, we must have access to information about the issues and the capability to comprehend and act on that information. Likewise, to perform effectively as employers or employees, we must be able to understand instructions or report results.

Illiterate persons are held back in crucial ways from exercising effectively their rights in the political arena and in the marketplace. Worse still, they are held back in myriad small ways from functioning as independent persons in our society. They are dependent on others to read them the instructions on a bottle of medicine. They are at the mercy of the loan shark in truly under-standing the terms of a loan agreement. They cannot even read well enough to take the test required to obtain a driver's license. And when all these small hindrances build up so that they can barely support themselves and their families, they cannot even read the forms necessary to obtain the assistance to which they might be entitled. In short, the inability to read imprisons the illiterate in demeaning dependency.

That is why the National Right to Read Effort was established with the goal of eliminating illiteracy in the United States in this decade. For only 1 per-cent of our people is there a bona fide medical reason why they cannot learn to read. The rest of us are able to read, and must read to enjoy productive and successful lives. There is no national standard of reading achievement involved in Right to Read, merely the simple goal of helping people to read to their own desired level of ability, in order to fulfill their own personal goals.

Those goals, of course, vary. Some want to perform better on the job, or seek job advancement, or just get a job. Some want to be more informed and effective parents. Some want to be able to seek advanced education. As the goals vary with the diverse motivations of why people want to learn to read or read better, so too do the approaches to reading instruction and the materials used in teaching reading.

Since its inception in 1970, the function of the National Right to Read Effort has not been to be prescriptive. Rather the function has been to find the best and most successful methods of reading instruction that can be employed in a wide variety of situations—schools, community centers, factories, even prisons—to meet the needs of the nation's nonreaders. At the same time, it has been Right to Read's function to communicate proven methods of reading instruction to educators and others who can implement them; to offer technical assistance in establishing and evaluating reading programs; and to motivate the private sector as well as the academic sector to recognize the importance of reading in our society and create the opportunities for reading improvement necessary to achieving the goal of eliminating illiteracy.

Often the most effective method of reading instruction, especially for adult illiterates, is one-on-one. There is no doubt the National Right to Read Effort will be labor intensive, requiring thousands of volunteers and the commitment of businesses, civic groups, and service clubs, as well as the educational community, to succeed.

There are those who say that kind of commitment will never materialize, that it is a dream to think we can wipe out illiteracy in this country in this decade. The answer to them is, yes, it is a dream.

So too did the realists of the eighteenth century think it a dream for a ragged army of colonists to try to wrest their independence from the greatest empire of its time. Even more visionary, they considered it a dream to establish a form of government that assumed the ability of people to govern themselves. Yet during our bicentennial, we celebrated not only the endurance of that dream, but its accomplishment.

Suggested Readings

Allen, James (U.S. Commissioner of Education). *Right to Read* (pamphlet). Washington, D.C.: Department of Health, Education, and Welfare, September 1969.

Freire, Paulo. *Pedagogy of the Oppressed.* New York: Seabury, 1971.

Weinstein, Gerald, and Fantini, Mario (Eds.). *Toward Humanistic Education.* New York: Praeger, 1970.

James V. McConnell

Grades: feedback at its best, or elitism at its worst?

15

This chapter by Dr. McConnell deals with the aspect of education that best exemplifies the attitude of many educators toward their students. In the process of grading we usually see an approach that is directly counter to that advocated by people who believe in a humanistic approach to education. It will be very interesting for you, I am sure, to discuss the grading practices in your class in light of the material presented by Dr. McConnell.

James V. McConnell

Dr. McConnell was born in Okmulgee, Oklahoma, in 1925. He did his undergraduate work in psychology at Louisiana State University, and took his M.A. and Ph.D. degrees from the University of Texas. Since 1956 he has taught at the University of Michigan, where he holds professorial degrees both in the Department of Psychology and in the Department of Psychiatry. Since 1959 he has edited and published both the *Journal of Biological Psychology* and a humorous scientific magazine called *The Worm Runner's Digest*. His best-known book is *Understanding Human Behavior*, an introductory psychology text published in 1974 by Holt, Rinehart & Winston. In 1976, Dr. McConnell was given the Award for Distinguished Teaching in Psychology by the American Psychological Foundation.

I hate grades. I hated them when, as a student, I was on the receiving end, and I hate them still as they are used by most teachers. At their best, as I will try to explain, grades can offer a most rewarding kind of performance feedback from professor to pupil. But at their frequent worst, grades can be used as a tyrannical tool by teachers who wish to demonstrate their own superiority to most of their students. After giving considerable thought to the matter, I have concluded that we must either make radical changes in the ways that we teach and award grades, or we must abandon the present grading system completely. Let me first tell you a brief story from my own life, and then describe how I use grades in my own classes.

When I was a graduate student at the University of Texas, a friend of mine talked me into taking a course in anthropology. The teacher, a brilliant scholar, came on in class as a "softy." He said that it did not matter whether we attended his lectures or not and that he wanted lively, creative conversations; hence, he encouraged us to contradict and challenge what he said. Unfortunately, I took him at his word. One day, he began pontificating about psychology and muttering how useless experimental science was in uncovering truths about human behavior. I challenged him so vigorously that he said angrily, "If you think you know so damned much about this, why don't you teach the class today?" Never the shrinking violet, I took the stage and talked for thirty minutes. By the time I finished, the professor was nearly apoplectic, and one of the students became so enraged that he stalked out of the room. (Smart fellow—he was the only person who passed the course!)

I soon forgot the incident, but the teacher obviously did not. At the end of the term, when the final exam had been graded, I had the highest score of all. The teacher was so furious that he promptly subtracted points from my score for each class meeting I had missed. (I was the only student so penalized.) He thus got my score below that of the lad who had marched out in a huff. This student got an A; the rest of us received failing grades. I could laugh off this man's fit of pique because the course did not matter to me. But I felt very sorry indeed for the dozen or so other students (most of them graduates in anthropology, for whom the course was required) who had to suffer because I had shot off my mouth in class. I got even with this man by "killing him off" in a science fiction story I published shortly thereafter. Some of the other class members dropped out of school because this man chose the only revenge available to him.

Of course, not too many teachers deliberately punish rebellious students the way this professor tried to punish me. But by "grading on the curve," or by using exams to "weed out inferior students," teachers may unconsciously be promoting a kind of academic elitism designed to prove how superior they are to everybody else. Perhaps the time has come for the academic establishment to re-examine our "theory of grading" to see if it is really yielding the results we pretend we desire.

What Purpose Grades?

If you ask most teachers why they give grades to their students, the teachers will usually come up with a mix of three reasons: (1) grades motivate pupils to study hard and to learn; (2) grades give performance evaluations to the students so that they can correct their mistakes; and (3) grades are a traditional part of the educational process, and besides, the dean requires that grades be assigned so that the world can tell the good students from the poor ones. At first glance, these reasons may seem legitimate. A closer inspection might suggest otherwise, however.

Do grades motivate students to learn? Certainly they do. Most of us love success and fear failure. In many academic settings, however, only a small fraction of the students are allowed that ultimate success symbol, an A grade. If one is limited to giving As to no more than 10–15 percent of one's students (as I was when I first came to Michigan), then 85–90 percent of the students must perforce be considered partial or complete failures. To put it more bluntly, if one grades on the curve, then no matter how much the majority of the students study or learn, they will fail to achieve complete success. Little wonder that so many young people hate school, become depressed, and depart the academic scene as rapidly as they can.

Worse than this, the system is self-perpetuating. Those students who get the top grades typically are so rewarded that they stay on to become teachers or professors. Thus they have a vested psychological interest in continuing to grade on the curve; after all, the system picked them out as stars, so it must be a pretty good system, right? My own suspicion is that the curve has caused more human misery (and yes, let us admit it, more suicides) than any other aspect of the educational process.

The second reason for using grades has to do with performance evaluations. Surely it is true that we all need feedback on what we are doing in order to become better human beings. However, as B.F. Skinner and his followers have long since shown us, positive reinforcement is a far more effective and humane feedback than punishment or criticism. There is a strong sentiment in the academic environment that learning is chiefly a matter of correcting one's mistakes. The data—both from animal experiments and from studies on human learning—suggest otherwise. Pointing out someone's faults typically makes that person annoyed, defensive, and unhappy; criticism seldom leads to any kind of positive behavior change. The best strategy for getting someone to abandon an inappropriate response is almost always that of rewarding a competing behavior rather than merely punishing what the person is doing wrong.

The behavioral literature is full of examples of the superiority of positive reinforcement over punishment strategies. But let me give you an illustration from my own experience. Dr. Chauncey Smith and I have a private clinic in Ann Arbor called the Institute for Behavior Change. Much of our work is with obese people who want to lose weight. Most of our clients have seen one or more physicians about their weight problems. The usual response of the physician is to tell the person, "You've got to lose weight or you're going to die!" The usual response of the clients is to become so depressed that they go home and eat a large meal to soothe their psychological distress. At our institute, we assume that it is more important to encourage people to acquire good eating habits than to punish their inappropriate responses to food. So we do everything in our power to encourage our clients to gain self-control. We help them decide on realistic goals (usually a loss of one to two pounds per week), we get them to keep accurate charts that will graph their progress, and we reward every step the clients make toward their goals. The graphs are particularly important, since they act as impersonal and objective monitors that the people have in front of them continuously. And whatever else we do, we never, never criticize. As a consequence, our clients typically report rather marked changes in their own self-images. They also lose a tremendous amount of weight. According to the American Bariatrics Society (that group of physicians dealing with weight problems), the national success rate for the medical treatment of obesity is about 5 percent. Our long-term success rate at the Institute for Behavior Change is well above 70 percent.

What do you think might happen in our classrooms if teachers adopted the same sort of behavioral technology that Dr. Smith and I use at our clinic? Or to put the matter another way, what might happen if we started marking the answers that students got right on exams rather than just putting a big red mark on the answers they got wrong?

The third reason that most teachers give grades has to do with what I call academic elitism. Although the United States is a democracy, and we are all supposed to be equal before the law, most of our cultural traditions came from Europe. There are still kings and queens in Europe—nobility who *by birth* are somehow superior to the "common folk." We carry on this cultural tradition in many ways—by discriminating against minority groups, by repressing those individuals who are culturally deprived or perhaps merely deviant, and by grading on the curve.

Academic elitism is easy to defend; it's always been with us, it allows us to heap rewards on people who think and act like us, and it makes certain selection processes very easy. When I talk about this matter to businesspeople, they often tell me that they are in favor of the present grading system because it allows them to hire "only the best." In fact, that is not so; as Harvard psychologist David McClellan pointed out years ago, there is almost no connection whatsoever between school grades and performance in the business world after graduation (that is, the correlation is practically zero).

There is, however, a very high correlation between IQ scores and school grades, and between undergraduate grades and graduate performance. At first blush, this correlation might seem an argument in favor of grading on the curve. But think about the matter for a moment. Does not this correlation tell us that IQ tests merely give high scores to those people whose cultural backgrounds are similar to those of the psychologists who devised the IQ tests, and that the academic curve merely selects those students whose motivations, rewards, and work habits are similar to the teachers'? I can't think of a much better example of what Robert Rosenthal has called "the self-fulfilling prophecy" than the academic curve.

The Pursuit of Happiness

Let us make three wildly improbable assumptions about the academic process, just to see where these postulates might lead us. First, let us hypothesize that learning is the purpose or goal of an education. Our second assumption is that any living human being is capable of learning. Our third hypothesis is that some teaching techniques or ways of learning are better than others. Now, most teachers and students would probably agree with all three of these hypotheses. At least, there would be agreement at a verbal level. But as Freud pointed out a long time ago, you can tell more about a person's *real* beliefs by observing the person's actions than by listening to the person's verbal outpourings. So let's inspect the logical consequences of these three assumptions to see if teachers really practice what they preach.

Most college bulletins or brochures state that the major goal of collegiate education is to equip students to survive better after graduation. That is, a college should somehow impart to the student those facts, attitudes, skills, and behaviors that are necessary for lifelong success. Now to tell the truth, we do not really know what all these attributes for survival are, because no one has ever measured them scientifically. We do know, however, that most of the piddling little facts that teachers try to pound into students' craniums are forgotten within weeks or months. We also know that students who find school a joyous experience continue to read and learn and grow afterwards, while those students who are punished or who feel themselves failures tend to avoid further contact with anything intellectual. Thus if we really believed that school was for learning we would do everything possible to make it the most rewarding, thrilling, successful experience possible for everyone. Do you really think that grading on the curve helps inculcate the right sorts of attitudes and desires into our students?

Second, while we pay lip service to the belief that all humans are capable of growth, we do not always act that way. Recent studies with severely brain-damaged children prove that even a child without most of its cortex can still learn simple tasks—if and only if it is reinforced for improvement rather than being punished for failure. My own students and I often work with these terribly handicapped youngsters. In the spring of 1975, for instance, we attempted to teach a very retarded nine-year-old boy to read and write. This lad had been given at least two IQ tests earlier; his scores led the staff of the institution the boy was in to label him as "uneducable." So the staff had not bothered to give the boy any intellectual training. By rewarding the youngster for each tiny response he made that was directed toward progress, and by using comic books rather than standard texts, we were able to get the child to read and write simple words within a few weeks.

Now, most college students have IQs that are well above "average." If there is anything at all valid about these so-called intelligence tests, we must conclude that any college student is bound to be capable of learning to master almost any academic subject. Yet when students fail, teachers typically blame them for being "stupid" or "lazy" or "unmotivated." Should we not realize instead that it is usually the teachers who have failed, not the students?

Our third assumption was that some teaching techniques are better than others. All data I know of suggest that when we give individualized attention to our students, they learn better than when we do not. That is, to maximize learning, we must discover what motivates each student, what his or her entering skills and behaviors are, and what each individual has as his or her personal goals. We can then make use of this information—*even in large classes*—to reinforce positively each bit of learning that each student shows. This approach requires teachers to do a lot more than just prepare lectures or give examinations, of course; but are we paying educators to lecture or to *teach*?

As I suggested earlier, those students who succeed under the present educational system are those young people whose goals and values closely approximate those held dear by most educators. But our Constitution gives us the right not only to life and liberty, but to the pursuit of our own brands of happiness—that is, the right to our own goals and reinforcers. Teachers often tell me that "learning should be its own reward." What they mean is that everybody ought to be turned on by what the teacher likes. And anyway, if our system guarantees that most students will fail to get the highest grades, how can we pretend that learning is really rewarding?

In brief, if we are to make our schools more humane and efficient places, we must start learning what really motivates our students, and then give our students what they want in return for their giving us what we want, namely, *learning*.

Feedback and Effective Teaching

I believe that grades should always be considered a type of feedback to a student about that student's performance in a course. Implicit in this belief is the assumption that teachers know what goals their students should reach in each class, and that teachers are able and willing to measure the progress that each student makes toward these goals. Unfortunately, many of us claiming to be teachers have only vague notions of what it is we want from our students. We may say, "I want the kids in my class to learn psychology, or to learn to think, or to be creative." But what in the world do we mean by such terms? Sadly enough, if we cannot state our pedagogical goals in measurable terms, we do not have a prayer of achieving them. And if we *can* state our goals clearly, then why in the world do we not do so the first day of class, giving our students written models or examples of exactly what we expect of them? If our expectations are concisely stated, not only will each student know how to achieve the goals (and hence earn a good grade), but also each student will be able to measure continuously during the course how he or she is doing.

In my own undergraduate courses at the University of Michigan, the students (from one hundred to three hundred of them) are given on the first day of class a list of activities, behaviors, or accomplishments that will earn them points. They are also told how many points they must get to earn a C, a B, an A, or an A+ grade. Included on the point list are such things as passing the mid-term and final exams with a grade of 80 percent or better, attending and participating in discussion sections, doing projects that will demonstrate that they can apply what they have learned, writing book reports, doing experiments, and so forth. The student then signs a contract with his or her discussion leader in which the student specifies what grade he or she wants and how that grade will be earned. If the student does not like the list we provide, the student is encouraged to negotiate a substitute list of "acceptable behaviors" with the discussion leader that will demonstrate mastery of the material we want learned. Once the contract is signed, it becomes a quasi-legal document. Students either fulfill the contract by the end of the semester, or they take an incomplete grade and finish the work later, or they must withdraw from the course (without penalty).

Everyone associated with the course goes out of his or her way to make sure that all of the feedback given the students is positive and encouraging. If the student turns in an unacceptable book report—despite the "model" that we usually provide to show what we want—then that student is told both what is good about the paper and also how to improve it so that it will be acceptable. We are not interested in proving how inferior the student is—we want all our people to learn how to succeed at complex intellectual tasks. In like fashion, our exams are all pass/fail. If the student gets a score below our 80 percent cut-off point, he or she is allowed to take the exam again (although we require a higher score the second time around). We have no desire to fail a certain percentage of the students. Rather, we have an urgent desire to help them all master the material. And, perhaps because it is a nonthreatening challenge, about 95 percent of them do pass the exam the first time it is given.

It is my belief that if we are really effective teachers, and if all our students are theoretically capable of learning, then all the students should not only deserve an A grade but get one as well. And if almost all the students did not earn that A, should not the teacher be encouraged to learn a bit more about how people actually learn? In my classes, I feel I have personally failed if more than 90 percent of the students do not contract for and earn an A. What is the percentage of As in the courses you know about or are associated with?

Objections to Good Teaching

The contract-grading system we use was first developed by Fred Keller (an educational psychologist), and in almost every instance in which it has been compared rigorously to other teaching techniques it has come out a winner by any and all criteria. We call it *contracting for mastery.*

But not everyone in academia approves of this approach to education. For example, in the October 10, 1975 issue of *Science*, Columbia sociologist Amitai Etzioni raises a number of objections. Giving too many students As leads to what Etzioni and others call "grade inflation." Fortunately, what Etzioni most objects to is the indiscriminate giving of As, where the grade in no way reflects mastery of the material offered in the course. I would object to this sort of grade inflation as strongly as does Professor Etzioni. However, Etzioni apparently has not seriously considered the alternative of grade-contracting, for he writes as if he is opposed to giving all students good grades *even if the students earn what they get.* One of his major arguments is that the Phi Beta Kappa organization would have to raise or change requirements for admission if too many students get As—an elitist position if ever there was one!

Another position advanced against contracting for mastery is this: life is harsh. Some people live, some die, some succeed, some fail. The sooner the student learns these nasty facts of life, the better off the student will be. This hopelessly dismal view of life fails to impress me very much, for the same argument could be used to keep poor people in the ghetto or to restrict good medical attention only to the rich. If we have discovered a better way to teach, should we not make it available to everyone?

The third argument happens to be true, and I say thank God! It is a fact that some people agree with Vince Lombardi, the famous football coach, that "Winning isn't the most important thing, it's the *only* thing!" But Lombardi was speaking of what scientists call a "zero sum game," in which somebody else must lose if you win. But is education a zero sum game? When one grades on the curve, of course, that is just what education becomes. Students look on each other as competitors, and cooperation is minimized. But is that the sort of society we really want to train our young people to live in? In many courses, cheating is rampant because the course criteria are so vague and the teacher so insensitive to reinforcement strategies that cheating is the only possible way a student can succeed. I sometimes wonder if the Watergate mess was not in large part a consequence of our elitist, "teacher knows best," curve-grading, competitive sort of school system.

The fourth objection to contracting is based on a mythical belief that students will slack off and stop working if you do not goad them into performing by beating on them physically or intellectually. Our experience is just the opposite. The students in my course, by actual measurement, do almost twice as much work as they do in other similar classes where curve-grading is employed. The students give my courses high ratings, and they usually state that they learn more than in other classes. In the last decade I have taught some three thousand students using the contracting-for-mastery technique. More than 92 percent of them state that they prefer this approach to any other they know and wish it were used in their other classes. Parenthetically, those students who do not like grade-contracting are mostly the "grinds," who are annoyed that everyone else can do as well as they, and the Vince Lombardi types whose major motivation seems to be winning at the expense of others.

The fifth difficulty that people raise about contracting is that the technique penalizes the "brighter" students. We can all learn, but some of us require less time to master any given material than do others. In contracting, the bell-shaped curve does in fact appear, but as a measure of the time students spend working, not as a measure of their final accomplishments. In fact, the contracting approach rewards quickness rather than punishes it, for the fast students now have the freedom to spend more time on their own pursuits. And if the rapid learners choose to indulge themselves in athletics, cultural events, politics, or socializing instead of reading more books, do we have the right to object? After all, we can guarantee that they are learning as much in class as we demand.

A related objection also has to do with fast learners. If some students can master all the material required in a course in just a few hours, do they not in fact "owe" us more work? In response, let me tell another true story. Here in Michigan there is a very large automobile company that produces trucks and buses. These vehicles are so big that their drive trains—the motor and transmission—must be hand-assembled. For years, the agreed-upon work standard for the drive-train assembly group was 70 units per hour; the actual output was but 55 units per hour. The workers claimed it was physically impossible to produce more than 55; management claimed the workers were lazy and irresponsible. Management frequently tried to punish the workers into producing more, but the union always protected the men.

Not too long ago, a new supervisor took over the group. Knowing that he would be fired if he could not increase output, he tried a different approach. He asked the men how he might reward them for "making quota." The men suggested that if they could produce 70 units in less than an hour, they be given the time left in the hour for a smoke break. The supervisor agreed. Within a week, production reached 70 per hour; within two weeks, the men were working so hard they were getting a 35-minute smoke break each hour!

The supervisor was pleased, but horrified. The men were proud of themselves, but worried. They offered to renegotiate, and voluntarily pushed the output up to 85 an hour. Even so, the men still had a 15-minute smoke break every hour. The supervisor was even more pleased, but the divisional vice-president was now horrified. "If the men can produce 85 drive trains in 45 minutes, they can produce 100 in an hour," he said. "Stop giving them smoke breaks. We pay them for a full hour's work and that's what we ought to get." So the supervisor had to end his noble experiment. As you might guess, production immediately dropped to less than 55 units per hour, and has remained there ever since.

Teachers, like this divisional vice-president, sometimes believe that our students "owe" us their undivided and full-time efforts; and like that corporate executive, we all too often try to punish students who do not meet our sometimes unrealistic expectations. So think about it. We know that we can almost double the time most students work by using the contract method. Do we really want to kill the goose that laid the golden egg by demanding too much?

The seventh objection to contract teaching concerns quality versus quantity. Many of my colleagues in the physical sciences here at Michigan refuse to use contracts because they say contracts merely reward the *amount* of material the students turn in, not the goodness or badness of what the students produce. These colleagues insist that they wish to reinforce creativity, or at the very least reinforce high-quality thinking and problem solving. How can one do that by assigning points, they ask? The answer is—quite simply. Creativity, at one level or another, involves the production of new or novel responses. If we can identify or recognize any part of creativity, we can measure it. The same may be said of high-quality thinking and problem solving. Anything measurable can be assigned a point value of some kind. And if we cannot measure something, how can we grade it or reinforce it? However, there are literally hundreds of studies and anecdotal reports suggesting that most teachers do not really care much for creativity responses and, like my anthropology professor at Texas, tend to punish "new" thinking should it happen to contradict their own. Albert Einstein, for example, stated that once he had obtained his doctorate, it took him three years to forget or repress all the nonsense that his highly uncreative teachers had insisted he learn so that he could get back to work on his theories.

In my classes, we give students models of what we think are high-quality papers and reports. If the students' work fails to measure up to these models, we encourage them to rework their papers until the quality is up to snuff. Thus *each student* must meet or exceed our standards for both quantity or quality.

Also, we try to show great excitement on those rare occasions when students do, in fact, come up with bright-and-shiny new thoughts. Perhaps our approach helps to explain why, at Michigan, there are presently more undergraduate majors in psychology than in all the physical sciences put together.

The eighth argument against contracting for mastery is that the technique requires a great amount of work on the part of the teacher. To some extent this is true. However, it is my experience that in the long run, teaching by contracting actually saves time and effort. The changeover from the present system of aversive control does demand the expenditure of additional thought and the learning of new habits. But once a contracting system is set up, it tends to take care of itself. For instead of trying to shape student behaviors and attitudes through constant threats and punishment, one actually gives most of the course management over to the students. That is, contracting can be used to teach students self-control. Since pupils know at any given instant how many points they have earned and what they must do next, they are able to pace themselves without external interference. It may surprise many teachers to discover that students are quite good at this sort of self-control, if they are given a chance to exercise it and rewarded appropriately for doing so.

Why Change?

Most of us resist change, particularly if we are thereby forced to act or think in new ways. So let me offer other teachers a positive inducement to at least try this rather different way of conducting their classes. Professors need positive feedback from students as much as vice versa, for teaching is often a dull and unrewarding profession (particularly when our pupils do not really learn). Since I have shifted to using contracting for mastery, my life has been much more pleasant than I could have imagined. Students sign up for my courses by the hundreds. They give me and the rest of my staff a lot of affectionate and very positive attention. The students appear to learn and to grow and to enjoy themselves tremendously. They come to see me in my office or after class, not to argue about grades or to raise trouble, but rather to tell me how important they think my ideas are. It is very rewarding to look out on a sea of smiling faces when I lecture; it is also nice to be liked. Any teacher who is not getting that kind of response from his or her students might do well to consider shifting to the contract method of teaching, and all students should consider encouraging their teachers to do so.

Thomas D. McSweeney

Social psychology in the classroom

16

This chapter by Dr. McSweeney stresses the importance of responding to the student as an individual. It gives a number of illustrations of how the principles of social psychology can be applied directly to the classroom. If such an approach as that suggested here were to be implemented in the educational system, many of the problems in contemporary education that were discussed in earlier chapters could be solved.

Thomas D. McSweeney

Dr. McSweeney is currently a full professor and Executive Director of the Educational Psychology Program at the University of San Francisco. He obtained his doctorate from the University of California, Berkeley, in the area of counseling psychology. He has held important positions in many professional groups, including president of the Northern California Personnel and Guidance Association; president of the California Personnel and Guidance Association; chairman of the Western Branch, Council of the American Personnel and Guidance Association; and senator to the APGA from California.

When we speak about social psychology in the classroom we are describing the very core of the teacher's function. As Elliot Aronson defines it, social psychology is the influences that people have on the beliefs or behavior of others.[1] These influences are what teaching is all about. As a teacher, I must have a permanent and positive effect on the beliefs and behavior of my students. If I do not have that influence, I am really a poor teacher no matter what else is going on in my classroom. I may have a room bustling with activity, my students may be busy as bees, but if my goals and purposes are not being achieved then it is all just busywork. My plan must be to influence what my students are doing and how they feel about doing it. If I cannot realize these objectives, if I cannot have an impact on my students, then I am truly failing as a teacher.

The teacher cannot hope to be a major source of influence by serving just as a role model. The stream of time is flowing all too swiftly to bridge the generation gap. We can no longer impress students by our ability to dispense knowledge. It is certainly true that the teacher is the knowledgeable person and the student has a genuine need to know. But the classroom process is not filling empty bottles. Nor can it be seen as planting seeds for future harvest. Students do not and should not set emulation of the teacher as their goal. Students are persons in their own right and, of necessity, must be their own persons.

Being one's own person assumes that students have a need for a "now" existence. Not only have they needs that must be met in the present but they must also live in the present if they are to enjoy the fullness of life. The concept of students as immature adults who must suffer through childhood to reach the full status of maturity is a totally unacceptable view of human life. It is as if we must deny ourselves the pleasure of spring blossoms if later we are to eat the fruit of the trees. As living persons, all of the students' moments of consciousness are of value. In their present state of learning they are leading as full lives as human beings as they will ever live in any future condition of being learned or competent or qualified persons.

In today's world teachers may exercise influence over the behavior and belief of their students only if the teachers are *credible*. Today there is a questioning of all our institutions and the roles of those who serve these institutions. Sputnik challenged the academic credibility of our teachers, *Brown* v. *Board of Education* challenged their social credibility, and Vietnam challenged their political credibility. Credibility has been transferred from the *role* of the teacher to the teacher as a *person*. It is now an individual contract between the teacher and the students. Unless the teacher can demonstrate to the students that the interaction is authentic and genuine, there is little room for credibility. There have been too many instances in the past when students have been asked to accept institutions that have been revealed as mere facades.

Credibility with students is established through personal interaction. Personal interaction already exists in the living environment of the classroom. So necessary is this personal interaction that we may describe it as a *living imperative*. If a teacher tries to carry on interaction in a classroom without personal involvement it is similar to the problem of an organ transplant. If identified as incompatible with the living processes of the classroom, the teacher will be increasingly a source of sensitivity to the students. The students, like the living organism, will reject the teacher as a foreign, noninteractive substance in their midst.

What is the living imperative for teachers if they are to achieve credibility with their students? Simply stated, they as people must relate to their students as people during the time they are in the classroom. They are part of the institution, but as persons and not facades. They openly bring their feelings and attitudes and explore the feelings and attitudes of students. This demands self-awareness of what they are experiencing, of what is available to them from their flow of consciousness. They must not deny themselves the feelings they are experiencing as people.

When teachers perceive the students as "trainees" to be rewarded and punished, neither the teachers nor the students are given any personal role in the process. The students are treated as "objects" to be manipulated by the classroom operators, the teachers. When teachers offer a role to be imitated by the students, there is no person-to-person interaction. It is only when teachers acknowledge that they bring to the classroom their total persons and interact with the students that teaching takes place. Teaching is not reaching out to the individual student. Rather it is reaching out to the *person* of the student as a significant individual. We can teach only on a person-to-person basis.

The credibility of the teacher will depend to a great degree on the manner in which the behavior of the teacher is seen by the students. The teacher may not feel comfortable in relating to the students on a person-to-person basis. The teacher may choose instead to relate to the students from the position of roles, the role of the teacher interacting with the role of students. This places a kind of impersonal barrier between the student and the teacher, and certainly makes the teacher much less vulnerable in terms of self-exposure. This idea is very much akin to the idea that has been developed in the area of transactional analysis. As developed by Eric Berne, in *Transactional Analysis and Psychotherapy*[2] and, later, *Games People Play*,[3] and Thomas Harris in *I'm OK—You're OK*,[4] people may relate to other people in a number of different roles they have learned.

Eric Berne discussed this relationship from the point of view of three basic roles. The first was that of the self as we became aware of it in terms of the way that our parents treated us and the way we learned to behave in relation to our parents. This is called the "child," and is generally described as the behavior that is based not on reasoned activity but on emotional activity. In the development of the role of the child, a person was really not called upon to make responsible decisions about his or her behavior; rather the decisions were made by the parents. The child was encouraged to accept these decisions. The parents—by praise, reward, or threats of punishment—induced the child to take a particular course of action that had already been decided; therefore, it is almost like prejudiced behavior. The child is motivated by feelings rather than by an analysis of the situation or by any attempt that might be called responsible behavior.

The second role that Berne developed was that of the parent. In this case the person grew up and imitated the manner in which the parents behaved. In other words, the value system, the belief system—the conscience, as it were—of the parents became a model for the child entering into adulthood. Again, the behavior of the person was not to be controlled by insight and clear decision making, but rather by the lifestyle or the type of life that the person wished for herself or himself. The person was motivated to fit his or her behavior into a preconceived scheme of how the world should be. The person was to shape that world according to her or his conscience.

The third role that Berne postulates is the role that grows out of the person's gradual achieving of maturity. The person comes more and more to examine the implications of his or her behavior in terms of the kind of person he or she wants to be. The person looks at the effects of this behavior on herself or himself and on other people. He or she looks at the appropriateness of behavior in terms of what he or she feels is going to produce a fuller, more effective life. Therefore, we say that the third role the person learns to live is the role of the adult, characterized by the reasoned, thought-out kind of behavior that we associate with people who are growing up in a mature fashion.

Now, we certainly cannot limit the teacher to only these three roles. However, these three roles are indicative of the kind of credibility that the teacher can create. A teacher who, as a person, is authentic, open, and adult in dealing with herself or himself and with the students establishes a person-to-person relationship. To quote Berne:

> The teacher is no longer a child, seeking to have his own way, seeking to have his own emotional needs fulfilled. Nor is the teacher the parent, seeking to control the behavior of the students in the classroom, seeking to set up a situation which flatters and conforms to the view of the world which is seen by the teacher. Rather, the teacher has to let go, to let the class atmosphere become one akin to which an examination of behavior is made to see if it is appropriate, to see if it is fulfilling, and most of all, to see if it furthers the emotional and intellectual growth of the student.

In terms of the classroom setting, then, we may move to what Thomas A. Harris has described as the transaction between the teacher and the students in terms of how they see each other's role. Harris has indicated that little children often perceive their parents as "OK" but they themselves, because they are scolded, reprimanded, and in other ways controlled by their parents, see themselves as "not OK." Thus you have an interaction between the "I'm OK" parent and the "I'm not OK" child.

Often this kind of perception of roles is carried over into the classroom, and the child perceives the teacher as "OK" and perceives himself or herself as "not OK." Therefore, the relationship between the teacher and the student is a crossed relationship. Going back to the Berne analogy, the student will be functioning in the role of a child and ascribing to the teacher the role of the parent, so there could not be clear and open communication between the two.

A second relationship that Harris talks about in terms of the interplay between the teacher and student is when the student perceives herself or himself as "not OK" and also perceives the teacher as "not OK." This becomes a very disorganized and nonrewarding relationship. Again going back to Berne, the student really sees himself or herself as a child in terms of the kinds of emotional satisfactions he or she is demanding in interacting with the teacher. But the child also sees the teacher as a child in terms of the emotional satisfactions the teacher demands of the students. Therefore, because the interaction is seen as basically self-serving, and the teacher is seen as a person encouraging emotional dependency, the student really cannot ascribe any credibility to the teacher. What is required in terms of the classroom interaction is that the student perceive herself or himself as "OK" and also perceive the teacher as "OK." From the point of view of transactional analysis, the student would see himself or herself behaving in what might be called the adult fashion; that is, in an authentic, genuine, reasoned manner. The student would also see the teacher behaving in an adult manner. The transaction or communication between the two would be open and forthright, with no hidden agendas. The open, forthright communication then becomes the basis for the credibility of the teacher. When the student sees the interaction between himself or herself and the teacher as one that is free of personal prejudices on the part of the teacher, the teacher is perceived as a credible, believable person the student can trust. The interaction is seen as free of a demanding, punitive kind of attitude on the part of the teacher. It does not demand that the student revere the teacher in his or her role in much the same way as the student is expected to display filial devotion to his or her parents. When the student perceives that this is not the relationship that exists with the teacher, but rather that the relationship between them is an open one, in which the freedom to explore feelings is pleasant and there is a genuine search for a reasonable understanding of themselves and their environment, then the student does perceive the teacher as a *credible person* and does accept the relationship between the teacher and himself or herself in a trusting and straightforward manner as person to person.

Let us now deal with the manner in which teachers should present a belief system or should present what is worthy to be believed by the students. From our study of the manner of human learning, we can cite a number of significant principles or rules of action that must be incorporated in the presentation by teachers of things to be believed.

The first of these rules or learning principles is the application of what has come to be known as the *interaction* effect. In short, the interaction effect is the response given when a person is involved as a person in the working through of an innovative or experimental process. In the classroom, if the teacher is asking for feedback from the students, is interested in the their attitudes and reactions, and explores their difficulties, if any, in determining the learning process, then we have the application of the interaction effect.

We have described discoveries of human learning as principles or rules, and they are indeed that. Just as with the application of such rules or principles in the physical sciences, so also the application of such rules or principles in the social sciences determines the condition of a given process. The interaction effect requires that there be an interactive process between each individual in the classroom and the teacher. This interactive process may be in the form of some group consensus or group communication, but in every instance the individuals in the classroom must feel that they have a share as persons in determining the communication or decision that they and the teacher are innovating. The implication of this interaction effect is that the teacher, to be truly credible, truly effective in motivating behavior or influencing behavior in the classroom, must communicate with every student in the classroom as a unique person. The student must not only experience this but also be aware of it. As a teacher I must make certain that to fully realize the contribution of each student not only must I recognize the uniqueness of each individual as a person, and elicit the responses and feedback of that person, but I must also make certain that in the process the individual student is fully aware that the teacher is trying to relate to students person to person, and that this is the teacher's contribution to the overall creation of an innovative learning environment. This I believe is what has been the background of the more general principle that every child is a unique individual and must enter into the classroom learning process as a unique individual. It is not only a recognition by the teacher in the development of classroom procedures, activities, lessons, and so forth that each child is a unique individual, but more important, it is in the process of classroom management that the teacher acknowledges and makes the child aware in a clearly demonstrated fashion that the individual child as a person plays an essential part in the classroom learning process. The opportunity for the individual child to contribute her or his feelings, attitudes, understanding, and decisions with respect to the classroom learning process must not only be present and offered to the child, but must also be participated in by the child as a person. This participation in the activity of building better classroom learning produces the interaction effect, or the involving process of a member of a group in innovation or problem solution.

A second principle essential to the impact of the teacher in the classroom learning situation is referred to as the *Premack* principle.[5] There are a number of classroom activities that do not ordinarily tend to be involving, interesting, or providing of any satisfaction in their accomplishment. Many of the routine learning activities, such as becoming adept at the process of carrying or borrowing or at the use of the multiplication tables, do not lend themselves to ordinary types of involvement. However, the Premack principle suggests that these types of noninvolving activities may be carried on by the students if they are associated with types of activities that produce satisfaction and do have involvement. A good example of this is the old-fashioned spelling bee. The students were encouraged to attempt to spell words correctly and were willing to make this attempt not because the activity of spelling words was interesting of itself but because of the Premack principle. The activity of spelling words was associated with the excitement and pleasure of being acclaimed the winner, or receiving praise and recognition; these later activities became highly motivating circumstances that could be associated by the Premack principle with the process of spelling words. Many other examples of the use of this principle in classroom management can be cited. Good teachers were aware of this phenomenon even though they had not, in their own minds, reduced it to the Premack principle. What they had done was to design an overall activity that incorporated the Premack principle and was a demonstrable motivator for learning. The key element in the application of the Premack principle is to discover what is a reward for a given student. We cannot generalize and state that certain activities are equally desirable for all children. Rather we must discover the *personal* likes and dislikes of each child. This will enable the teacher to select an activity that has high desirability in order to elicit a related activity that has little or no desirability for a given child. The Premack principle can be successfully applied only on the level of person to person.

We can move now to a third principle that is effective in a classroom organized around a teacher-student, person-to-person relationship. This third principle is the *feedback* process.

Because the teacher is a believable person with whom the student wishes to interact, feedback becomes very important in the operation of such a classroom. The feedback process is necessary because the teacher and the student are in a continually interactive process and are establishing a human relationship in which the teacher expresses not only the fact that she or he can be believed, but also and more important the fact that he or she believes in the student.

It is because the teacher is seen in this positive, supportive role that the commentary on the process becomes so very important to the student. The student does, in fact, wish to live up to the planned goals and successes that the teacher and the student incorporate into the learning process. We said that the interaction effect was important in such a classroom because the teacher demonstrated a willingness to believe that the student as a person could positively affect the outcome of the learning process. The credibility of the student as a learner was incorporated into the classroom process. The input and reaction of the student as a person to that process was considered to be a significant aspect and an essential part of the teacher's samplings of what was happening in the classroom.

In like manner, the feedback process from the teacher to the students is an important aspect of the learning process in the classroom. Because the teacher is believable, the student does not infer that she or he is being manipulated or in some way coerced or enticed into some aspect of defining the classroom process. Rather, because of the openness of the teacher and the credibility that the teacher has established, the student sees the teacher's behavior in offering commentary and feedback as further developing the learning process. It is, in effect, providing the student with one more tool by which he or she can grapple with learning. The student does not see this as some form of extrinsic motivation whereby the teacher is outside of the student learning process and is attempting to manipulate the student's behavior through some kind of external recognition, praise, or reproof. Rather, the student sees the feedback process by the teacher as an intrinsic part of the learning process. It is as if the teacher were an extension of the student's own anatomical system.

If feedback by the teacher is to be effective, there are certain conditions that must be met. The first of these conditions is that the feedback process must be continuous and not periodic. It cannot be assumed that the teacher knows what is occurring if at the end of the week the student is required to complete a spelling test, or some other gross measurement of the student's total involvement in the course. Rather, the student must be aware that there are certain activities that will be evaluated and will be assumed to have greater impact in the determination of his or her progress. However, there must also be a number of other significant signs that the teacher and the student exchange in terms of creating a more effective learning process. These signs are indicative of both the student's and teacher's awareness of their mutual efforts to create an optimum learning process in the classroom. This interactive process is cyclical in nature. The credible teacher is seen by the student as being aware of what is actually occurring and therefore the credibility of the teacher is heightened. Because the credibility of the teacher is heightened, every comment, observation, or interaction of the teacher takes on greater significance, has greater impact for the student. The person-to-person dialogue becomes more meaningful and this in turn increases the further credibility of the teacher.

In the beginning of this chapter we stated that it was the work of the teacher to influence not only what the students were doing, but also how the students felt about doing it. We have developed credibility as the primary motivation and person-to-person interaction between the teacher and the students as the manner of establishing credibility. We have tried to show some of the ways in which credibility influences the learning process in the classroom. We cited the examples of the interaction effect, the Premack principle, and the feedback process as three ways in which the credibility of the teacher does in fact influence not only what the child learns but also how the child feels about learning. These three ways that the teacher may influence the learning process in the classroom are simply illustrative of the type of person-to-person exploration that each teacher should be carrying on for herself or himself.

In the last analysis, the effectiveness of the teaching process depends on the credibility that this process has for the student. Reading, for example, must be seen as a learning process that is being designed and implemented in that classroom. Reading is not simply being taught. The teacher must also see teaching as a truly effective process that not only influences the behavior of the students but also influences their beliefs, their plans, and what they feel for themselves. This awareness of the personal influence that the teacher has on the life of the student as person is what teaching is all about. Teaching is social psychology in a classroom application.

References

1. E. Aronson, *The Social Animal* (San Francisco: W. H. Freeman, 1972).
2. E. Berne, *Transactional Analysis in Psychotherapy* (New York: Grove Press, 1964).
3. E. Berne, *Games People Play* (New York: Grove Press, 1967).
4. T. A. Harris, *I'm OK, You're Ok* (New York: Avon, 1967).
5. D. Premack, "Toward Empirical Behavior Laws: 1. Positive Reinforcement," *Psychological Review* 66 (1959), 219–233.

Suggested Readings

Buber, M. *I and Thou*. New York: Scribner's, 1958.

Festinger, L. *A Theory of Cognitive Dissonance*. New York: Harper & Row, 1957.

Gendlin, E.T. *Experiencing and the Creation of Meaning*. New York: The Free Press, 1962.

Heider, F. *The Psychology of Interpersonal Relations*. New York: Wiley, 1958.

Jourard, S.M. *The Transparent Self*. Princeton, N.J.: Van Nostrand, 1964.

Kelly, G. *The Psychology of Personal Constructs*. New York: Norton, 1955.

Laing, R.D., Phillipson, H., and Lee, R. *Interpersonal Perception: A Theory and a Method of Research*. New York: Harper & Row, 1972.

Maslow, A.H. *Toward a Psychology of Being.* Princeton, N.J.: Van Nostrand, 1962.

Schutz, W. *Joy.* New York: Grove Press, 1967.

Szasz, T. *The Myth of Mental Illness.* New York: Harper & Row, 1961.

Van Kaam, A. *Existential Foundations of Psychology.* Pittsburgh: Duquesne University Press, 1966.

Weinstein, G., and Fantini, M. (Eds.). *Toward Humanistic Education.* New York: Praeger, 1970.

Michael Scriven

The necessity for evaluation

17

This concluding chapter by Dr. Scriven deals with the importance of evaluation. We have spent billions of dollars on educational research without achieving the spectacular improvements in educational practices that educators and social scientists had hoped for. This inability to produce the desired improvements has focused attention on the role of evaluation in determining what kinds of research get funded, and how to assess the real contribution that a particular study can make to the improvement of our educational system. Dr. Scriven is one of the foremost educational evaluators in the United States and his chapter offers us some penetrating insights relating to the evaluation process.

Michael Scriven

Dr. Scriven is Professor of Philosophy and Professor of Education at the University of California, Berkeley. He received his B.A. and M.A. from the University of Melbourne, and his doctorate from Oxford University. He runs a small evaluation consulting and training company, and has given numerous workshops for administrators, teachers, and researchers—in rural (values) education as well as evaluation. He has about two hundred publications in a wide variety of fields, including philosophy, mathematics, ethics, religion, logic, and science, as well as education.

Introduction

Evaluation is something like medicine—it's a nuisance to take, it costs money to get, it frequently has a bitter taste, and you often suspect you would have got well without it. But, like medicine, it can save you time, trouble, and money in the long run. And unlike medicine, you do not have to be sick to need it. In this chapter, we look at some ways in which even the most advanced sciences, and certainly applied ones like education, need evaluation.

The Strict and the Sloppy Sense of Evaluation

A member of the board of the National Science Foundation (NSF) said something in a discussion recently that expresses a very common feeling about proposal and project evaluation. "To be frank," she said, "our problem is that we have so many good proposals coming in, proposals to support work that we know is of high scientific value, that we hate to take money out of that inadequate pool in order to pay for evaluation, when we know that doing so will mean turning down even more of the good proposals than we have to anyway."

In a strict and sensible meaning of the term evaluation, what she said is of course a contradiction in terms, although the contradiction would not occur to many people. For it is clear that she is speaking of a situation that can occur only *after* evaluation, not before it. A series of evaluative judgments has been made about the scientific merit of a set of proposals, judgments about whose reliability she is extremely confident ("work that we *know* is of high scientific value"). Consequently, *further* evaluation (which is what *she* identifies as "evaluation") seems—plausibly enough—to be a needless expense.

And she might well be right. But confidence alone is not exactly evidence. When we start looking at the peer-review panel process that provides her (and NSF) with these rock-solid evaluations, it is not at all clear they deserve her confidence—on the evidence available. We will come back to some details of that issue later. Here we just want to note that her conceptualization is highly prejudicial. Evaluation must not even be thought of as an add-on, probably redundant, footnote to a satisfactory funding process. *If* she could justify her claim to knowledge of the scientific value, then the conclusion is not that evaluation is unnecessary, but that it has been done, and doing any *more* would cut into scarce resources unjustifiably.

Her use of the term "evaluation"—probably the most usual one in the scientific/educational/business community—essentially identifies "evaluation" with "surplus evaluation" or "some bothersome and rather dubious *extra* evaluation." Or perhaps it means "what evaluators do" as opposed to "what scientists do." We constantly manipulate terms in this rather prejudicial way—scientists are perhaps more prone to it than they realize. One often encounters, in a respected text, or in discussions, the remark by a scientist that "we" do not need philosophers to tell us what scientific truth or scientific explanations are, since it is clear that scientific truth is just high probability, or that scientific explanations are just deductions from laws, or some other hopeless old wreck of a philosophical theory. Or perhaps the claim is that of course we do not make value judgments in science—doing so would be *bad* (!) scientific practice. The claim that we do not need evaluation in educational or scientific development is the claim that we do not need to distinguish between good and bad scientific or educational work or hypotheses; that is, it amounts to the absurd claim that the difference between the scientific and the unscientific approach has no significance. Whether one needs the services of an evaluation *specialist* is indeed a good question, but it is a sloppy use of the term to identify all evaluation with the work of specialists. For one thing, it makes it a little hard to explain what you are doing when you are trying to decide among these specialists, not all of whom are equally competent or useful for your purposes. Are you not *evaluating* them? Then you are *not* just using the term "evaluation" for what *they* do. You are using it to mean "determining the worth or merit of something."

This basic sense of evaluation is inescapable. It is the only correct sense and it makes nonsense out of the worries about whether evaluation is necessary, since every effort to avoid evaluation in that sense abolishes the very standards on which science is based, the standards of *good* evidence, *sound* arguments, and so forth.

But now let us look at the problem of whether we commonly need the kind of special and separate activity by people called *evaluators*, which is what is often referred to as "evaluation," in a sloppy sense of that term.

The Role and Functions of Professional Evaluation

The professional evaluator exists for partly the same reason as the professional statistician; namely, to render visible what cannot be seen with the unaided eye, to detect significance. While the statistician does this with regard to (typically) numerical data, and has to convert these data into *scientific* significance, the evaluator does it with regard to typically quantitative data, and must convert *these* data to educational or social or economic or philosophical or scientific significance. The evaluator may well need statistical skills or the aid of a professional statistician; but equally well, the quantitative data he or she handles may be cash-flow or depreciation schedule figures and the required expertise may be that of an accountant. And there are many other skills and types of knowledge that the professional evaluator should have or know how to get—knowledge of tests and scales of measurement for difficult concepts such as need and effect, of available and effective alternatives, of typical delays in development, of the magnitude of Hawthorne and John Henry effects, of ingenious unobtrusive designs, of the costs of not randomizing, of process observation procedures, of presentation media, of combinatorial procedures for hybrid data and peaches-and-pears comparisons, and so on.

Now when is that kind of expertise necessary; that is, when do we need evaluation in the sense of a professional service? And when is it an extravagance or imposition?

It is highly instructive to examine the way in which this necessity gradually emerges as we move from pure scientific research toward either applied scientific research (in one conventional sense), or toward educational materials development in, say, science education, to take a slightly less obvious example of applied science.

The scientist working on a research problem such as developing new models for the biological dynamics of a coastal headland is of course engaged in scientific evaluation of the hypotheses, predictions, explanations, classifications, and (hence) models that emerge. This kind of evaluation is an integral part of scientific method and is one reason why the claim that science should be free of value judgments has to be defined rather precisely in order to avoid immediate absurdity. But I did not appeal to this kind of evaluation to show that the quoted argument with which I began this essay was mistaken. That would have been quite unfair, since the speaker was talking not about this kind of *internal* (to science) evaluation—that is, the evaluation of the constructs of scientific methodology itself—but about the evaluation of proposals and projects.

Notice, however, that the line here is not a sharp one. It might well be said that the evaluation of the scientific merit of a scientific paper is an essential skill for a scientist. Such papers often begin with a review of related research; and competence in evaluating as well as doing that overview (which is a project itself) is a sign of scientific competence in the field. Similarly, the capacity to evaluate experimental designs is an essential quality of a good scientist. Now a proposal for support of scientific research has as its chief and certainly its crucial components exactly these two elements (a review of the literature and a proposed experiment), typically linked by a rationale that suggests that a significant gap in the research field can be filled by actually doing the proposed experiment or investigation. Hence, one might conclude it makes very good sense to use the peer-review approach to evaluating proposals, since scientists are essentially using their scientific skills in the evaluation procedure. Not *quite*, of course, and not *fully*. Not quite, because a proposal contains certain other important elements such as a budget and a time line and an analysis of resources available and needed, the criteria for which go beyond the scientific skills—though usually not beyond the practical skills acquired by the working scientist, who learns to be a project manager, and hence not beyond the capacity of a peer-review panel of experienced scientists. So it has seemed to many scientists, and to the director of the National Science Foundation, that the very tough standards that are applied in judging the merit of scientific work, and thus of scientists, provide a firm foundation for the selection of panels and thereby the selection of proposals.

So far we appear to have provided a rather solid justification for the peer-review approach. But I shall now argue that there are two major respects in which problems of competence nevertheless emerge, problems that require the skills of the professional evaluator. One set of them arises even with regard to the pure science case; the other, as we move toward the applied areas.

Suppose that we view the peer-review panels as *themselves* objects for scientific study. As soon as you realize that they are simply information sources, providing information about (as it happens) the merit of proposals, this stance is a natural one. But if you continue to be befuddled by the idea that assertions about merit are "value judgments" and hence *not* part of the concern of science, you will be inhibited from adopting this investigative, scientific approach—an approach that every scientist regards as mandatory about the other information sources with which he or she interacts, from thermometers to computers. Approaching panels as information sources, one would naturally raise the general question of their reliability and objectivity. The dazzling argument of two paragraphs back notwithstanding, no scientist in his or her right mind is going to accept a plausible *argument* over direct *evidence* (1) when both can be obtained at reasonable cost, (2) when the issue is of great importance, or (3) when the field where it arises is his or her home territory. But scientists are hard put to carry their scientific training over into other fields, even fields that are quite close (think of psychologists reacting to parapsychologists, doctors to psychosomatic medicine, and so on). And when it comes to applying scientific method to the study or management of science itself, the gap proved to be too great to be bridged by the excellent scientists who manage the National Science Foundation. Systematic studies have as far as one can determine *never* been made of panel reliability, consistency, or objectivity. Even the few accidents that have provided part of the anecdotal "wisdom" about panels' reliability have never been systematically collected and analyzed; or if so, they were never publicized widely enough to reach the attention of the director or board of the NSF.

Although a few of us have been arguing for such studies for some time, it has taken political pressure to bring even the slightest responsiveness to these complaints. That the scientific establishment has been unresponsive to criticisms that have such obvious scientific justification is an unwelcome sign of the continued failure to apply the standards of the discipline to the discipline's own practices, a failure that has haunted the history of science and shown itself most recently in the phenomenon of bias against women as leaders of funded research.

But perhaps these criticisms are still too abstract for it to seem sinful to ignore them. It sounds very grand to call for "checking the objectivity" of review panels, but what would it mean to practice? Here is exactly the point—or one of the points—where a professional evaluator, whose job includes the scientific study of evaluation procedures, should be able to translate that abstract demand into particular experimental designs. We will devote the whole of the next section to exactly this challenge. But first I want to develop the rest of the argument.

I suggested that as we move toward applied research, the relevance of the apparently plausible argument for the peer-review procedure will diminish, and the necessity for help from the professional evaluator will emerge for independent reasons. Let us distinguish between applied research in the sense of "research developing the consequences of a general scientific theory for particular instances," and applied research in the sense of "research aimed at the solution of a problem originating in the practical world outside science." An example of the first type would be the three-body problem—a problem in applied math; an example of the second kind would be the design of an "electronic fog" generator to confuse enemy naval radar—a problem in applied electronics. For our present purposes, the first kind of problem can be treated as pure science; the second raises distinct problems.

In the example given, for example, the Navy may let the contract to a private firm and may give rather detailed specifications in the contract of the characteristics of the required device. Somewhere or other in the system, however, there will be arrangements for extremely careful field trials of the resulting product. These may or may not reveal *contractual* default; what they must examine more carefully is the question of the real *practical* utility of the fog generator. It may well be that circumstances have changed since the contract was let—for example, the enemy may have developed "perspective radar" that can penetrate the usual electronic fogs. Or it may be that the original specifications were an inadequate translation of field needs. This review of the product is an evaluation, and in the case described it may be done by naval officers from the vessels that would be using the product, or it may be done by evaluation specialists from the procurement division, using field officers as consultants. The choice between these options is one that should be based on an empirical study of the relative success of the two approaches. In the example chosen, it is clearly possible that the results of such a study might go either way; thus, not *all* applied research, even in the restricted sense, is likely to require professional evaluators. But it is easy to give examples of product evaluation where the results will be entirely unclear without professional help.

For example, the relative merits of the various audio preamps or FM tuners or cassette recorders on the market can only be assessed competently by a professional evaluator of such devices, such as CBS Labs or Hirsch-Hour, or perhaps Consumers Union. The ordinary consumer, even one with considerable experience with similar equipment, is simply lacking in the test equipment, comparative experience, and skills required to avoid various biases that would give misleading results. Even the advantage of better knowledge of the *particular* needs the equipment will be called upon to serve (namely, your own) does not overcome these handicaps—especially because these evaluators carefully describe the performance test results in such a way that one can match the "performance quality profile" to one's needs.

Notice also that *the original designer* or the *manufacturer/producer* of the product is no longer even the *kind* of expert we turn to for evaluation. Naturally, one reason for this is lack of independence—one indicator of objectivity. But another is simply one in expertise difference. Julian Hirsch of Hirsch-Hour does absolutely nothing except test hi-fi equipment and develop better ways of doing it. He does not have to worry about ease of production, distribution networks, quality control on the assembly line, the reliability of suppliers, and so forth. He does not particularly care how those problems are handled, though he may make some incidental mention of the solutions; all he cares about is how well the resulting product performs. And, apart from his half-dozen professional colleagues, nobody else can match his skill in that, as we find out from our own experiences, the reports of others, and the follow-up surveys of owners as well as manufacturers. (The same situation applies to audiovisual educational products, obviously enough.)

What happens as we move toward this "externally oriented" applied science is simply that the task of translating needs and performance into technical specifications that adequately and comprehensively represent them, and the task of synthesizing the results, especially comparatively, becomes sufficiently complex and technical to generate a specialist. Not just in fact, but of necessity.

As soon as we look at the field of education, thinking now of programs and products other than audiovisual devices and systems, we realize that it fits this description very well; for example, the need for sampling (because of the large numbers often involved), the need for special tests (because of the lack of reliability of judgments), the need for rather sophisticated cost analyses (because of the relative importance of indirect costs), the subtlety and size of side-effects that require special techniques for identification and measurement—all these requirements rule out the ordinary educational consumer (student, teacher, principal, parent, or taxpayer) as an adequate judge of merit. Hence the need for a professional evaluator: in principle, at least.

Another feature of these applied fields is of such importance as to distinguish them from the pure scientific areas. As the contractor or developer is working toward a solution of the external problem, there will be a stage at which a *tentative* or *partial* solution will be available. This will have to be tested. It is desirable that at least some of this testing (the last phase of it, that is, the phase that will terminate further development if satisfactory results eventuate) match as nearly as possible the testing that will eventually be employed by the evaluator of the final product. Consequently, whenever there is a case for the use of a professional evaluator in the latter situation (often called the summative evaluator), there is usually a case for the use of a professional evaluator during the developmental process (often called the formative evaluator). The so-called R&D process (research and development) is therefore sometimes the "RDD&E process," where the E stands for evaluation, explicitly introduced (and the second D stands for dissemination or diffusion); but any R&D process involves cycles of successive (alleged) *improvement*, the improvement being judged by a process of evaluation. The more seriously that process of evaluation is done, the better the final product is likely to be. Hence serious developers often involve independent outside evaluators even in this formative evaluation because they need the best reading they can get on their own progress and they know that evaluators on their own staff cannot easily avoid "co-option"—becoming biased in favor of the "home team."

The scientist searching for a theory of course goes through this process of successive approximations and improvements. But at each stage he or she needs only the basic scientific skills to evaluate the candidates. Not that this is intellectually any easier than the task of the professional evaluator in the applied areas; it is just different. There is no need for the use of a second professional. The same may, of course, be said of other fields, using other skills, either intellectual (the attorney polishing a brief), or aesthetic (the painter reworking a portrait), or kinesthetic (the carver or calligrapher or engraver reshaping a scroll).

Thus we see two points at which the need for professional evaluation arises with regard to the "externally oriented applied scientists"—the *formative* and the *summative* stages.

There is another reason for using professional evaluators, one that applies to both the pure and the applied science areas. This reason is what gives rise in a different context to the difference between an accountant and an auditor—it arises from considerations of *credibility*. We shall turn to this as soon as we have expanded on the practical aspects of evaluation as applied *to* (rather than *in*) the peer-review procedure.

The Evaluation of Evaluation

Whereas the kind of evaluation we have been talking about in the preceding paragraphs is the evaluation of products or proposals or programs, the kind of evaluation that is being called for with regard to the funding of *pure* scientific research is the evaluation of evaluation procedures themselves. I coined the term *metaevaluation* for this discipline—Tom Cook has used the term *secondary evaluation* for the one-on-one version of it (that is, the evaluation of a *particular* evaluation, especially by reevaluating the original data).

What, then, might one expect the big federal science and education agencies (for example) to do if they wanted to determine whether their evaluation procedures were sound? Here are a few components that should be included in any comprehensive metaevaluation study of procedures like NSF's. A more detailed plan would be necessary in practice, but these examples should serve as illustrations of the real content of the complaint that we are still practicing an unscientific approach to the management of science.

It is easiest to grasp these procedures if they are thought of as responsive to specific hypotheses about bias, since evaluating the advice of panels is very largely a matter of determining the extent of their bias.

First, then, the problem of personal bias. It can scarcely have escaped the notice of anyone serving on peer-review panels that the final judgments often appear to be considerably influenced by one or two powerful and persuasive members of the panel. And these people may be influenced by (and influence others with) nonscientific considerations, such as the probability of high social payoff, or getting work done that would help their own work, assisting a friend—all possibilities that weaken the apparent plausibility of using scientific panels. There are many variations on this theme that make the point more acute. For example, a panel will usually represent a range of subspecialties. This is deliberate and appropriate, but it has the result that a proposal falling into *one* of these subareas will often be judged—technically speaking—by only one panelist. Even more often, only two people on the panel can claim relevant expertise. In a general spirit of mutual respect, the rest of the panel goes along with the recommendations of the "resident experts." But the much-vaunted objectivity of science simply does not transcend the immense differences of opinion as to the promise and professional expertise in proposals that one can get among individuals—and among pairs of individuals, to a lesser extent.

Few of us find it difficult to recall fights over appointments, or promotions, in science departments (or education, or engineering, and so on) that illustrate that radical differences of opinion can exist even with regard to the scientific merits of an intimately scrutinized colleague and his or her work. The chances for disagreement about a single sample of work are probably even higher. Hence (subject to direct investigation) a single person's judgment cannot be regarded as very reliable in all such judgments, and a pair's judgment is only somewhat better.

Moreover, where the whole panel *is* deciding on some issue of common concern, such as the general allocation procedure, a single person of great eminence or eloquence (or stubbornness) can often have a very great effect. And the judgment of that person on such issues simply cannot be *assumed* to have great reliability. To put the matter scientifically, an evaluator familiar with the research on the power of social group pressures and on the unreliability of global judgments could not put much money on the claim that a second panel with equally well-qualified members would produce essentially the same results in nearly all cases. While it is quite likely, in my view, that one could reasonably *hope* for a moderately high correlation coefficient between the rankings—perhaps as high as .75—one should not allow this to conceal the fact that even then a substantial number of important and expensive projects would be recommended for funding by one such committee and flunked by another. And a closer examination may reveal that one of the committees is making serious systematic errors in its ratings. Moreover, it is quite possible that the correlation is nearer .5. But these speculations should not be at issue—we should long ago have found out, and taken steps to improve, the range of reliability for these judgments. The two most obvious ways are to use duplicate panels, working independently and preferably without knowledge of the existence of each other, or to use some common proposals for panels that overlap in expertise, these proposals being from the overlap area. A more radical design would involve putting in panel members with instructions to play a particular role. The reactive effects of such experts (whose existence in general though not in a particular case would, for ethical reasons, have to be known to prospective panelists) might be to improve the process of panel discussions. Or it might be detrimental. Such an experiment should not be done idly—that is, not unless necessary to determine the truth of a particularly crucial hypothesis—and it need not in any event be one of the early experiments.

The second procedure concerns *procedural* or *managerial* bias. Canny division heads in various agencies have long known about and often used procedural control over panels. One version of this operates—so it is believed—as follows. Program managers or division heads normally send out materials, including copies of the proposals, relevant priorities, and guidelines, in advance of a panel meeting. They can *either* ask that panelists send in (or bring to the meeting) preliminary recommendations that are then circulated to all panelists or perhaps put up on a display board before discussion begins; *or* they may simply suggest reading the materials as preparation for the meeting. The second approach usually has two effects. First, less reading of materials is done, since no proof of reading is required. Second, the influence of the powerful individuals on the committee (or the program administrator, who usually attends the meeting) is made much greater because the others are not in the position of having to defend a judgment that they have already made. (This effect is still further enhanced if they have not read the materials.) When time pressure is acute, the second procedure may be chosen by the manager because it reduces conflict. When someone is on the committee with whom the manager does not agree, but whose power precludes bumping him or her off, the first method will be chosen, to offset that power.

The extreme example of the range of procedural possibilities is often forced on the manager when funds for paying travel and *per diem* expenses run out when there are still proposals to be processed. Mail solicitation will then be used exclusively and, of course, the entire procedure for combining conflicting recommendations is then in the hands of the program manager, who thus usually controls the major decisions about where to spread the support.

It should be obvious to all that these procedural variations could make very considerable differences in the pattern of funding. If, for example, it is less common for "advance registration" of tentative evaluations to be required, then it is quite possible that a strong repressive effect on the more unconventional proposals is at work, since such unconventional proposals make it much easier to convert one panelist than to achieve majority support. And that one ambassador, if he or she has to fight to defend a prerecorded grade, will find that there will be a number of occasions when the pressure of argument will bring around a committee that this ambassador would simply not have taken on when it became obvious that the general opinion was unfavorable. It seems clear, then, that we need some serious studies of the effects of different procedural modes.

Third, there is the group version of the old-school-tie, or cronyism bias. Senator William Proxmire's version of this has more political punch—he is concerned about geographic elitism, about a heavy concentration of funding on the East and West coasts. In his honor, I will call this the problem of *political* bias. It is likely that the panelists, as well as the funded proposals, would show a nonrandom distribution favoring the same areas. It is of course possible that this merely reflects a quality distribution. But it is also possible that it reflects a kind of self-perpetuating bias system. Especially in rating younger applicants, panelists are usually quite influenced by the institution of origin, and that kind of influence is very slow to adjust itself to real quality shifts. We may have a serious problem there, and it is not going to go away without scientific investigation. It is easy enough to see experimental procedures that would get a fix on this, either the use of faked institutional affiliations or—less objectionably—a comparison between results when the affiliations are blanked out with the results from another panel where no information is deleted. Interesting questions can be raised about the legitimacy of the influence of the proposer's list of publications, and so forth, that could be handled in a similar way.

Fourth, there is the *paradigm* problem—the problem of systematic bias due to the influence of fashion on science; for example, to the bandwagon or underdog effects. Those familiar with Kuhn's thesis in *The Structure of Scientific Revolutions*, and indeed with the history of twentieth century science in any form, will be well aware that bias from this source is extremely likely. Detecting it is another matter. However, we can sometimes suggest procedures for improving evaluation as soon as we see possible sources of bias, without necessarily being able to measure the size of the bias. For example, as soon as we see the possibility of procedural bias, we can suggest that panels use a calibration procedure; that is, that two or three pseudo-proposals (perhaps drawn from dead files) be rated by *every* panel and discussed before rating the live candidates. Data on the evaluation of calibration examples by a series of several different panels (in the relevant area) would be likely to show up any significant shifts in baseline, which might correlate with the procedure used. Later, one could feed the results of previous evaluations of the calibration cases to a new panel after they had made their own preliminary judgment, in order to encourage stabilization of a baseline (except, of course, where the panel felt they had good reasons for a significantly different evaluation). In time, it would even be possible to develop some measures of the reliability of given panelists, and so forth.

Nothing quite so straightforward appears possible with regard to paradigm bias, since paradigms tend to be pervasive within a whole specialty. But there are two suggestions that deserve consideration and possibly a trial run. First the "mad-money" plan. We reserve 5 percent or 1 percent of the funds available, distributing the rest by the usual panel procedure. Then we change the rules slightly: the reserve funds are to go to projects where the chance of success is seen as small but the pay-off (for example, in terms of a scientific breakthrough) is seen as very high. In this way, we would partly counterbalance the tendency to stay with the safe paths, which means the ones seen by the scientific establishment as well-tried; the "revolutionary" would get more support. Moreover, the existence of such a system would probably have a substantial effect on the kind of research *proposed*—an effect of preventing premature "hardening of the paradigm." A second system (which has been tried but not studied seriously) is the "white-ball" or "wild-card" plan. Where a single panel member could not persuade a majority to support a proposal he or she felt to be of great significance, then he or she could cast one absolutely overriding vote per, say, forty proposals considered. Fairly strict care to avoid any sort of nepotism or other exploitation of this plan would be required, and would be part of any evaluation of a trial run. The point of this plan is to pick up "flyers"—the proposals far from the mainstream that still "speak" to a first-rate scientist. The reactive effect of the second plan might be undesirable unless panel membership is not widely known (pressure tactics might result), but each plan has advantages, and the failure to do something like this strikes one as a real failure to provide the possibility of support to the kind of independent, breakthrough thinking that characterizes so many of the heroes of the history of science.

Fourth, and last on this brief list, there is a nasty *self-protective* feature of the present system that makes an evaluator extremely nervous. There is *some* follow-up of proposals that are supported, through the ordinary grapevine of professional contacts and publications. But the follow-up on proposals that are rejected is much less effective (because they are often not undertaken and hence do not result in papers, and so on). In either case, however, the follow-up simply is not used systematically to detect and correct the biases of panels or procedures. By the time the follow-up data, such as they are, have surfaced, the panel that made the original decision has been replaced. We can do much better than this, in half a dozen ways. For example, we should make some efforts to do a follow-up that looked for "false negatives" among a sample of rejected proposals that did find alternative funding. We should include some rejects that did not get alternative funding in the proposals to be considered by the panel the next time its membership is changed (with the proposer's permission, of course). We should also systematically collect data on the numbers of false positives (funded proposals that did not prove successful) and look for any significant correlations with (1) procedural arrangements on the panel, (2) division or agency constraints, or (3) the opinion of individual panel members who may have recorded an individual evaluation. There is no reason why the track record of evaluators, mentioned earlier, should not be refined in this way and the better ones used and/or paid more. Of particular importance is the longer-term follow-up (five to ten years), which could give us an idea of the extent of paradigm prejudice or mere faddism in the evaluations. It would be especially important to do a follow-up on the mad-money or wild-card plans, again with the idea of improving our score-card records for individual evaluators and learning more about our overall procedures.

It is possibly an additional point, or perhaps just a symptom of the general need for self-study, that the key instruments in all these panel-rating activities—the form to be used by the raters, and the form used by the proposer—are still in a state of total primitivism. They are not coordinated, neither is well thought out (of the dozens I've seen), and they vary enormously among divisions and agencies without any justification. This is not a matter of division and agency preferences; this is a matter of professional instrument design.

Evaluation for Credibility and Accountability

Evaluation often serves a certification, accreditation, or official recommendation function. In this role, it is clearly a necessity as far as certain consumers and/or regulatory agencies are concerned. Even if what an evaluation did *could* be done as well by the producer or manager or individual whose work is to be evaluated (and it cannot, because of the improbability that one can avoid bias in evaluating one's own work any more than one's own children), the results could *not* be as, or even nearly as, *credible*. Credibility is conceptually distinct from validity—but it is not empirically distinct, for it is the well-known probability of invalidity in self-evaluation that makes external evaluation necessary for credibility. With the best will and the most honest heart in the world one can scarcely hope to avoid all blind spots about one's own work.

Hence the project manager, looking for new grants or extensions of grants, or for a market, has little choice (when dealing with rational funding agencies or consumers) but to go to a professional evaluator not on the program payroll. Of course, many agencies and consumers do not operate rationally and can be conned into high levels of support by the use of self-evaluatory, or anecdotal, data. Fortunately, Congress has begun to wake up to this source of errors and wastage and is putting on fairly heavy pressure to upgrade evaluation in a professional direction. Here then we have the demand for an auditor, not a report by the staff accountant. (Legal analogies abound.)

The accountability movement reflects some of the same legislative concern, and it often requires the use of evaluators not only for external credibility but for technical skills in writing objectives and measuring progress toward them, detecting side effects, and so on. But to say that professional evaluations are sometimes necessary is not to say that every professional evaluator is adequate for each, or indeed any, of the jobs described. Evaluation is a new and difficult field; there are no credentialing procedures and almost no training programs. Who and what there are vary widely in quality. No evaluator is competent in all areas of evaluation, and even a competent evaluator is capable of making a fatal blunder. The use of teams reduces but does not eliminate these problems. But I would make this claim: a small group of evaluators chosen by their record can virtually always greatly improve the performance of a management system. There is now a very substantial repertoire of well-tried standard procedures that make this a safe bet—in my view. But I do not think that judgment, by an evaluator, is more than a claim for investigation as far as others are concerned.

Despite these needs for external professional evaluation, it should be stressed that any suggestion that evaluation's *place* is in the hands of the external evaluator would be most unhealthy. Evaluation *is* quality control, and one cannot leave that to someone else; one must *also* do it oneself. Professionally competent internal evaluation is just as necessary as external evaluation and that will mean a great deal of training of administrators and developers/researchers in the basic skills of evaluation.

Conclusion

In the proposal form we use for certain grant programs at the University of California we have the usual final section calling for an evaluation plan. In the past, this has been a pro forma request, and the reports of the results of the evaluations have been as scarce as the evaluations have been feeble. This year we have introduced one that spells out the reasons for good evaluation designs, investigations, and reports, as well as giving brief guidelines as to what an evaluation should involve. The new form essentially says: you have to submit an evaluation plan that will perform three functions, and in some cases a fourth. It must (1) demonstrate accountability for the use of public funds; (2) set up a track record to be considered when future applications are made—it being explained that a successful track record is a big plus, and an unsubmitted evaluation a wipe-out minus, but that a thorough evaluation showing that the project was not successful does not count against you; and (3) establish grounds for the committee to make a decision about arranging for dissemination, either by means of further grants to the producer for that purpose or by appropriate information-provision by its own agents to potential users. In most of these dimensions, the use of a professional evaluator can be expected to be reasonably worthwhile, for both technical and credibility reasons. It should be noted that some of these reasons have become good reasons for the applicant to take evaluation seriously *only because* the institution has taken a particular stand. Since that stand has good independent justification—that is, reasons (1), (2), and (3) make good sense for an institution—evaluation becomes much more than paying lip service to an inflated type of final report. It becomes the only avenue to future funds from this source, the only way to reach large numbers of consumers, and (which brings us to the fourth reason, the formative role) the only route to optimal performance. I think that is a more appropriate view of evaluation. This fourth need for evaluation occurs only when development of new materials or procedures is involved, in which case the evaluation plan must (4) explain how this formative evaluation is to be done.

Is not the kind of evaluation advocated here a serious add-on cost? And as such, is not the "necessity" for it pretty empty, for education in particular, since the dollar option just is not there? First, evaluation is a necessary part of responsible cutbacks, so declining fortunes do not eliminate the need for it. Second, evaluation should be treated as a money-saving investment. By providing good advice about where money is to be spent or saved, it should normally save its own cost,[1] just as the use of any other kind of management consultant should. And that is not a bad note to end on in hard times.

References

1.   See Michael Scriven, "Cost Analysis in Evaluation and the Doctrine of Cost-Free Evaluation." In W. James Popham (Ed.), *Evaluation in Education* (Berkeley, Calif.: McCutchan, 1974).

Suggested Reading

Popham, W. James (Ed.). *Evaluation in Education*. (Berkeley, Calif.: McCutchan, 1974.)